THE DETACHED RETINA
Aspects of SF and Fantasy

BRIAN W. ALDISS

The Detached Retina
Aspects of SF and Fantasy

SYRACUSE UNIVERSITY PRESS

First Edition 1995

95 96 97 98 99 00   1 2 3 4 5 6

Published in the United States by Syracuse University Press,
Syracuse, New York 13244-5160, by arrangement with
Liverpool University Press, Liverpool, United Kingdom.

Library of Congress Cataloging-in-Publication Data

Aldiss, Brian Wilson, 1925–
   The detached retina: aspects of SF and fantasy / Brian W. Aldiss.
—1st ed.
      p. cm.
   Includes index.
   ISBN 0–8156-2681–9.—ISBN 0–8156–0370–3 (pbk.)
   1. Science fiction, English—History and criticism.   2. Fantastic
fiction, English—History and criticism.   I. Title.
PR830. S35A39   1995
823'.087609—dc20   95-133

Manufactured in the United Kingdom

**Dedicated
to Marshall B. Tymn**

and to my esteemed friends of the IAFA team, especially Robert A. Collins, Nick Ruddick, Leonard and Lillian Heldreth, Carl Yoke, Don and Scilla Morse, Donald Palumbo, Bill Senior, Rick Wilber, Bob and Linda Haas, Mary Pharr, President 'Chip' Sullivan III, and Gary K. Wolfe and Deedee Richmond.

Not forgetting David Hartwell and Charlie Brown, who remember everything.

I find I can excite ideas in my mind at pleasure, and vary and shift the scene as oft as I think fit. It is no more than willing, and straightway this or that idea arises in my fancy: and by the same power it is obliterated, and makes way for another. This making and unmaking of ideas doth very properly denominate the mind active . . .

Bishop Berkeley: *A Treatise
Concerning the Principles of Human Knowledge*

Humankind uniform throughout

CONTENTS

ACKNOWLEDGEMENTS

This book owes its origins to two volumes published by Serconia Press in 1985 and 1986, *The Pale Shadow of Science* (hereafter PSS) and . . . *And the Lurid Glare of the Comet* (ALGC). The former volume was designed for my appearance as Guest of Honour at Norwescon, Seattle, March 1985. Both were the brainchild of Jerry Kaufman of Serconia Press.

Almost all the original articles have been greatly revised, thrown out, supplemented, or at least tampered with. New articles have been added. Their provenance is as follows:

'Thanks for Drowning the Ocelot'—as Afterword in *Orbit Science Fiction Yearbook Two* (1989), edited by David S. Garnett.

'A Robot Tended Your Remains . . .'—new.

'Between Privy and Universe: Aldous Huxley (1894–1963)'—expanded from an article in *Nature*, August 1994.

'The Immanent Will Returns—2'—new, but based on 'Olaf Stapledon' in *The Times Literary Supplement* (1983) and the Foreword to Robert Crossley's *Olaf Stapledon: Speaking for the Future* (1994).

'A Whole New Can of Worms' (PSS, expanded)—published in *Foundation* (1982).

'Science Fiction's Mother Figure' (PSS, expanded)—developed from 'Mary Wollstonecraft Shelley' in *Science Fiction Writers* (1981), edited by E. F. Bleiler.

'Sturgeon: The Cruelty of the Gods' (ALGC, expanded from 'Sturgeon: Mercury Plus X')—as an obituary in *Isaac Asimov's Science Fiction Magazine* (1986).

'The Downward Journey: Orwell's *1984*' (PSS)—in *Extrapolation* (1984).

'Peep' (PSS, expanded)—as Introduction to James Blish's *Quincunx of Time* (1983).

'Culture: Is it Worth Losing Your Balls For? (ALGC, expanded from 'When the Future Had to Stop', *Vogue*, 1986). Plus Introduction to *The Alteration* (Easton Press ed., 1993).

'Wells and the Leopard Lady'—lecture given to the International Wells Symposium (1986) and in Parrinder and Rolfe, eds., *H. G. Wells Under Revision* (1990).

'The Adjectives of Erich Zann: A Tale of Horror'—new.

'Jekyll'—new.

'One Hump or Two'—lecture given at IAFA Conference of the Fantastic #12. Reprinted as 'Fantasy: US versus UK' in Damon Knight's *Monad* (March 1992).

'Kafka's Sister'—Introduction to Brian W. Aldiss, ed., *My Madness, The Selected Writings of Anna Kavan'* (1990).

'Campbell's Soup'—new, based on a review in *SFRA Review* (1993).

'Some Early Men in the Moon'—based on 'The Raccolta of Filipo Morghen' in *Life on the Moon in 1768* (1990).

'Kaliyuga, *or* Utopia at a Bad Time'—a talk given at the annual MENSA meeting, Cambridge, August 1994. Based in part on an article appearing in *Locus* (1994).

'*The Atheist's Tragedy* Revisited' (PSS)—revised.

'The Pale Shadow of Science' (PSS)—address to the British Association for the Advancement of Science, 1984.

'Decadence and Development'—new.

'The Veiled World'—based on a talk given to The Oxford Psychotherapy Society, 1991.

'A Personal Parabola'—adapted from a speech delivered in Madrid, January 1994.

INTRODUCTION

WARNING: These essays are written by a man who produced his first SF short story at the age of eight. Writing has brought him joy and possibly saved him from a life of crime. The unifying theme here is his belief that all literature is a criticism of life, or someone's life. Even when that was not the intention behind it.

Among the great range of talented artists working in the SF/fantasy field, the name of Jim Christensen is particularly cherished. Not only is he marvellously inventive, he is a man of great charm and courtesy. And an obsessive.

I watched him during a signing session at a conference in Houston. As people came up to his desk with a book to be autographed, Christensen gave them something extra, something more than the bare signature we novelists extrude. He would swiftly draw beside his name a cameo: a fish, or a boat, or a dwarf, or a boat-fish, or a fish-dwarf-boat, or something entirely new. That's obsession!

This particular IAFA conference was being held at the Hobby Aiport Hilton Hotel in the mid-eighties. The Conference of the Fantastic is organized by the International Association for the Fantastic in the Arts, for many years under its energetic president, Marshall B. Tymn. Another obsessive.

The term 'obsessive' is used in complimentary fashion, since I must clearly be obsessive myself. My involvement with creative writing and criticism and science fiction has led me into the shallows of academia. Being a creative writer and a critic at one and the same time is somewhat convoluted, but I have certainly learnt from the academics, not least from the dedicatees of this volume.

The two similar writing processes impede but also cross-fertilize each other. I rejoice that it is so, and late in my writing career—if career it is—wish to give grateful thanks to the IAFA, one of the two major bodies to which SF academics belong. The other, and longer-established, body is the SF Research Association.

Before these two well-organized bodies set up shop, a certain amount of chaos reigned. The teaching of science fiction was in its infancy, with no one clear as to what to teach or how. Early SF curricula were described as Utopian Studies, or Futurism in Literature, or went under similar disguises. Most of the thought on the subject could best be described as muddled, though early lecturers on the subject, such as Jack Williamson, Tom Clareson, and Willis E. McNelly were fighting the good fight by dawn's early light.

In 1971, when my wife and I were staying in California with Harry Harrison and his wife, I was called upon to lecture at the J. Harvey Mudd College. SF had become all the rage as a degree option, and unqualified persons were being coerced into teaching courses for which they were ill-prepared.

A woman came to me in distress. 'I was due to hold a course on Dryden', she said. 'But no one enlisted. It was cancelled yesterday. Now I have to teach Science Fiction. Can you tell me anything about a writer called Robert Heinlein?'

Billion Year Spree was devised to attend to such problems. My hope was, by a little clarity of thought, to supersede some of the sillier theories of SF then floating about, and by so doing to focus on the intrinsic nature of the beast. Also, of course, I wanted to write of SF from my own experience as writer and reader with a half-lifetime's enjoyment behind him. While preserving as much detachment as I could muster.

The IAFA—I hope I have this right—was founded in the late seventies, by the revered Dr Robert A. Collins of the Florida Atlantic University, among others. Their first conference was held in Boca Raton, Florida, at the University, in 1979—a year after the SFRA presented me with a Pilgrim Award for Distinguished Contributions to Science Fiction. Dr Collins invited me to the third conference (referred to in the Sturgeon chapter). Since then I have attended all conferences bar two, and have attained the valued status of Special Permanent Guest.

The conference moved to Houston in the eighties, and is now (1994) convened in Fort Lauderdale, Florida. It has become the most pleasurable event of the SF year. I owe a great debt of gratitude to the executive board, whose skills I view with awe. This annual plunge into the rather hard-pressed academic world of American scholarship acts like a refresher course, while the continuity of the relationship, with all its challenges, is invaluable.

The board invited me in the first place because of the SFRA precedent, and also because I was one of the few writers actively to support the idea of academic criticism and study. In England, by contrast, there seemed to be only one lone scholar of SF, the feisty Tom Shippey, and in Scotland Colin Manlove. If SF is to be a literature, clearly the scholarly side must thrive. Nowadays, others writers, such as Joe Haldeman, John Kessel, Jane Yolen, Tom Maddox, and Stephen Donaldson, and of course Frederik Pohl and his wife, Betty Anne Hull, write and teach. And attend the IAFA conferences. Veteran editors such as David Hartwell and Charles Brown are generally present, to remind scholars that SF also has to be lived right down to the toenails. Writers as diverse as Doris Lessing, John Barth, Stephen King, Leslie Fiedler, and Richard Ellman have proved successful and popular visitors.

In the nineties, science fiction has spread into media other than the printed word. Into movies and videos, and into all the ramifications of the still proliferating electronic world, towards that digital time in the twenty-first century when the entire globe is on Internet and we all have access to everything.

Billion Year Spree proved an asset to scholars. It gave them *carte blanche* not to have to study texts a million miles from the real thing unless they wished; they were not forced to lead their students through Gilgamesh or Dante; they could narrow their sights on *Frankenstein* and all the amazements which have poured forth since. That proved good news for all concerned.

Billion Year Spree delivered a dialectic in which SF could be studied as a literature dealing with mankind's attempts to come to terms with new powers and to overcome those aspects of nature reckoned to be impediments to progress.

The success of the book meant that I was called upon to update it in the eighties. By that time, the field had greatly expanded and its parameters had become even more blurred than previously. I could not manage the task without my colleague, David Wingrove, another writer/critic, and the most diligent collaborator a man could wish for. So we produced *Trillion Year Spree* in 1986, with the able editorial assistance of Malcolm Edwards, then an editor at Gollancz.

Trillion met with less opposition than *Billion*, and even won a Hugo Award. It might be argued that this change in attitude was due to the establishment of academic bodies in the States like the SFRA and IAFA, where discussion is taken for granted.

In succeeding years, critics have perceived an increasing difficulty in writing what is referred to as 'hard SF' — that is, SF closely involved with technology and the sciences. The fantasy aspect has become predominant. As I try to indicate in the essay entitled 'Some First Men in the Moon', it is not always easy to separate scientific speculation from fantasy. Our wishes and fears are wild horses not easily tamed. The one often comes wrapped in the other, as truth in an ordinary novel can arrive, as Iris Murdoch has said, in an ambush of lies. Kepler, the great Kepler, used the one to enliven the other, in his *Somnium*.

This is my fourth selection of essays and reviews to appear in print. In *This World and Nearer Ones*, the essays were deliberately diverse. I had in mind as a model two small collections of essays which delighted me at a time when I was even more ignorant than I now am. Both books were by minor British poets: *Tracks in the Snow* (1946) was by Ruthven Todd, and *The Harp of Aeolus* (1948) by Geoffrey Grigson.

Todd introduced me to a number of artists I should have known and did not, such as Henri Fuseli and John Martin, both early exponents of the Romantic and the Fantastic. Todd's volume also included a reproduction of that marvellous painting, Joseph Wright's *An Experiment with an Air Pump*, which David Wingrove and I were to use many years later in *Trillion Year Spree*. It represents the introduction of a scientific principle to ordinary people—some of whom appear more interested in the medium than the message.

Grigson talks about a painter, Samuel Palmer, a favourite of mine—a man who turned the Thames Valley into Biblical illustrations. Grigson claims that Palmer, and the poets John Clare and Alfred Tennyson were the first people to admire the horse chestnut. Before their day, in the eighteenth century, that century of the landscape gardener, the horse chestnut was despised as 'a heavy, disagreeable tree', much like an overgrown lupin.

Later in the nineteenth century, we find Coventry Patmore remarking admiringly how

> quiet stood
> The chestnut with its thousand lamps.

Tastes change—and not only in trees. Perhaps even mad Fuseli is not fashionable any more. And perhaps in time the writings of certain science fiction writers—not all of them, not all of those 'thousand lamps' we find lighting current publishers' lists, by any manner of means—will come to be admired and studied as we study, say, the prolific Balzac.

I mention painters only because, for me, much of the pleasure of

SF lies in its imagery, in the bold pictures it paints. The ancient woodland invading the mansion in Holdstock's *Mythago Wood*, the alien landscapes of Earth at the end of Bear's *Blood Music*, the infernal city of Dis rising up from Death Valley in Blish's *The Day After Judgement*, the wonderful forbidding planets and moons in which we all indulge from time to time—this visual side of SF is apt to be neglected by critics, and taken for granted by readers. Even a poor SF movie can generally be relied upon to deliver visual fillips. Isn't this techno-romantic sense one of the special developments of our century?

The big question is, as ever, why is SF not more readily absorbed as part of the general diet read by a literate public? It is accepted that that audience may read crime novels without thereby losing status. Police procedure is an interesting subject: but is it really more interesting, of greater worth, than the procedures of planets, or the future of mankind? To which critics might respond, 'Is SF about the future of mankind? And if it is, is a popular literature the proper place in which to discuss such a serious subject?' Popular literature has always been about serious subjects: courage, love, adultery, failure, heroism, death. The argument that because something is popular it must be in some way debased gets us nowhere; it is a statement merely of prejudice.

Science fiction is not so much a forum for new topics, as some claim; rather, it is itself a new way to discuss old topics. The sense of the alien. The unease generated by religion and the failure of religion. The quest for meaning. Notions of the Sublime. A hope for the better miscegenating with a misgiving about the worse. Our ambiguous feelings concerning technology. The longing for security and its obverse, adventure. And more recently the importance of gender roles.

And science fiction seems to offer an elusive something more, a Martian sense of looking at things and finding the familiar strange, of finding novelty in this world, and nearer ones. For this it needs the SF writer's gift, a detached viewpoint, a detached retina. Perhaps ordinary readers are not comfortable with detached retinas. As Samuel Delany pointed out, you have to train yourself or be trained to appreciate the tropes of SF.

We in the West worry about the blemishes in our societies, and about their failures, remedies for which can be perceived but not applied. To paraphrase Percy Bysshe Shelley, we enslave much of nature, yet ourselves remain slaves. Horse chestnuts may go in and out of fashion, and the drawings of Fuseli likewise, but war is always with us, destroying humans, homes, monuments, histories and environments. Our societies become increasingly politicized; yet as politicians become increasingly a part of showbiz and mediabiz they grow less and less able to offer leadership. Engendered by this situation, alternating fits of exhilaration and depression pour into science fiction.

Cool reflections on the state of play are offered by many contemporary writers. Karen Joy Fowler, for instance, in her novel *Sarah Canary* (1991), has this to say:

> Sanity is a delicate concept, lunacy only slightly less so. Over the last few centuries, more and more of those phenomena once believed to belong to God have been assigned to the authority of the psycho-analyst instead. Some of the saints can be diagnosed in retrospect as epileptics. St Teresa was almost certainly an hysteric. St Ida of Lorraine seems to have suffered from perceptional insanity . . . The prognosis for such cases in our own age is excellent; saintliness can often be completely cured.

The essays which follow might seem not to deal with such weighty matters. I no longer attempt to emulate Todd and Grigson. My belief is that much of SF's interest and importance lies in what it does not say. Or rather, that we like mainly what it *corporately* has to say about what it sees through that detached retina. Hence our addiction. It scratches where we itch.

I am no academic, as these essays show. For that reason, I use my own experience when it illuminates an argument. Academics do not behave like that; unlike me, they have careers to protect. I can scratch in public . . .

And, just as opinions may change regarding the attractions of the horse chestnut, so the place where we itch changes. I remember the days when all we needed to stir our imaginations was to read of a landing on the Moon. The very idea challenged the limits of what was possible. Then men went and landed there, and spoilt everything (maybe they spoilt it even for themselves, because I notice they've not been back since . . .).

So nowadays a Moon landing must have a different emphasis if it is to scratch in the right place. Terry Bisson would presumably concur with Fowler, as quoted above. In one of his deceptively relaxed stories, *The Shadow Knows*, he tangles up his Moon landing nicely with other contemporary elements. The major is homing in on Station Houbolt:

> Situated on the far side of the Moon, facing always away from the Earth, Houbolt lies open to the Universe. In a more imaginative, more intelligent, more spirited age it would be a deep-space optical observatory; or at least a monastery. In our petty, penny-pinching, paranoid century it is used only as a semi-automated Near-Earth-Object or asteroid early-warning station. It wouldn't have been kept open at all if it were not for the near-miss of NEO 2201 Oljato back in '14, which had pried loose UN funds as only stark terror will.

Here's our old familiar Moon landing, wonderful as ever. But nowadays it crawls with social commentary.

We devotees of SF enjoy its diversity of opinion, the bustle of bright and dark, the clash of progress and entropy, the clamour of theories about the past, the future, the ever-present present, everything.

We doubt: therefore we are.

B. W. A.
Boars Hill
Oxford
November 1994

THANKS FOR DROWNING THE OCELOT

~~~~~~

England, 1989

Dear Salvador Dali,

It's a real sorrow that you died in January of this year, and I expect you were upset as well. I wanted to say thanks to you; let's trust I'm not too late. I hope this letter will reach you as you rest in Abraham's Bosom. Rough luck on Abraham, though.

But that can't be right. You must be in some surreal place—perhaps in the heaven the ancient Egyptians dreamed about, by the summer stars. Or simply in orbit. Somewhere unorthodox. You liked breaking taboos.

Remember you once tried to prove that 'the whole universe comes to a focus' (as you put it) in the centre of the railway station in Perpignan? That was a good stunt. Perhaps you're there in Perpignan, awaiting a celestial diesel to somewhere.

You were crazy. Or you acted the part. The remark about Perpignan railway station came in an article you wrote in 1965, extolling the virtues of the great Salvador Dali. Like Caesar, you referred to yourself in the third person—though in your case you were the first and the second person too: there were scarcely any others.

Your article involves the miraculous flies of Gerona, the cleanliness of Delft, the visceral eye of Vermeer, van Leeuwenhoek's invention of the microscope, several revolutions, the atomic bomb, and a swarm of priests dressed in black. It's incoherent. You never wanted to make sense of the world; that had no part in your 'critical paranoia' method. Yet there was a tawdry magic. Take one sentence from that article:

> Thus the blood of the dragoons and the hussars who hibernated at Beresina mixing directly with the blood of the new technologists of the always Very Holy Russia caused a historic mutation, producing the true and new mutant beings—

the astronauts who, propelled by the templates of their genetic code, could not have a more positive way to direct themselves toward heaven than to jet straight toward the moon, which we will see happen from one moment to the other.

Even van Vogt couldn't manage prose like that. So let's just think of you in orbit somewhere in the summer stars. Greetings to Hieronymus Bosch.

You may not remember this, but we met on one occasion; an event was held in the London Planetarium, when you and I helped to launch a book of Fleur Cowles's poems and paintings. You were working hard on giving an impression of great eccentricity. Without wishing to complain, I was slightly disappointed—only, I hasten to add, in the way that one is generally disappointed by meeting one's heroes in the flesh. It's the Napoleon-was-a-bit-short syndrome. When I met Jeffrey Archer, another of the greats, the same thought flashed across my mind. There was a kind of rotting Edwardian stylishness about you. Whereas Archer's unmitigatedly eighties; the Hush Puppy school.

But you were a hero. At my school, in Form IVA, it was taken for granted you were the great artist of the age. We liked rotting carcasses, elongated skulls, soggy watches, crutches, and the rest of your props. One of our number, now a Labour back-bencher, could act out your canvas, *Spectre of Sex Appeal*, naked, with the aid of a couple of hockey sticks. We chortled over your *Life*, so full of disgusting facts or fantasies that it would have meant expulsion had we been caught with the book in our lockers.

It was the confusion of fact with fantasy which caught the imagination. I have cooled down a bit since those days in IVA, when the class debated whether you had an exceedingly large whatnot, a laughably small one, or possibly none at all. Since then, you have sunk down the list of favourite artists in my estimation, whereas Kandinsky, Gauguin, Tanguy, Max Ernst and de Chirico in his early period, remain firm. Odd how all the century's most exciting art was achieved before World War II was spent.

We'll return to the confusion of fact with fantasy later, because that is where your connection with science fiction comes in, but first, at the risk of disturbing that great calm into which you have flown, I want to remind you of what George Orwell said. Orwell wrote that your two unquestionable qualities were an atrocious egotism and a gift for drawing. Many of us have aspired towards either, or both. As a kind of corollary to that remark, Orwell said 'one ought to be able to hold in one's head simultaneously the two facts that Dali is a good draughtsman and a disgusting human being.' It is an oft-quoted remark. You must be proud of it.

Although he belonged to the NUJ, Orwell was a little, well, prudish. He objected in print to the way in which you consummated your love of Paul Eluard's wife. That certainly must have been a Gala event: you covered yourself with a mixture of goat's dung boiled in fish glue. *Chacun à son goat*, I say. It must have made something stick, since Gala remained your idolized companion for fifty years. Orwell has no comment on that aspect of your life.

To be honest—Orwell was another hero of mine—the author of *1984* is wearing no better than you. A new world has come up over the skyline since your heyday in the thirties and forties. Your paranoid harp-players and flaming giraffes have acquired period charm. You got too rich. You became religious, in a florid, Murillo-like, Madonna-worshipping way which sickens us more than the necrophilia sickened Orwell. It's a common tragedy, outliving your epoch.

Still, you did paint *Soft Construction with Boiled Beans: Premonitions of Civil War*, and several other canvasses which will remain icons of their time.

You must always have worked very hard. Kept working, even when—towards the end—you turned to the kitschy religious subjects. Is Dali perhaps Catalan for Doré? Like Doré, you illustrated numerous books. But it was the early paintings which fed a young imagination, the images seen through a dry, pure atmosphere—some of them, like *Sleep*, where an immense sagging face is propped precariously above the desert, are now fodder for Athena posters, alongside Beardsley and Escher, other masters of illusion.

Your titles too took one into a new imaginative world. *The Ghost of Vermeer of Delft which can be Used as a Table. Average Atmospherocephalic Bureaucrat in the Act of Milking a Cranial Harp. Paranoic Astral Image.* Convincing, as only the preposterous can be.

Some of the paintings held even more direct links with a mentality which questions what is real. *The Invisible Man*, for instance. Various visual puns where things appear and disappear, such as *Apparition of Face and Fruit-Dish on a Beach, Slave Market with Invisible Bust of Voltaire*, and the hallucinatory *Metamorphosis of Narcissus*, another of Athena's victims. Well, I won't auto-sodomize you with lists of your own canvasses, but doesn't it strike you, as you take your astral ease, that it's the past which is rich with life? It's the future that's dead, stuffed with our own mortality?

Naturally, all these whims and excesses of your imagination can be put down to revolt against upbringing, revolt against Catholicism, revolt against traditional dull nationalism. There was just a little too much showbiz. All the obits followed Orwell in speaking of your egotism. After obit, orbit—and there you swing, moody among the summer stars. We who remain Earth-bound look up. You probably have for company the Japanese Emperor Hirohito, once proclaimed a god, who achieved escape velocity a mere two weeks before you.

What a patriot that man was! Your very opposite. Never showed off. Kept a low profile. Good family man. Responsible for perhaps millions of deaths.

And even your egotism was relieved, or probably I mean made more roccoco, by your sense of humour. Perhaps you recall a stuffy English BBC type—it can't have been a young Alan Whicker, can it?—coming to interview you in your retreat in Port Lligat, near Figueras? You sat with Gala by your blue swimming pool, your pet ocelot lounging on a cane armchair beside you.

The interview went on. You spoke English of such beauty and density that the BBC found it necessary to run sub-titles at the bottom of the screen. The interviewer, as I recollect, was just slightly critical of your notoriety, for in those days—this was in Harold Wilson's time of office—we rather used to fawn on failure; whereas, now that Mrs Thatcher holds office, we have learnt to suck up to success.

So the interviewer came to his most devastating question. He had heard, he said, that Dali was unkind to animals. Was that true?

Do you remember how your music-hall moustache curled in scorn?

'Dali cruel to ze animal?' you exclaimed. 'Nevair!' And to empha-size the point you seized up your ocelot by the scruff of its neck and hurled it into the swimming pool.

That indeed is the way to discomfit the English.

We SF writers, in our own humbler way—for we live in Penge and Paddington and Pewsey, not Figueras—the very names shout the difference—we also try to discomfit the English. It is what SF is designed for, what Mary Shelley and H. G. Wells used it for.

Of course, we never discomfited the English very much; we have no luck at all in that respect.

I suppose you know that while you were posturing on your death bed, in a leg-over position with mortality at last, Salman Rushdie was having trouble here with his latest phantasmagoria, *The Satanic Verses*. It's a fantasy which now and again makes fun of the Christian God and of Mohammed. The English dutifully bought their copies at Smith's and Waterstone's, to display them prominently so that friends would think they had read the book, and maintained a calm almost indistinguishable from catatonia. Not so the Moslem community in Britain (or in Bradford, which is near Britain). The Moslems descended on W.H. Smith with flaming brands, in the manner of those exciting final scenes in a Frankenstein movie. It's the Spanish temperament, I suppose. The British are full of phlegm. Sometimes it makes you spit.

Far more worthy of expectoration was the medieval behaviour of the Ayatollah Khomeini in pronouncing the death sentence on Rushdie for his novel. Even in World War II we never witnessed such behaviour. The situation is far more bizarre that even Rushdie's mind could think up—bizarre and horrifying.

It was my misfortune to appear on the BBC TV programme 'Kilroy' which discussed Khomeini's death threat. I felt very strongly that both the freedom of speech and Rushdie must be protected—the former on principle, the latter from his foolishness. The majority of those appearing in the Kilroy-Silk bear-pit were Muslim. The atmosphere was thunderous. Many, though not all, of the Muslims present agreed vociferously with the Ayatollah that Rushdie should be killed. Some of these men held high positions in the Muslim community in Britain. When asked directly if they would murder Rushdie themselves, the men fought shy, knowing the television cameras were upon them. Two women had no such qualms. Both said they would murder Rushdie themselves.

To have to listen to such madness was almost unbearable. Fact and fantasy were again confused. No one in the vociferous belt could—or would—distinguish between a novel and a theological work. These people and millions like them, had surrendered their consciences into the keeping of the mad old man in Teheran. The most recent similar case we experienced was the fever of the Cultural Revolution under the Great Helmsman (you didn't meet him, did you, Dali?), when two million people stood in Tienanmen Square and waved their Little Red Books.

Rushdie began his writing career with *Grimus*, once categorized as SF. I tried to give it the award in a *Sunday Times* SF Competition, but it was withdrawn. Later, I tried ineffectually to bestow the Booker Prize on D. M. Thomas's *White Hotel*, rather than on *Midnight's Children*. No one then imagined that Rushdie's name would become more widely known over the face of the globe than any author since Rosetta wrote his Stone.

In the matter of freedom of speech, writers must be for it. On the whole I'm also for blasphemy—it proves the god spoken out against is still living. You can't blaspheme against Baal or the Egyptian goddess Isis.

Some of the bourgeois like being épated. As I enjoyed Henry Miller's writings when he was forbidden, so I enjoyed your carefully executed shockers when they were disapproved of. To my mind, some of them have a long shelf life. Longer than yours.

Your old friend Luis Buñuel proceeded you into the realms of darkness. He too did his share of shocking us out of apathy, and would have recognized in the bigotry of the Ayatollah the intolerance he mocked in the Roman Catholic Church in Spain. With Buñuel, if you remember, you made that celebrated surrealist film, *L'Age d'Or*. It certainly opened a large door in my consciousness.

But it's a silver age. 'The New Dark Age', as a headline in our beloved *Guardian* calls it today (1 February 1989). Singing yobs are in vogue, Dali. Pre-pubescent voices. Tribal drumming. Over-amplification. Your exit was well-timed.

And for SF too it's a silver age. True there is some sign that a few of the younger writers are impatient with the stodginess of their elders. (During the time of President Reagan, patriotism became a way of life and patriotism is always a blanket excuse for stifling the critical faculty, as if there were no other use for blankets.) Paul di Filipo and Bruce Sterling are names that spring to mind in this connection, and the group of writers who centre round the magazine *New Pathways*, with their subversive artist, Ferret.

You weren't particulary patriotic. When the Civil War hit Spain, you sensibly refused to take sides—though you had a good precautionary word for General Franco—and went to live in Italy, continuing to flirt with psychoanalysis and sunlight. When Europe sank down on its knees in the fury of World War II, you hopped over to the New World, where the Americans embraced your flamboyance and dirty mind with open purses. Orwell blamed you for those two desertions. Silly of him, really—such an English chap, he should have remembered the words of another Englishman, 'Patriotism is the last refuge of a scoundrel'.

Those words were quoted in 1973 in the pages of *Analog*. (Did you ever see *Analog*, Dali? In its better days, the covers might have appealed to you.) They were quoted by the late Robert A. Heinlein in a guest editorial. He referred to Johnson's cautionary remark as 'a sneering wisecrack'. Johnson never sneered. Heinlein then compounded his philistinism by referring to Johnson as 'a fat gluttonous slob who was pursued all his life by a pathological fear of death'. Several readers cancelled their subscription to *Analog* on the spot.

You see what I'm getting at? It is a mark of civilization that one criticizes one's own country. Hemingway said that a writer should always be against the government in power. Whatever their faults of exhibitionism, your paintings spoke out against the mundane, the dreary, the received. Like the other surrealists, you were up in arms, though you preferred yours covered in mink and diamonds.

American SF writers have not been slow to write about their Vietnam War. The British have had little to say about their adventure in the Falkland Islands at the start of this decade. A thousand pardons—as a Spaniard you probably think of those shores as Las Malvinas. Our neat little war!—won through the bravery of the common man and because the French sold the Argentinians dud Exocets.

We captured the Falklands from you Spaniards back in Johnson's time. And what did Johnson have to say about that victory, in his ponderous, humorous fashion?

> . . . What have we acquired? What, but a bleak and gloomy solitude, an island thrown aside from human use, stormy in winter, and barren in summer; an island which not the southern savages have dignified with habitation; where a garrison must be kept in a state that contemplates with envy the exiles of Siberia; of which the expense will be perpetual, and the use only occasional . . .

How the words ring on!

Garry Kilworth has gone to Hong Kong. Perhaps we shall have a similar devastating bulletin from him in the next *Yearbook*. SF in England has settled down to comfortable squalor, relatively unmoved by dirty needles, inner city decay, and the prospect of union with Europe. At least you preserved the clean contorted rocks of Figueras and the drypoint desert as background. Your air was clear.

You may not have been in the very front rank, Dali, but you stood up to be counted. At the least, you kept us amused throughout a lifetime, like Richard Burton and Elizabeth Taylor rolled into one. You replenished that small vocabulary of images which shapes our imaginative life. You are the great international SF writer in paint.

And you chucked that bloody ocelot into the water.

All the best in the summer stars,

Your admirer,
Brian Aldiss

'A ROBOT TENDED YOUR REMAINS . . .'
The Advance of the Mega-machine

Every so often, someone writes a heart-rending book about science fiction. To say how bad it is. Perhaps to say how good his or her writing is and how little appreciated. That needs courage.

The most academic journal in the field, *Science-Fiction Studies*, in its issue #61 (November 1993) listed my name among the five or six most neglected names of authors. So I suppose I am also entitled to lament. However, cheerfulness keeps breaking in.

There remains that comment of Samuel Johnson's in his letter to Lord Chesterfield, which no doubt speaks to the hearts of many authors: 'I had done all I could', Johnson writes, 'and no man is well pleased to have his all neglected, be it ever so little'. The elegant English art of litotes! All the same, I have had a fair run for my money. More particularly, perhaps, in the United States than in my own country. Three books on my writing, plus a wacking great 360-page bibliography of an unprecedented accuracy (being the work of my wife Margaret Aldiss) have been published—in the States, but not the UK.

In that same *Science-Fiction Studies* article, Gary K. Wolfe, one of our most acute and active critics, lists topics he feels are neglected, such as the contributions of SF editors other than Gernsback and Campbell.

Another topic rarely discussed goes to the very roots of SF—the drift towards the impersonal, towards humans as units, as machines. Towards rule by machine. Towards the sort of giantism in corporations and architecture such as Nazi Germany preferred. Towards anything which rules out of court the quiet dissident voice of the individual. Towards crushing the anima. Towards the immense—which is always cruel.

Towards metropolis and megalopolis.

Towards galactic empires.

Towards artificial intelligences taking over from us.

Towards, in sum, most of the gaudy goodies on the front counter of SF's supermarket . . .

Are not these items which reinforce anomia and spiritual impoverishment among the prevailing dreams of SF? Approached ambivalently, yet rarely rejected out of hand. Our SF culture springs from nations with most power. So power is naturally a prevailing theme.

A Czech playright by the name of Vaclav Havel spoke out on this threat in the days before his country threw off the Communist yoke, and before he became president of the Czech Republic. Here is an extract from what he said:

> In my view Soviet totalitarianism is an extreme mani-festation—a strange, cruel, and dangerous species—of a deep-seated problem which equally finds expression in advanced Western society. These systems have in common something that the Czech philosopher Vaclav Belohradsky calls 'the eschatology of the impersonal'. That is, a trend towards impersonal power and rule by mega-machines or colossi that escape human control.
>
> I believe the world is losing its human dimension. Self-propelling mega-machines, juggernauts of impersonal power such as large-scale enterprises and faceless governments, represent the greatest threat to our present-day world. In the final analysis, totalitarianism is not more than an extreme expression of that threat.

My first SF novel, *Non-Stop*, aired this theme. The big battalions, the grandiose ideas, have taken over from individuals and, in the words of the prologue, 'gobbled up their real lives'. The theme finds expression in much of my fiction since then. Less than a decade ago we were being confronted by that 'eschatology of the impersonal' in one of its most dreadful guises, Armageddon brought about by nuclear destruction, and by the belief that the Enemy was evil and had to be destroyed.[1]

My fondness for Orwell's old novel, as noted elsewhere, is because

1 Here is an opportunity to recommend H. Bruce Franklin's 1988 *War Stars*, the sub-title of which is *The Superweapon and the American Imagination*.

for him utopia is just a note saying I LOVE YOU, a rather seedy bedroom, a girl, and privacy . . . great things to set against a mega-machine. Clifford Simak was against the mega-machine; time and again, his characters seek something better—in *City*, his best-loved novel, it is a place where men do not have to be humans or dogs dogs. Philip Dick also fought against the mega-machine. His novels were for so long more popular in France and England than in the USA.

Every decade, SF changes as the world changes. The most popular SF/Fantasy author of the nineties is Terry Pratchett, with his wonderful Discworld comedies. They adroitly side-step any mega-machine back to the invention of the wheel.

More typically—SF is a solemn business—the novels of the nineties often strive to accommodate themselves within 'the eschatology of the impersonal', perhaps in an attempt at domestication. The machine manifests itself as cyberspace in the popular novels of William Gibson and others. Cyberspace has become a popular buzz word, with the Internet a manifestation of its neural structure. In Tom Maddox's novel *Halo*, several characters are ingested by Aleph, a controlling artificial super-intelligence installed on an orbiting satellite.

Jerry Chapman is one such character. He asks Aleph what became of his body.

> 'It was . . . recycled. A robot tended your remains with loving grace.'
> 'So I am nowhere.'
> 'Or here. Or everywhere. As you wish.'

Here the limits of human individuality seem to extend to infinity—but within the limits of the machine.

One of the unspoken divisions in the SF field lies between those who delight in the mega-machine and those who mistrust it. Rich and acclaimed authors, the L. Ron Hubbards of this and other worlds, are generally those who subscribe to and propagate the easy belief that bigger means better, that larger is lovelier. Happily, we know how God despises wealth, since we can see the sort of people on whom he bestows it.

Well, friends, there is much in the world to lament. What tales we could all tell about our involvement with SF! Which brings us to Barry Malzberg—unafraid to say how bad he believes SF to be, unembarrassed to use SF as his wailing wall. I admire Barry (since we're speaking personally, like individuals) and also somewhat dread encounters with him. We always fear those who speak truth. Or even half-truths.

Should not Barry Malzberg rank among the great neglected on the *Science-Fiction Studies* list of martyrs? He has many books to his credit, including two books which reach right to the heart of the field—in order to stab it and himself to death. One book is a novel, *Herovit's World*, one is a collection of essays, *The Engines of the Night*. These are the books to read in order to understand something about the pains of a writer's life—not necessarily an SF writer's, or a New Yorker's, or a Jewish writer's life. Or even a writer's life.

Malzberg once took my wife and me on a literary tour of Manhattan, showing us where each incident in his novel occurred. Here's the doorway where Herovit masturbated himself. That's the window of the room where X shot himself . . . How we laughed as we drove along!

Particularly poignant is the last essay in *The Engines of the Night*, a piece called 'Corridors'.

Ruthven is an SF writer, accorded the honour of being made Guest of Honour at an SF Convention. He delivers the GoH speech. For the first thirty-two minutes of his thirty-five minute address, he sticks to the script. His anecdotes of such editors as H. L. Gold and Campbell are appreciated. There is applause when he speaks of the Apollo landings on the Moon. 'We did that', he says. 'We did that at three cents a word.'

Then Ruthven loses control and deserts his text.

'We tried [Ruthven says]. I want you to know that, that even the worst of us, the most debased hack, the one-shot writer, the fifty-book series, all the hundreds and thousands of us who ever wrote a line of this stuff for publication: we tried. We tried desperately to say something because we were the only ones who could, however halting our language, tuneless the song, it was ours.'

He rants bravely on. And then—'in hopeless and helpless fury, Ruthven pushes aside the microphone and cries'.

But I have become carried away from my main theme. One admires the music of protest, at least when played on such a fine instrument as Barry Malzberg.

I have produced about thirty anthologies of other people's stories, many of them with Harry Harrison. The most successful is the *Penguin Science Fiction Omnibus*, which began life in 1961 and has rarely been out of print since. Something of a record, I would imagine. I have written well over three hundred stories, and published several novels, maybe thirty, among them—as mentioned earlier—*Barefoot in the Head*, so kindly referred to by Lester del Rey. I would be less 'neglected' if I always wrote the same book; but that choice was made long ago.

In the seventies, Harrison and I produced a series of three anthologies, dividing up SF by decades. The third and last was *Decade: The Sixties*. It dealt with the SF of that anarchic, sublimish decade when we discovered the Present, and therefore it featured the New Wave. If there was ever a blind spot among American SF readers, and many British ones, it concerned the New Wave, even though American writers such as Norman Spinrad, John Sladek, Pamela Zoline, and Thomas Disch came to England at the time and were involved with it and with its flagship, the magazine *New Worlds*. The New Wave aroused as much hatred as if it had been a Commie plot; in reality it was only a revolution. There was even a move afoot to boycott any New York publisher who dared publish New Wave authors; the names of Sam Moskowitz and Isaac Asimov somehow became involved in this shamingly practical zoilism, which happily got nowhere. If ever there was a time to weep in the Malzberg way, it was then.

Perhaps those various people were right to be suspicious of us. It was all a bit of a snow job. We danced on the firn of old stories. Iceflows in society were breaking up. One thing uniting the loosely coherent group centring round *New Worlds* and its flamboyant editor, Michael Moorcock, was an aversion to that vast impersonal mega-machine of which Havel speaks. Nor were they alone. That aversion, and the embrace of personal fulfilment, were hallmarks of a memorable decade, the sixties.

I was writing such stories as 'Poor Little Warrior' and 'The Failed Men', and novels like *Report on Probability A*, some while before the New Wave was a ripple, yet somehow I became entangled in its coils, and was on a sinister blacklist.

However that might be, only two of Harrison's and my decades anthologies were published in the States. The third one, the sixties anthology, was turned down. Looking through my Introduction to that volume, it still seems a fair summing up in two thousand words of how we viewed the whole matter then. By far the best book on the subject is Colin Greenland's scholarly *The Entropy Exhibition: Michael Moorcock and the British 'New Wave' in science fiction* (1983). It is a key document in the history of that brief epoch.

I attempted to bring that Introduction (which follows) up-to-date, but finally considered it must stand as it was when first published in 1977.

The eighteen stories in the anthology, to which the Introduction makes reference, are:

J. G. Ballard: The Assassination of John Fitzgerald Kennedy considered as a Downhill Motor Race
Harvey Jacobs: Gravity
Kurt Vonnegut: Harrison Bergeron
Gordon R. Dickson: Computers Don't Argue
Will Worthington: The Food Goes in the Top
Mack Reynolds: Subversive
Thomas Disch: Descending
Brian Aldiss: The Village Swindler
Keith Roberts: Manscarer
Keith Laumer: Hybrid
Pamela Zoline: The Heat Death of the Universe
Roger Zelazny: Devil Car
Michael Moorcock: The Nature of the Catastrophe
Robert Silverberg: Hawksbill Station
Frederik Pohl: Day Million
Philip K. Dick: The Electric Ant
Norman Spinrad: The Last Hurrah of the Golden Horde
Kingsley Amis: Hemingway in Space

Of all these stories, it is only the Zelazny I would discard today. The Ballard, Zoline, and Pohl stories remain brilliant, and are among the best to emerge from those few brief years before the Oil Crisis of 1973—another manifestation of the world machine—when the world took another of its not infrequent turns for the worse. (More litotes!)

All the stories would get a clean bill of health under the Havel edict. None pays a subscription to the glamour of power. They are fine SF for all that.

INTRODUCTION

Suppose you want to boil yourself a perfect egg, the kind in which the white is hard and the golden centre still fluid like a medium-consistency honey. You are alone in the kitchen, there is no clock, you have lost the egg-timer, and your watch has stopped. How can you time the egg exactly?

One answer is that you could put a record of Mozart's overture to *The Marriage of Figaro* on the record-player. The overture lasts four minutes. At its conclusion, remove your egg from the pan and it will be done to perfection.

We recognize that this useful culinary tip has nothing to do with music. It is a misapplication. It is using Mozart as a utility; we are amused by the inappropriateness of the idea, or perhaps we think it is vaguely immoral.

Literature is a bit different from music, and maybe science fiction is a bit different from literature. For science fiction authors, among them some of the best known, like to claim practical applications for their fiction. Not that their fiction boils eggs—although of course there is a fortune awaiting a man who writes the story which will boil the first four-minute egg—but, less modestly, that it changes opinions, that it turns them into scientists, or even that it helps Man on his Way to the Stars.

Other authors would claim the opposite, that their fiction can have no justification unless it succeeds as fiction. This would seem to them glory enough. In imaginative literature and in poetry, the human spirit has risen to some of its greatest heights. To turn fiction into propaganda is to demean it.

The two opposed views can best be exemplified by a juxtaposition Mark Adlard made (in an article entitled 'The Other Tradition of Science Fiction') of statements by Isaac Asimov and C. S. Lewis. In a film he made about the history of magazine SF, Asimov says in essence that the SF of the 1940s (when Asimov's SF was in full spate) became the fact of the 1960s. He went on to imply that when Neil Armstrong stepped on the Moon it justified the work done by Campbell's stable of writers in *Astounding* (see *Decade 1940s*).

In *Of Other Worlds* (1966), Lewis by contrast has this to say: 'If some fatal process of applied science enables us in fact to reach the moon, that real journey will not at all satisfy the impulse which we now seek to gratify by writing such stories'.

The argument about the role of SF is highly germane to the sixties. It was a period of tremendous popular intellectual ferment, when everything was called into question. The great issues of the day found SF writers divided, whether on Vietnam, on the Space Race, on Marxism, on drugs, or on race. The question of one's life-style became crucially important; beards were political.

It was a highly political decade, starting promisingly with a glamorous president in the White House and the dandyish Macmillan in 10 Downing Street, and continuing with ominous vibrati from all over the world. The two great communist countries, China and the Soviet Union (with its luckless satellites), turned their arts from aesthetic purposes to expressions of political intention, and many people in the West were prepared to do the same thing. But there is a gulf of difference between personal belief and state-imposed belief; certainly SF authors, whose very material has of necessity economic and political implications, often forsook aesthetic goals for the causes in which they believed. The Third World lay uneasy on their consciences. In the United States, despite its racial upheavals, some people found time to wonder at the justice which permitted a small number of people to consume something like ninety per cent of the world's resources. There was reason to think of SF as ammunition in a global battle.

As change was inevitable in the world at large, so it was inevitable in the realm of SF. Each decade shows a changing pattern, although the basic arts of story-telling are perennial and less susceptible to alteration than readers may imagine. The forties was Campbell's and *Astounding*'s decade. The fifties saw the great change in taste which brought in *Galaxy* and *The Magazine of Fantasy & Science Fiction*, with emphasis on sociology and human values. The sixties re-emphasized this swing; in addition, it was the decade in which space travel and the future became less of an overriding concern.

The point needs some examination. Before the first Sputnik sailed up into the skies of the fifties, magazine SF seemed at times to have turned itself into a propaganda machine for space travel. Wernher von Braun was one of the heroes of this machine, as he laid before Congress and the general public grandiose plans for a fleet of ships to annex Mars. Yet, according to the mythology, sales of SF magazines declined with the launching of the first satellites. If this is what really happened, it justifies C. S. Lewis's dictum and provides an argument for SF as an imaginative literature, SF as reverie rather than prophecy; its proper subject is the things that may be, not the things that will be.

Many of the older SF writers held as an article of faith the belief that space travel was possible. When the possibility became actuality, a sense of *déjà vu* set in. And more than that. In the context of the times, aspirations foundered. The multi-million-dollar and -rouble programmes aimed at getting men into space contrasted gratingly with the mess they left behind on Earth. Arguments were sometimes short-sighted on either side. The 'space race' eased an emergence from the Cold War which had dominated the fifties, as well as proving a tremendous and undeniable success in its own right, a technological miracle on a scale we may not witness again for many years.

And yet . . . Had the natural aggressiveness of mankind merely stumbled on a new arena for its working-out? Commenting on man's arrival on Luna, J. G. Ballard said, 'If I were a Martian, I'd start running now'.

The tremendous process of which journeys to the Moon are part has by no means unfolded fully. And yet . . . Propaganda apart, the brilliance of the success served to emphasize to one half of the world how grandiosely the other half lived.

Disenchantment or curiosity made many writers look away from space and the future to the world about them. There was plenty to explore, from computers to over-population, from injustice to the Pill, from heart-transplants to emergent nations. The sixties was the decade in which SF discovered the Present. It is no coincidence that it was also the decade in which the general reading public discovered SF.

A few milestones are in order.

In 1961, Kingsley Amis's survey of SF, *New Maps of Hell*, was published in England. It had been condemned in some quarters; Amis wrote lightly and amusingly about a subject on which he felt deeply, and some people understand only the ponderous. But *New Maps* remains a shrewd, reliable guide to what it's all about, and certainly paved the way to more general acceptance of the genre. Amis emphasizes the satiric aspects of SF at the expense of the fantastic side; there he was merely being prophetic. As this antho-logy shows, the decade following his book relied heavily on forms of satire—including satires on prose styles.

Within forty-eight hours of the death of President Kennedy in 1963, two writers died whose names, for all their other achieve-ments, are still closely associated with the upper pastures of the science fiction field: Aldous Huxley and C. S. Lewis. Huxley's *Brave New World* (1932) has long ranked as SF; so does the neglected but equally penetrating *Ape and Essence* (1948); while his last novel, *Island* (1962), is a remarkable utopian novel which repays careful attention. Lewis, a connoisseur of romances and science fiction, wrote the beautiful trilogy which begins with *Out of the Silent Planet* (1938).

In 1965, Professor J. R. R. Tolkien's great trilogy *The Lord of the Rings* was published in paperback; it went on to become the cult book of the sixties. While not in itself SF,[2] its enormous success has directed attention towards the enchantments of alternate worlds to ours. During a period when SF was expanding and becoming increasingly departmentalized, the Tolkien syndrome encouraged alternate-worldery, so that alternate worlds have increasingly become a part of SF. Other cult books included Frank Herbert's *Dune*, which began life as a serial in *Analog* and won the first Nebula Award for the best novel of 1965, and Robert Heinlein's *Stranger in a Strange Land* (Hugo award-winner 1962), a campus favourite for some years. Other award-winners of the decade included Daniel Keyes' *Flowers for Algernon* (Nebula, 1966), Samuel Delany's *The Einstein Intersection* (Nebula, 1967), Ursula Le Guin's *The Left Hand of Darkness* (Nebula, 1969), Walter Miller's *A Canticle for Leibowitz* (Hugo, 1961), Philip K. Dick's *The Man in the High Castle* (Hugo, 1963), Fritz Leiber's *The Wanderer* (Hugo, 1965), Roger Zelazny's *Lord of Light* (Hugo, 1968) and John Brunner's *Stand on Zanzibar* (Hugo, 1969).

One interesting thing about this list is that few of the award-winners can be classified as adventure or action novels. Their equivalents only a decade earlier would have been so classifiable. After all, magazine SF largely grew out of men's adventure fiction. In the sixties, a more meditative mood set in.

Another milestone of the decade was the Stanley Kubrick-Arthur C. Clarke film, *2001: a space odyssey*, which had its European première in May 1968. Significantly, it is cast as an adventure, but it concludes with a psychedelic trip followed by meditation.

Another comparatively new feature of SF was that it began to stand outside itself and look at itself. 'Heat Death of the Universe' (included here) is not so much traditional SF as a story which takes SF for granted and uses its vocabulary. Among the great successes of the decade are two novels by my collaborator on this series, Harry Harrison. Both his *Bill, the Galactic Hero* and *The Technicolor Time Machine* make ingenious fun of all the clichés of the genre—the former with particular reference to the novels of Heinlein and Asimov.

It was hardly to be expected that changes which infiltrated every facet of life should not have their effect on the way the writers wrote

---

2 Although the jacket of the first hardcover edition in 1954 quoted the perceptive Naomi Mitchison as saying, 'It's really super science fiction'.

as well as what they wrote about. The mood became dispassionate, hard-hearted at least on the surface. To be 'cool' was the height of fashion.

In the mid-sixties, London was the height of fashion. For a few years—which now seems as remote as the Ming Dynasty—London was the place where culture lived and thrived as it had done in Paris in the twenties. An electricity was generated. We all felt it. The time and the place acquired a label which was instantly mocked: Swinging London. But the phenomenon needed a label, however absurd.

Behind the ballyhoo, the hippies, the Flower Power, and the youth cult, many dark things lurked. Writers have always been abnormally aware of dark things. They did not forget them as they made hay with the rest while the sun shone.

This go-where-you-please, do-your-own-thing, turn-on-freak-out mood found particular embodiment in the pages of a British SF magazine, *New Worlds*.

New Worlds was the oldest-established British magazine. Under its editor E. J. Carnell it had achieved regular publication and modest success but, as the sixties dawned, its sales were dwindling and illness afflicted the dedicated Ted Carnell. Also, it must be said, its formula was growing somewhat threadbare. Although most of its fiction was by British writers, many of them copied American models of some vintage and assumed a Transatlantic tone of voice. Not infrequently, the stories were rejects from the more profitable American market.

It seemed as if only a miracle could save *New Worlds* and its companion *Science Fantasy*, also edited the Carnell. He handed over editorships to Michael Moorcock and Kyril Bonfiglioli respectively. Moorcock had already made a name for himself as a writer of fantasy and his hero Elric was well established, although not taken too seriously (least of all by the genial Moorcock himself). Kyril Bonfiglioli was a hitherto semi-respectable antiquarian-book- and art-dealer and *bon viveur* residing in Oxford.

Bonfiglioli was an important influence in the life of several new authors, among them Johnny Byrne, who went on to write *Groupie* with Jenny Fabian (a real sixties-flavour book) and to work on the TV series *Space 1999*; Thom Keyes, who went on to write *One Night Stand*, which was filmed; and Keith Roberts, who became editor of *Science Fantasy* when Bonfiglioli changed the name to *SF Impulse*, and did much of the excellent artwork as well as contributing stories. The best known of these stories were those which formed the novel

Pavanne; in that book and others since, Roberts has shown himself master of the alternate-world story, pitching his tone deliberately in a minor key. He is represented here by 'Manscarer', a story of artists in an over-populated world, which was first published in *New Writings in Science Fiction*, the paperback magazine started by Carnell when he left *New Worlds*; *NW in SF* still continues, with even greater success, edited by Kenneth Bulmer who, like Carnell before him, has shown himself generous, reliable and discerning.

SF Impulse faded out, but *New Worlds* went from strength to strength. Aided by a dedicated editorial team, including such lively men as Charles Platt, Mike Moorcock kicked out the old gang and installed the new. Galactic wars went out; drugs came in; there were fewer encounters with aliens, more in the bedroom. Experimentation in prose styles became one of the orders of the day, and the baleful influence of William Burroughs often threatened to gain the upper hand.

The revolution was inevitable. The bathwater had become so stale that it was scarcely to be avoided if the baby sometimes went out with it. When an Arts Council grant was secured for *New Worlds* and it became glossy and filled with illustrations, it was the only SF magazine in the mid-sixties which looked as if it belonged to the mid-sixties. All the others seemed like fossils. Life was where *New Worlds* was.

Of course, individual issues were often disappointing. But the ritual of a magazine, its layout, its expectations, its continuity, its hazardous pact with readers and authors, elevates it to a sort of protolanguage which speaks as strongly as its actual fiction content. The ritual suggested that the future had arrived with a flutter of colour supplements and mini-skirts and was securely nailed to *New Worlds'* editorial desk. The rather twitchy hedonism of *New Worlds* had no need to look ahead, and the galaxy began in Ladbroke Grove.

In the decidedly more sombre mood of the seventies, all this may sound silly. Naturally, it was easy to hate *New Worlds*, which often opted for trendiness rather than depth—though trendiness in those days was almost a philosophy in itself. But the feeling that the future has happened is not as perverse as it seems. Our Western culture has in many ways fulfilled the targets established in the early Renaissance: to take control of our world through observation and understanding and application. Enormous benefits have accrued to us. The life of the average man in the West, as regards both his physical and his mental horizons, has been much enhanced by the impetus of that aspiration. Now the bills for our astonishing performance, centuries long, are coming in. We see that progress and pollution, medical discoveries and over-population, technical development and nuclear escalation, improved communications and terrorism, social care and public apathy are sides of the same coin. Further advances are increasingly hard-won; moreover, the Oil Crisis in the early seventies rang like a tocsin through the West, reminding its citizens that the hour grew late and Toynbee's Civilization Number Twenty-Two was losing autonomy. Our alternatives grow fewer. *New Worlds* was the first SF magazine in the world to abandon the idea that technological progress could be extrapolated for ever; as such, it may be honoured for having been truly prodromic.

Hardly surprising, then, that it often radiated a hard shiny surface of scepticism, the cool of slight desperation. Boiling eggs to Mozart—the whole comedy of misapplication—was *New Worlds'* thing. The dominant figure here was J. G. Ballard, with his postlapsarian guilts and a genuine power to embody the landscapes of subtopia in skeletal fiction. It is possible that *New Worlds* ultimately damaged Ballard's development by overlauding the sadistic side of his work; but he is and remains a genuine original and an acute observer. Ballard threw away the old pack of cards. His new ones may not be to everyone's taste, but they are his own. He has the courage of his convictions, and his best stories remain the best. If he often seems to use other authors as models—Jarry, as in the piece we anthologize here, Kafka, Greene, Conrad, Burroughs—the benefit of a post-Renaissance period is that we are heirs to all styles, and Ballard moulds each to his own purpose.

Moorcock rightly seized upon Ballard, but also forged his own fictional hero, Jerry Cornelius. Cornelius is in fact neither hero nor anti-hero, but a sort of myth of the times. He can be male or female, white or black. Moorcock encouraged this ambiguous aspect by persuading other writers to chronicle the adventures of Cornelius; included here is Norman Spinrad's Jerry, in the typically cool and comic account of the 'The Last Hurrah of the Golden Horde'.

Spinrad was one of a number of American writers who found the English cultural climate more congenial than the American one. His chief contribution to *New Worlds* was *Bug Jack Barron*, serialized at inordinate length; its use of four-letter words, together with a modicum of sexual intercourse, oral sex and other pleasures, led to a banning of *New Worlds* by W. H. Smith and the denunciation of Spinrad in Parliament as a degenerate—the sort of accolade most writers long for. *Barron* is a powerful novel about the role of television and government, powerfully over-written.

Among other expatriates who drifted through was Thomas M. Disch, a distinguished writer whose stories move easily between being flesh, fowl, and good red herring. Disch's greatest contribution to *New Worlds* was the novel *Camp Concentration*. A friend of his, John Sladek, settled in London, and has become one of SF's leading comedians and parodists. Pamela Zoline, primarily an artist, also came over and settled here; we reprint her fine story 'Heat Death of the Universe'.

Among the English authors encouraged by Moorcock were Langdon Jones, Hilary Bailey, David Masson, Robert Holdstock and Ian Watson. Moorcock has gone on to greater things and is a legend in his own time. With the maverick *New Worlds*, he brought British SF kicking and screaming into the twentieth century.

News of the English revolution percolated back to the United States, where it had imitators who seem mainly to have thought the issue rested on writing as wildly and fuzzily as possible. But the times they were a-changing rapidly in the States as elsewhere, and many authors emerged with genuine fresh approaches to experience. One of them was Harvey Jacobs. Comic writers are always welcome in a field which frequently inclines to the ponderous; but Jacobs found he was most welcome by Mike Moorcock. Among the other new names were Will Worthington, who showed, like Disch, some kinship with the Theatre of the Absurd; he came and went all too fast, but shall be remembered here by his excellent story, first published by Ted Carnell, 'The Food Goes in the Top'.

Roger Zelazny came and stayed. A genuine baroque talent, often too much in love with the esoteric, but shining forth clearly here with 'Devil Car'. His story is a persuasive embodiment of the sixties' passion for the automobile.

Keith Laumer rose to great popularity in the sixties, when his name was associated with Retief, his hero whose military adventures had a satiric edge. He is represented here by 'Hybrid', a good safe space story of the kind *New Worlds* ceased to print.

The other authors include Kurt Vonnegut, Jr, Gordon R. Dickson, Philip K. Dick, Frederik Pohl, Robert Silverberg and Mack Reynolds—distinguished names all, and old hands at SF. All manifest the spirit of the sixties in one form or another—Reynolds in his enquiry into capitalist economics, Vonnegut in his satire on equality, Pohl in his sparky creation of Day Million, Dickson in his preoccupation with

the blindness of computers. Silverberg re-creates the past, the far
past. Dick does his own thing on the Dickian subject of reality.
Reality trembled in the sixties. As many of us discovered, when
things settled back into place again and the music died, life ceased to
be quite so much fun.

B.W.A.

BETWEEN PRIVY
AND UNIVERSE
Aldous Huxley (1894–1963)

> The ambition of the literary artist is to speak about the ineffable, to communicate in words what words were never intended to convey . . . In spite of 'all the pens that ever poets held'—yes, and in spite of all the scientists' electron microscopes, cyclotrons, and computers—the rest is silence, the rest is always silence.

Thus claimed Aldous Huxley, in a small book entitled *Literature and Science*, published in the year he died, 1963. The silence needed many millions of words in explanation. Even on his death-bed, Huxley was busy explaining Shakespeare, 'a human being who could do practically anything'. In *Literature and Science*, he is busy making connections, and in this case entering the debate between Snow and Leavis on 'The Two Cultures'. As ever, Huxley builds bridges. 'The precondition', he tells us, 'of any fruitful relationship between literature and science is knowledge.'

Which is all very well, but few of us set out in life with such cultural advantages as Huxley. He was the grandson on his father's side of the great Thomas Henry Huxley, while his mother was the grand-daughter of Dr Arnold of Rugby, niece of Matthew Arnold, and sister to Mrs Humphrey Ward, the novelist. Aldous grew up in a house full of books and the intelligent conversations which spring from (and into) books: where knowledge is as routine as good meals.

This privileged English existence, with its Eton and Balliol background, was to end on the coast of California, fading out in gurudom, on an LSD injection. The pop group 'The Doors' named themselves after Huxley's short work, *The Doors of Perception*, advocating use of mescalin.

Here lie mysterious connections between the world of experience

and the world of conjecture and speculation. Huxley took his title—
he was always brilliant at fishing for titles—from William Blake:

> If the doors of perception were cleansed,
> everything will appear to man as it is, infinite.

Yet in the text, he makes reference to a different kind of writer,
when speaking of our longing to transcend ourselves: 'Art and
religion, carnivals and saturnalia, dancing and listening to oratory—
all these have served, in H. G. Wells's phrase, as Doors in the Wall.'
The reference is to one of Wells's most poignant short stories. So, via
the pop group, the expression passed into popular life, and into the
drug culture of the sixties.

Alas, behind the doors of Haight-Ashbury, the broken dreams and
dead babies piled up. Even the Flower Children were only human.
Transcendence is hard work, as Huxley himself was aware. He says,
'To be enlightened is to be aware, always, of total reality in its
immanent otherness—to be aware of it and yet to remain in a
condition to survive as an animal, to think and feel as a human being,
to resort whenever expedient to systematic reasoning.'

Behind this modest but complex statement, compassionate yet
uncompromising, lies an extraordinary trajectory of a twentieth-
century life, the long trek from Eton to the Mojave, prompted in part
by that fearless curiosity which Christopher Isherwood called 'one of
Aldous's noblest characteristics'.

Curiosity spells diversity. The diversity of Huxley's life is echoed in
his writings. These engage readers of many kinds, since even the
novels, for which he was most renowned, touch upon religion,
science, politics, literature, art, music, psychology, utopianism,
and—to use the title of one of his most remarkable books—the
human situation. Through them all flow Huxley's wit and his adroit
use of language. Huxley's early distaste for bodily functions, in his
Bright Young Thing phase, develops into a passion for mysticism.
Henry Wimbush's comic discourse on sixteenth-century privies in
Crome Yellow ('the necessities of nature are so base and brutish that in
obeying them we are apt to forget that we are the noblest creatures of
the universe') later becomes a preoccupation with enlightenment,
and with the hazardous position between privy and universe which
we occupy.

Thousands of individuals have had their spirit of enquiry shar-
pened by Huxley's cultured tour of 'the ineffable'.

His preoccupation took many forms. Advice on how to see, for instance, in Huxley's little valuable book, *The Art of Seeing*, in which one notes a typical observation concerning the eye: 'its peculiarly intimate relationship with the psyche' . . . For Huxley, all things connected.

Concern with quality of life, and with any new thing which might conceivably alleviate the human condition, pointed a way to the future, from hydroponics to Scientology. Like a true Californian, Huxley embraced many crank cults in his time. (In her biography of Huxley, Sybille Bedford relates how L. Ron Hubbard and his wife, 'stiff and polite', went to dinner with the Huxleys. They presented the Huxleys with two pounds of chocolates.) So—discounting the marvellous cruel joke of *After Many a Summer*, with its speculations on evolutionary longevity—Huxley's three utopian novels appear.

None was received with great understanding by a literary world partial to country houses, stories of the wealthy, large doses of characterization, and even larger doses of nostalgia. Such is the fate of novels of ideas, at least in England.

The utopian trilogy consists of *Ape and Essence*, reviled on its appearance in 1946, perhaps because Huxley does not treat the human species with the respect it believes it deserves; *Island*, his last novel (1963); and *Brave New World* (1932), Huxley's most famous work. Huxley was a connoisseur, some might say victim, of unconventional ideas. *Brave New World* shows us what happens when mass production is applied to biology. Promiscuous sex helps preserve immaturity; immaturity reinforces superficiality. 'When the individual feels, the community reels.' Drugs keep everyone happy. The workers get four half-gramme tablets of soma every day after work. It can readily be seen why thousands have longed to live in such a utopia, from which Huxley himself would have recoiled, at least in part. The privy may not be abolished, but at least the universe is obscured.

In *Ape and Essence*, the theme of sexual promiscuity is reintroduced. Nuclear bombs have fallen on LA. What remains of mankind has reverted to savagery. Womankind has reverted, ape-like, to oestrus. For religion, a kind of perverted bogomilism is practised. The Narrator (the novel takes the form of a film script) says, 'Thanks to the supreme Triumph of Modern Science, sex has become seasonal, romance has been swallowed up by the oestrus, and the female's chemical compulsion to mate has abolished courtship, chivalry, tenderness, love itself'.

In this respect, *Ape and Essence* is an extension of the evolutionary idea, so splendidly defended by T. H., Aldous Huxley's grandfather, parodied in *After Many a Summer*. There, down in the cellarage of his castle, the Fifth Earl enjoys near immortality, coupling perpetually with his housekeeper. But the foetal ape has had time to mature. The universe has disappeared; only the privy remains . . .

The two creatures coupling in the ancestral dark are literary cousins to the orgiastes presided over by the Arch-Vicar of Belial, Lord of the Earth, and Bishop of Hollywood, who presides over the post-war dystopia.

The codified society of *Brave New World* was the work of Mr Mond. In *Ape*, the ruined post-war world is the work of Belial. It's an emetic work, perhaps, but I persist in seeing both books as slyly sardonic, like *Gulliver's Travels*. If they are science fiction, they are Huxley's brand, not H. G. Wells's.

Huxley plays Jung to Wells's Freud. Huxley saw an escape from the human situation through mysticism, not politics; politics was Wells's thing, when, later in life, his closed mind produced the Open Conspiracy. So the least (but lengthiest) of Huxley's three utopias, *Island* reverses many of the assumptions of *Brave New World*. It shows a threatened utopia where soma and sexual freedom bring about genuine happiness. Alas, as Milton's *Paradise Regained* is less readable than its noble predecessor, *Paradise Lost*, so *Island* is less readable than its two mischievous predecessors. The devil—and Huxley knew it well—has all the best tunes. Mysticism and soil conservation challenge any novelist's repertoire.

If *Island* is a failure, it is nevertheless worth reading for the instruction it gives—which not all can follow—and for its courage. Huxley must have known when he was writing *Island* that he had to lay aside one of his best weapons, the blade of satire, to write about what he conceived of as the most desirable place. Philip Toynbee perceived as much when he reviewed the book in *The Observer* on Sunday, 1 April 1962. While admiring *Island* as 'an act of genuine virtue and love', Toynbee points out that the islanders address each other in preposterous language, and that much of the book belongs to what he calls 'the helpless language of inarticulate mysticism'.

To this charge, Huxley had earlier given answer. In *Grey Eminence*, he speaks of a book, widely available in England even a generation ago, which was written by a fourteenth-century mystic, and entitled, *The Cloud of Unknowing*. Commenting on *The Cloud*, Huxley says:

Ultimate reality is incommensurable with our own illusoriness and imperfection; therefore it cannot be understood by means of intellectual operations; for intellectual operations depend upon language, and our vocabulary and syntax were evolved for the purpose of dealing precisely with that imperfection and illusoriness, with which God is incommensurable. Ultimate reality cannot be understood except intuitively, through an act of the will and the affections.

And that is what *Island* is: Huxley's act of the will and the affections, to reach out beyond the privy to embrace the universe.

Unlike most utopias, *Island* is not about governance, but about Being. Whereas Wells came to believe that a group of good men and true could reorganize the whole world, Huxley mistrusted governments. 'Society', he said, 'can never be greatly improved, until such time as most of its members choose to become theocentric saints.'

This remark comes in *Grey Eminence* (1941), one of his most absorbing books, where his gifts are deployed in a study of Father Joseph, a Capuchin monk who became adviser to Cardinal Richelieu. Between them, Father Joseph and Richelieu prolonged the Thirty Years War, causing millions of deaths by torture, famine, disease and the usual appurtenances of war, including cannibalism. The Capuchin Father Joseph eschews the simian diversions beloved by the Fifth Earl, but falls into a different trap. Politics betrays the nationalistic religion, and vice versa.

The best of Huxley is scattered everywhere, perhaps most thickly in collections of essays; of the essay form he is one of this century's masters. *Adonis and the Alphabet* (1956) is a perfect example. The erudition, never obtrusive, carries us from psycho-industrial power, dirt and spirituality, and population pressures, to Martian language and literature . . . and much else besides.

The Human Situation (1978) gathers together a series of lectures delivered at the University of California, Santa Barbara, in 1959. They provide learned and unpompous summaries of Huxley's thinking on many subjects, answering such questions as, 'How should we be related to the planet on which we live? How are we to develop our individual potentialities?' No better handbook to our ongoing civilization could be devised.

In one of those essays, the one on 'Man and Religion', Huxley states that, because mysticism does not commit one to any cut-and-dried statement about the structure of the universe, there is no conflict between a mystical approach to religion and science. Nevertheless, it is noticeable that such gurus as Gurdjieff and Ouspensky commit themselves to wacko versions of the world. Ouspensky seemed to believe that the periodic table was somehow related to notes in music. Low man in the guru totem pole, Hubbard believed in vast intergalactic battles. Yet the universe as revealed by current science is wacko enough for most mortals.

However, Huxley also says that there is a sense in which it is no great matter whether myths are true or not: they are simply expressive of our reactions to the mystery of the world in which we live.

Huxley's personal myth was of this mystical union of something that existed beyond words. It produced his difficult, dedicated work, *The Perennial Philosophy* (1946). The possible connection of this myth with the death of his much-loved mother when he was fourteen is a matter for speculation, though it is scarcely to be imagined that such a traumatic event left no shockwave.

Huxley faded away on Friday 22 November 1963, with LSD in his veins. Within twenty-four hours, another wise man, another writer of SF who had lost his mother in childhood, C. S. Lewis, would also be dead. But it was Huxley who died on the day John F. Kennedy was assassinated.

Huxley's continuing influence was summed up by Isaiah Berlin, who said, 'He was the herald of what will surely be one of the great advances in this and following centuries—the creation of new psycho-physical sciences, of discoveries in the realm of what at present, for want of a better term, we call the relations between body and mind.'

Almost everything Aldous Huxley wrote was adversely criticized at one time or another. Everyone spoke well of the man himself, of his nobility and charm. His gentleness, sweetness and humour were remarked on by all those fortunate enough to know him.

Anita Loos, author of *Gentlemen Prefer Blondes*, was a personal friend. She has the last word. 'I shall always think of Aldous as smiling.'

THE IMMANENT WILL
RETURNS—2

〜〜〜〜〜〜〜〜〜〜〜〜〜〜〜〜〜〜〜〜〜〜〜〜〜〜〜〜〜〜〜〜〜

'What of the Immanent Will and its designs?', asks Thomas Hardy. The question forms the opening line of Hardy's vast drama, *The Dynasts*, and is answered by that phantom intelligence, the Spirit of the Years:

> It works unconsciously, as heretofore,
> Eternal artistries in Circumstance,
> Whose patterns, wrought by rapt aesthetic rote,
> Seem in themselves its single listless aim,
> And not their consequence.

To which the Spirit of the Pities joins, saying,

> Still thus? Still thus?
> Ever unconscious!

It is clear that the Immanent Will is a prototype of Philip K. Dick's VALIS, that Vast Active Live Intelligence System. Thinking the matter over after the carnage of the First World War, Hardy decided that he had erred on the optimistic side—thereby leaving the door open for Olaf Stapledon.

Stapledon sweeps away the human characters in whom Hardy delighted, to present us with a threadbare stage upon which humanity is all but lost. On that stage are unfolded the evolutionary histories of the Last Men and the soliloquies of the Star Maker.

Those two great dramas of Stapledon's, *Last and First Men* and *Star Maker*, were written over fifty years ago, in 1930 and 1937. They loom above the later oceans of science fiction like the immense rocks in Böcklin's painting, 'The Isle of the Dead', appearing and disappearing in the mist. That Stapledon, an Englishman, has not himself taken permanent sojourn on Böcklin's grim island is entirely due to the work of American scholars. *The Oxford Companion to English Literature* allows him no entry to himself.

In fact, Stapledon is a writer of a notably English kind, his attempts to establish an individual mythology somewhat reminiscent of William Blake (the sub-title of his novel, *Odd John* echoes a poem of Blake's, 'A Story Between Jest and Earnest'—though there's precious little enjoying of the lady in the book). His grandiosities recall Charles M. Doughty's six-volume epic poem, *Dawn in Britain*, with its quixotic attempt to restore Chaucer to modern English. Two other voices echo conflictingly through Stapledon's fiction, the voice of John Milton in *Paradise Lost* and the voice of that Victorian storm-trooper, Winwood Reade, author of *The Martyrdom of Man*.

In many respects, Stapledon is of his time. Born in 1886, he was torn by religious doubt, like many men of his day. Essentially a Victorian, he had trouble fitting into the post-war world. Together with many others, he flirted with pacifism, communism and promiscuity. And being outside the swim of London literary society, he knew few other authors and soon became critically disregarded.

The central premise of his work, that mankind is irrelevant to the purposes of the universe, proves unpalatable to many. His admirers honour him precisely for that unpalatability, so variously, so swoopingly expressed. We encounter in his work faith versus atheism, and the seeking for individual fulfilment versus communality, whether terrestrial or stellar. These remain painfully contemporary concerns. In his two great glacial novels, spanning the thirties, we encounter spiritual suffering and the surreal mutations which mankind must undergo at a Creator's command.

My first encounter with *Last and First Men* came at a time of suffering and mutation. I was part of the British Second Division, fighting back the Japanese Army which had invaded Burma and Assam and was planning to storm the gates of India. I was nineteen, brown as a berry, on half rations. We were about to advance on enemy-held Mandalay while shooting DDT down our pants and under our arms. Specifically, I was standing in a commandeered bungalow in the jungle outside Kohima, awaiting a typhus injection.

The medical officer had established his temporary HQ in the home of a tea planter who had fled—to India or England. In the room where I awaited my jab were book-lined shelves. Among the books were two blue Pelican books, together comprising a paperback edition of *Last and First Men*. The title caught my eye. I took them down and began to read.

I could not leave them behind when I was summoned to the surgery. I kept them. For the first and last time, I stole a book. Well, it was wartime . . .

While the great salvation and destruction of the sunlit world went forward, Stapledon's steady voice proved to be what was needed. In particular, his daring time-schemes appeased an urgent desire for perspective.

What sustained me then, as we advanced across the Burmese plains, was the bleak vision of humankind locked within the imperatives of creation. If Stapledon's name is to be preserved, it will be by science fiction readers. Quite apart from the intrinsic interest in his writing, there is also the wider question: why is not SF, or work which closely resembles SF, accepted into the general corpus of the century's literature? The writing is excellent; the subject under discussion is a central one; the author was not exactly a backwoodsman; nor did he write in obscure tongue; so how is it that he suffers a general neglect? Why is he not considered as is, say, Jorge Luis Borges or Mikhail Bulgakov or even William Burroughs?

These are perforce rhetorical questions. I cannot answer them. Nor, as far as I can see, can anyone else. *De gustibus non est disputandum.* And yet . . . we must continue to dispute . . .

I was instrumental in having Penguin Books reprint *Last and First Men* in 1963. The edition contains my Foreword, and was reprinted more than once. Harvey Satty, the active chairman of the Olaf Stapledon Society, published *Nebula Maker* in 1976, an interesting early attempt of Stapledon's to write *Star Maker*. Later, Satty, in collaboration with Curtis C. Smith, produced a comprehensive bibliography (1984). The volume contains an essay by Stapledon never before published. In 1982 came Patrick A. McCarthy's *Olaf Stapledon* from Twayne Publishers. This slender volume presents excellent summaries of Stapledon's novels. McCarthy collaborated with Charles Elkins and Martin Harry Greenberg to produce *The Legacy of Olaf Stapledon* in 1989.

In 1987, the Los Angeles publisher, James Tarcher, published an edition of *Star Maker* with my introduction and, in the following year, *Last and First Men*, with a Foreword by Gregory Benford and an Afterword by Doris Lessing. This is claimed to be the first complete edition of the novel to be published in the USA. In fact, Dover Books had published the complete text in 1968.

A curious player in the Stapledon game is the celebrated critic, Leslie A. Fiedler. Fiedler's *Olaf Stapledon: A Man Divided* was published in 1983.[1] Fiedler had shown interest in Stapledon some years previously. When Harry Harrison and I were editing a series of hardcover and paperback reprints of classic SF in the 1970s (SF Master Series), Harry persuaded Professor Fiedler to write an introduction to *Odd John*.[2] An excellent introduction it is too. The longer critical work is of more dubious value.

The authority on Stapledon is undoubtedly Dr Robert Crossley. Again an American weighs in to great effect. Crossley has a better grasp of British weirdness than Fiedler; he is familiar, for instance, with the deadly English habit of litotes; as witness his exemplary editing of *Talking Across the World: The Love Letters of Olaf Stapledon and Agnes Miller, 1913–1919*.[3] These gentle, humorous letters of courtship during a terrible war are touching and beautiful. They carry us closer than anything else to the private man, and far beyond the world of science fiction, though they are not without speculative content.

Crossley follows up with his massive biography, *Speaking for the Future: The Life of Olaf Stapledon*.[4] This will always remain the standard life.

The new biography brings out well Stapledon's sense of division within himself, manifest in his fiction. Even the august *Star Maker*— the very emblem of Stapledon's cogitations—is given, like the god Shiva, a dual nature, both mild and terrible. The opening sentence of *Last and First Men* makes the division clear: 'This book has two authors'.

Other examples of this division are not far to seek. The title of Stapledon's last book, clearly autobiographical in nature, and published only months before his death in 1950, is *A Man Divided*. In 'The Peak and the Town', the posthumously published essay included in the 1989 book mentioned above, one of the characters speaks of 'the double life' as 'a marvellous duplicity'. This submerged quality— Mary Shelley speaks poignantly of it too—manifests itself in the first of the letters Crossley preserves in *Talking Across the World*. In a letter declaring his love to the distant Agnes in Australia, Stapledon says, 'I fear lest you might in answering say there is no hope at all, and if you

1 New York, Oxford University Press.
2 London, Eyre Methuen, 1978.
3 Hanover, NH, University Press of New England, 1987.
4 Syracuse, NY, Syracuse University Press and Liverpool, Liverpool University Press, 1994.

were to say that I should only outwardly accept it, and inwardly go on hoping and acting as if there was a chance . . .'

Stapledon served as an ambulance driver in the First World War. For his courage he was awarded the Croix de Guerre. In that serving capacity, he observed the divided nature of his fellows, remorseless in enmity, at other times compassionate to friend and foe alike.

Mathew Arnold has a splendid poem, 'The Buried Life', in which he says how

> There rises an unspeakable desire
> After the knowledge of our buried life

This element in Stapledon drove him to extend the boundaries of conventional human sensibility.

Stapledon was in his fifties when *Star Maker* was published. So let's finally talk about this masterwork.

It is the most wonderful book I have ever read, while its central premise is the most difficult to accept. *Star Maker* is grander in theme than *Last and First Men*, more felicitous in style, and subtler in approach. And more overwhelming in its imaginative power.

It's not an abstract book. Rather, it's chock-a-block with great common agonies and private lonelinesses—often the lonelinesses of entire solar communities. Madness, that kith and kin of loneliness, is often present in Stapledon's mind. The intellect is threatened by the prospect of endless galaxies formed—for what?

> As we searched up and down time and space, discovering more and more of the rare grains called planets, we watched race after race struggle to a certain degree of lucid conscious- ness, only to succumb to some external accident or, more often, to some flaw in its own nature, we were increasingly oppressed by a sense of the futility, of the planlessness of the cosmos.

The sombre mood owes much to the pessimism of Schopenhauer. The conviction that God was dead is characteristic of the thinkers of the late nineteenth century. But we cannot call it unearned: this was a man who had been through the carnage of the Somme.

Pessimism unrelieved is not much to anyone's taste. The pessim- ism of artists is a different matter. We drink down the pessimism of Swift's *Gulliver's Travels* because of his and our delight in artifice. Stapledon is short on dialogue, but he keeps us reading by the prodigality of his imaginings, expressed in delicate imagery.

In one section of Chapter X, the journeying human soul, together with its spirit friends, observes the galaxy at an early stage of its existence. The passage concludes with an overview of the fully evolved galaxy:

> The stars themselves gave an irresistible impression of vitality. Strange that the movements of these merely physical things, these mere fireballs, whirling and travelling according to the geometrical laws of their minutest particles, should seem so vital, so questing. But then the whole galaxy was itself so vital, so like an organism, with its delicate tracery of star-streams, like the streams within a living cell; and its extended wreaths, almost like feelers; and its nucleus of light. Surely this great and lively creature must be alive, must have intelligent experience of itself and of things other than it.

And then follows one of those rapid contradictions which endow the narrative with its tensile strength and astonishment:

> In the tide of these wild thoughts we checked our fancy, remembering that only on the rare grains called planets can life gain foothold, and all this wealth of restless jewels was but a waste of fire.

Under the cool tone is an almost animist belief in conscious life everywhere, a marked Stapledon characteristic. One of his last fantasies, *The Flames*, postulates a madman's vision of fire with intellect.

Any similarity between Stapledon's sweep of cosmic events and conventional SF is coincidental. After discoursing with the minds of the nebulae, his questing spirit moves on to achieve a discussion with the Immanent Will, the Star Maker itself. The finely sustained climax of the book is the Maker's description of the series of universes with which he is experimenting, of which ours is but one in an almost infinite series. Where does one look in all English prose for an equivalent of the magnificent Chapter XV?

For here Stapledon describes a succession of flawed cosmoses, each one of greater complexity, yet each one in turn failing to satisfy its creator—who stows them away like old computer games on a shelf, their interest exhausted.

Our own cosmos is about to be shelved. The Star Maker resolves that the succeeding cosmos will be better. The beings who inhabit it will be 'far less deceived by the opacity of their individual mental processes, and more sensitive to their underlying unity'. One thing in particular in this sharply agnostic cogitation sets it apart from Christian doctrine: the ruthlessness of the Star Maker. The point is made more than once. 'Here was no pity, no proffer of salvation, no kindly aid. Or here were all pity and all love, but mastered by a frosty ecstasy.' And again. 'All passions it seemed, were comprised within the spirit's temper; but mastered, icily gripped within the cold, clear, crystal ecstasy of contemplation.'

No hope here, as with Hardy's Immanent Will, that 'The rages of the ages Will be cancelled' . . . We're getting cancelled—we and the whole caboodle.

It is this central perception, this refusal to compromise, this icicle in the heart, which makes Stapledon. C. S. Lewis, a charismatic Christian apologist (and author of memorable science fiction), rejected this viewpoint, which he regarded as shallowly scientistic. He pilloried Stapledon as the evil scientist, Weston, in *Out of the Silent Planet* and *Perelandra*. Stapledon never rose to the bait.

C. S. Lewis was a revered acquaintance of mine. But in this matter I must agree with Olaf Stapledon. It's cold outside.

So we have the curious situation. Stapledon's grand theme was communication. Communication between woman and super-beast, as in *Sirius*, between alien and human, between organic and inorganic, between soul and its creator, even between England and Australia. Yet we have to admit that—the world being what it is—he has largely failed to communicate. Not with the general public. Hardly with his fellow authors. And pretty rarely even with SF fans . . .

A WHOLE NEW CAN
OF WORMS

~~~~~~

Philip Dick made me happy. I loved and still love his novels. Why be made happy over novels which show all too plainly how awful the state of the world is? Because they did just that, without flinching, without having soft centres and sloppy endings. And because of the way they were written—with a unique tang.

Cowardly critics have sometimes found my novels gloomy, but I never managed as much sheer silent disaster as Dick. He should have had a Nobel prize.

When Dick died, we held a memorial meeting for him in London. It was a heat-wave time, with temperatures in the nineties. The dogs were crawling into dustbins to die. Nevertheless, the faithful turned up at the old City Lit rooms and crammed into the theatre. Even the molecules jostled each other.

I was one of the three speakers from the platform.

Here's what I said. And I hope you're still listening, Phil.

We're here tonight to rejoice. There is no reason to mourn—well, not too much. Bucket-kicking is endemic in the human race. Have you ever considered that it may be all of us who have gone, whisked into some terrible schizoid version of the present ruled over by Brezhnev, Mrs Thatcher, Pope John Paul, and the Argentinian junta, while Phil Dick remains where he ever was, in Santa Ana, still jovially fighting entropy and kipple with a new, eighth, wife by his side?

We rejoice because Dick is one of the few writers to defy the First Law of SF Thermodynamics. This law states that exploitation in the SF field is so great that the writers decay as they age instead of maturing, like bad wine, and that meaningfulness decreases in inverse proportion to number of words published.

Like all good SF writers, Dick was continually trying to figure out what made the universe tick. Even if there is a way to figure out the universe, it probably can't be done through SF, which forever throws in its own 'what ifs' to flavour the recipe. Figuring out the universe needs long scientific training, the mind of a genius, and years of zen silence; three qualities antithetical to all SF buffs. Nevertheless such an attempt is worth making, and for the same reason that never quite reaching the peak of Mount Everest is better than not having climbed it at all. There really were times when it seemed as if Dick had the Universe in a corner.

The more you try and figure out the universe, the more enigmatic it becomes. You know that ingenious U-bend in a toilet, which used to figure conspicuously in Harpic adverts: it keeps the stinks down the drain instead of in the room? Since the universe you are trying to figure out includes the mind doing the figuring, then—as Sir Karl Popper may have said in a back issue of *Planet Stories*—that mind acts as its own U-bend and refuses to let you get down to the real layers of fertilizer where growth and destruction begin.

All the same, Dick patented his own U-bend into ontology. Before our eyes, he kept opening up whole new cans of worms. Dick suffered from paralysing anxiety states which forays into the world of drugs did not alleviate; we see his mind constantly teasing out what is to be trusted, what let in, what discarded—and how far let in, how far discarded. The process applied alike to words, can openers, wives and worlds.

From this, anyone not knowing anything about Dick might conclude that he was a gloomy and terrifying writer. Well, he was terrifying, certainly, but the gloom is shot through with hilarity. The worse things got, the funnier. His literary precursors are Kafka and Dickens. Actually Kafka, Dickens and A. E. van Vogt: it's the secret schlock ingredient that makes Dick tick.

Let's just illustrate with a passage from *A Scanner Darkly*, one of Dick's best and most terrifying novels, where Charles Freck decides to commit suicide.

> At the last moment (as end-time closed in on him) he changed his mind on a decisive issue and decided to drink the reds down with a connoisseur wine instead of Ripple or Thunderbird, so he set off on one last drive, over to Trader Joe's, which specialized in fine wines, and bought a bottle of 1971 Mondavi Cabernet Sauvignon, which set him back almost thirty dollars—all he had.

Back home again, he uncorked the wine, let it breathe, drank a few glasses of it, spent a few minutes contemplating his favourite page of *The Illustrated Picture Book of Sex*, which showed the girl on top, then placed the plastic bag of reds beside his bed, lay down with an Ayn Rand book and unfinished protest letter to Exxon, tried to think of something meaningful but could not, although he kept remembering the girl being on the top, and then, with a glass of Cabernet Sauvignon, gulped down all the reds at once. After that, the deed being done, he lay back, the Ayn Rand book and letter on his chest, and waited.

However, he had been burned. The capsules were not barbiturates, as represented. They were some kind of kinky psychedelics, of a type he had never dropped before, probably a mixture, and new on market. Instead of quietly suffocating, Charles Freck began to hallucinate. Well he thought philosophically, this is the story of my life. Always ripped off. He had to face the fact—considering how many of the capsules he had swallowed—that he was in for some trip.

The next thing he knew, a creature from between dimensions was standing beside his bed looking down at him disapprovingly.

The creature had many eyes, all over it, ultra-modern expensive-looking clothing, and rose up eight feet high. Also, it carried an enormous scroll. 'You're going to read me my sins,' Charles Freck said. The creature nodded and unsealed the scroll.

Freck said, lying helpless on his bed, 'and it's going to take a hundred thousand hours.'

Fixing its many compound eyes on him, the creature from between dimensions said, 'We are no longer in the mundane universe. Lower-plane categories of material existence such as "space" and "time" no longer apply to you. You have been elevated to the transcendent realm. Your sins will be read to you ceaselessly, in shifts, throughout eternity. The list will never end.'

Know your dealer, Charles Freck thought, and wished he could take back the last half-hour of his life.

A thousand years later he was still lying there on his bed with the Ayn Rand book and the letter to Exxon on his chest, listening to them read his sins to him. They had gotten up to the first grade, when he was six years old.

Ten thousand years later they had reached the sixth grade. The year he had discovered masturbation.

He shut his eyes, but he could still see the multi-eyed, eight-foot-high being with its endless scroll reading on and on.

'And next—' it was saying.

Charles Freck thought, at least I got a good wine.

This unusual ability to mix tragedy with farce is matched by a paranoid's ability to scramble—if not always unscramble—plots. The result is an *oeuvre* which presents a large scale portrait of the incursions of technological advance upon the psyche of the West, and its shattering under a series of hammer blows. Occasional protagonists may survive, but Dick never leaves us under any illusions about the magnitude of the incursion.

Thus his work represents an unrivalled unity in the SF field, a unity only reinforced by the way in which most of the texts of that *oeuvre* are staged—not far away in the galaxy, which might have afforded some relief—but in one of the epicentres of the disintegrating psyche, Southern California.

With the disintegrating psyche, as some might expect, the disintegrating family. The one portrait of a family in all of Dick's *oeuvre* is four miserable junkies, spying on each other, dying or trying to die, together with their cat child-substitute, in *A Scanner Darkly*. With this absence of familial pattern goes a disconcerting absence of mother-figures, and indeed a certain lack of females all round. It's hard to imagine a Mrs Palmer Eldritch, and the policeman who wants his tears to flow has for a wife merely a devilish sister.

For three decades, Dick unfolded this schizoid portrait of the coming age. Again, one must repeat, we can observe in his writing a steady deepening of his understanding and capacities, as we observe it in Dickens.

During the first decade, the 1950s, we admire the surface glitter of his puzzles—*Time Out of Joint*—and all that. His prankish short stories become increasingly sophisticated. In the 1960s, profound change continues: what was devised becomes felt; complexity of plot becomes matched to a complexity of thought. The *weltanschauung* is not universally dark, though illusion is harder to disentangle. In this period stand three of Dick's surest memorials, *The Three Stigmata of*

Palmer Eldrich, *The Man in the High Castle* and *Martian Time-Slip*. Slightly later, also in the 1960s, is another group of three, though I think a lesser group, *Now Wait For Last Year*, *Do Androids Dream of Electric Sheep?* and *Ubik*. Here, unrealities have multiplied to such an extent that the result is a confusion we are tempted merely to reject as abnormal; the threatened illusions of the earlier group strike much nearer home.

The 1970s yield two remarkable novels in which the protagonists strive for reality, in one case finding and in one case failing to find it: *Flow My Tears, The Policeman Said* and *A Scanner Darkly*. The 'explanation' of *Flow My Tears*, whereby a group of people move into transposed reality because of another person's, Jason Taverner's, failings, makes no scientific and even worse theological sense, though for all that it is a sombrely glittering novel, the real hero being a corrupt police chief who does not enter until half-way through the book. But *A Scanner Darkly* is all too terrifyingly plausible, on both scientific and theological grounds, with the terrible drug, Death, which splits the corpus callosum, rendering the victim dissociated from himself. This, it seems to me, is the grandest, darkest, of all Dick's hells.

Dick at one time came to some kind of perilous treaty with various drugs, just as Anna Kavan did with heroin. Kavan never came off heroin; it was her *doppelganger*, her bright destroyer, killingly necessary to her. Dick's renunciation of drugs brought forth the 1980s group of novels, again a trio, *Valis*, *The Divine Invasion* and *The Transmigration of Timothy Archer*. It's too early to judge this group. The last novel is set in what for Dick is a curiously sunny Southern California, and opens on the day John Lennon is shot. It thrills with intimations of death—but when I said that to someone he replied, 'What Dick novel doesn't?'

I have to say, ungratefully, that I so vastly enjoyed Dick giving me bad news, opening up whole new cans of worms at every turn, that I become peevish when a can opens and angels come winging out. That the narrator of *Timothy Archer* is a lady called Angel hardly helps matters. Despite these reservations, it is a complex and interesting novel, fairly light and sunny in tone. It bears the hallmark of Dick, a hallmark discernible even in the minor novels, genuine grief that things are as bad as they are. That's a rare quality in SF.

So Dick began as a smart imitator of van Vogt and ended up as a wizard. Most careers in the SF field flow the other way about. Maybe it's the Hobart effect.

Dick said that it was not the possibilities of SF that appealed to him but the wild possibilities. Not just, 'What would happen if . . .' but 'My God, what would happen if . . .'.

This is partly why we like him. But ultimately the affection he inspires is beyond analysis. He had a way of dramatizing his inner fears which made you laugh. His novels are full of gadgets, sentient hardware and awesome entities, but nevertheless they are inward novels. He constantly invents new means of doom and destruction, but nevertheless a sense of gusto bounces up from the page. In some peculiar sense he was a world-league novelist, yet he meekly burnt two mainstream novels when Don Wollheim told him they were no good. There's the paradox. If it wasn't for Don Wollheim at Ace, we'd possibly never have seen any Dick novels ever, and the universe would have been different. And our inner lives, ditto.

Dick's first American readers appear only to have found Dick depressing. Was he too wild? Did they not dig his humour? Were there too many worms in his can? It was in Britain that he first found a more realistic and welcoming appraisal. Accustomed by national temperament to sailing through seas of bad news without turning a vibrissa, we appreciated Dick's ingenuity, inventiveness, and metaphysical wit. We taught the Americans to see what a giant they had in their midst, just as they taught us to admire Tolkien. If we do admire Tolkien.

The tide has turned. Hollywood made an over-heated, over produced, and over immoral film from a lovely book, and called it by an old Alan Nourse title, *Blade Runner*. (Then there was *Total Recall*. The rebarbative Stanislaw Lem said that Dick fought trash with trash. It looks like trash could win!)

Meanwhile, the SF world rallies round, aware that some awful grey shagged-out thing on Mars has now got Dick by the short hairs. I've never liked the SF community more. A real spirit of affection is in evidence. Hence this meeting.

The SF newspaper, *Locus*, put out an excellent Dick memorial number just after he disappeared, with tributes and memories from many hands. Perhaps I may quote here a paragraph from what I said then, writing in New York:

> Dick was never out of sight since his first appearances in those great glad early days of the fifties, when the cognoscenti among us scoured the magazines on the bookstalls for names that had suddenly acquired a talismanic quality: J. G.

Ballard, William Tenn, Philip K. Dick. Now he's gone, the old
bear, the old sage and jester, the old destroyer, the sole writer
among us who, in Pushkin's mighty phrase, 'laid waste the
hearts of men'.

The above was written in 1982. Some of us knew Dick was a
towering writer long before that date. We did not foresee that he
would be canonized after death, that even his rejected non-SF would
be published to acclaim. Looked at detachedly, the blossoming Dick
industry has its sad side. A writer needs appreciation in his lifetime;
praise goes unheard when you're six feet under.

For the purposes of this volume, I hoped to up-date the above, but
cannot see how. Dick is in a process of being deified. *Total Recall*
(1990) was a brutal and unscientific mess of a movie, which certainly
made it look as if trash had won. On the other hand, we have had
some excellent productions of Dick material. These certainly include
an elegant *Selected Letters of Philip K. Dick 1974* (1991), edited by the
energetic Paul Williams, who has done so much to tend Dick's
reputation, and Lawrence Sutin's brilliant and truthful biography,
Divine Invasions: A Life of Philip K. Dick, and, towards the rave end of
the spectrum, *In Pursuit of Valis: Selections from the 'Exegesis'* (1991),
edited by Lawrence Sutin.

Dick remains irreplaceable. One can name at least six of his novels
which are startlingly good, witty and dark, in which even what is
monstrous is treated with human sympathy: *The Three Stigmata of
Palmer Eldrich, Martian Time-Slip, The Man in the High Castle, A Scanner
Darkly, Flow My Tears, The Policeman Said*, and *Valis*. While they are
interesting, the non-SF novels are thinner; Dick needed the bitter
lemon of futurity in his potion.

With *Martian Time-Slip* in particular I have a rather long relationship. After protracted dealings, I secured for this beautiful complex
novel its first hardcover edition. That was in 1976. In the same year, I
was in contact with Stanley Kubrick, and suggested to him that
Dick's novel would make an excellent film. Nothing came of the
suggestion.

In the 1980s, having founded the small company of Avernus Ltd
with Frank Hatherley, I started negotiations with those at the top of
Paramount UK for a movie. The heads were keen: then the heads
started to roll. But I had opened protracted negotiations for an option
on film and TV rights in the book. These I eventually bought. We're
talking now about the 1990s.

As a bit of agitprop, or agit-pop some might say, I wrote the imaginary conversation, *Kindred Blood in Kensington Gore*, which Avernus published as a pamplet in 1992. This represents Dick in the Afterlife. I have performed this surreal piece several times on stage, with two gallant actresses playing the multiple roles of Dick's father, his sister, and VALIS itself. The ladies are Petronilla Whitfield in England and Colleen Ferro in the USA.

By this time, we had the TV Drama department of the BBC interested. More than interested, enthusiastic and involved, once they clearly understood this was not just a tacky length of sci-fi. *Martian Time-Slip* was to be a five-part mini-series produced with serious resources behind it. Given 250 minutes or so of air time, one can serve up more than one plot; characters and backgrounds get a chance to emerge. Not only were the BBC thoroughly behind it, but we managed to secure a considerable investment from Europe.

Hours, days, weeks, months, were taken up with various negotiations. Those who have written screenplays will know it is an elaborate, protracted business, not without its own dreadful attractions, every word being weighed in the balance, every page being written over and over.

Changes were overtaking the BBC as we wrote. Knowing how brilliant it was, knowing we already had the script editor's approval and support, we delivered the first of five episodes. This was late in 1993. We were informed after some delay that the drama department wished to take the development no further. *Martian Time-Slip* was out in the cold.

Of course Frank and I have not given up. But two years of my working time have gone down the drain. For this reason, I must return to my own work and leave this article unmodified. Sorry, Phil!

SCIENCE FICTION'S MOTHER FIGURE

I

My scrutiny of Mary Shelley's *Frankenstein: or, The Modern Prometheus* in *Billion Year Spree* in 1973 overturned a few old formulations and jerry-built temples. My argument was and remains that the beginnings of real science fiction can plausibly be identified in that novel. Here is no idle wonder; here is a man taking control of what was previously in the provenance of nature alone. Two decades on, and my once heterodox view has won wide favour.

Since *Billion Year Spree* was published, we have learnt more about the author of *Frankenstein*. Once regarded merely as the second wife of Percy Bysshe Shelley, Mary Shelley now shines forth as a vital part of the Romantic movement, and her most famous novel as a vital document of feminism.

Mary Shelley has become almost an industry. I list at the end of this article some of the most crucial books on and about the subject of the author and her circle.

The industry has also allowed us to know some of the other players better. The shelves are already well-filled with books on Byron and Shelley; now we can see more clearly the absent mother, Mary Wollstonecraft, and that far from absent Claire Clairmont, bane and bosom friend of Mary Shelley. Both remarkable women, living in times that often seemed against them.

A portrait of Mary Wollstonecraft by Sir John Opie shows a moody and passionate woman. Her Scandinavian letters are back in print again, to demonstrate her wild nature and descriptive powers. This true Romantic document, published in 1776, also contains a thought for the future which must have interested her daughter when she came upon it.

Wollstonecraft writes from the coasts of Norway. The passage, from Letter xi, runs as follows:

> I anticipated the future improvement of the world, and observed how much man had still to do, to obtain of the earth all it could yield. I even carried my speculations so far as to advance a million or two of years to the moment when the earth would perhaps be so perfectly cultivated, and so completely peopled, as to render it necessary to inhabit every spot; yes; these bleak shores. Imagination went still farther, and pictured the state of man when the earth could no longer support him. Where was he to fly from universal famine? . . . The images fastened on me, and the world appeared a vast prison.

Wollstonecraft bore two daughters. One, Fanny, was fathered by an itinerant American, Gilbert Imlay. The second was fathered by William Godwin, born in 1797, and named after her mother.

In Anthony Burgess's novel, *Beard's Roman Women* (1977), there is a passage where Beard, the central character, meets an old girlfriend in an airport bar. Both work in 'the media'; they discuss Byron and Shelley, and she says 'I did an overseas radio thing on Mary Shelley. She and her mother are very popular these days. With the forces of woman's liberation, that is. It took a woman to make a Frankenstein monster. Evil, cancer, corruption, pollution, the lot. She was the only one of the lot of them who knew about life . . .'

Even today, when our diet is the unlikely, Mary Shelley's *Frankenstein* seems extremely far-fetched; how much more so must it have appeared on publication in 1818. Yet Beard's girlfriend puts her finger on one of the contradictions which explain the continued fascination of *Frankenstein*. It seems to know a lot about life, whilst being preoccupied with death.

A preoccupation with death was undoubtedly an important strand in the character of the author of *Frankenstein*. Marked by the death of her mother in childbirth, she was haunted, at the time of writing *Frankenstein*, by precognitive dreads concerning the future deaths of her husband and children. By embodying this psychic material into her complex narrative, she created what many regard as that creature with a life of its own, the first SF novel.

Of course, it is a mongrel novel. But modern SF/fantasy is at its best when, like a mongrel, it runs barking down the road of present-day imagination. It's a mongrel art.

Frankenstein is generically ambivalent, hovering between novel, Gothic, and science fiction. To my mind, precisely similar factors obtain even today in the most celebrated SF novels. Heinlein's *Stranger in a Strange Land* contains magic; Anne McCaffrey's dragon novels hover between legend, fairytale, and science fiction. Is Greg Bear's *Blood Music* nanotechnological or allegorical? 'Pure' science fiction is chimerical. Its strength lies in its hybrid nature.

Where the central strength of *Frankenstein* lies is hard to say. We may admire the paintings of Picasso and feel intensely for them without knowing precisely why; some things lie beyond analysis. But just as many Picasso canvasses betray his ferocious anger, so a similar emotion burns in the darkness of Mary Shelley's pages. She rails against the injustice of the world.

The elements of fairy story are here; 'Red Riding Hood and the Wolf' comes to mind. Here are the same dark irrational codes: sex, death, domination, secrecy. Our fear of the monster fights with our pity, as our sympathy for Victor must struggle against our dislike of him. Will the wolf eat Red Riding Hood—or she him? What exactly is the disastrous nature of the relationship between Victor and his creature, that it must be fought out in the wild places of the earth?

The events of Mary Shelley's life (1797–1851) crowd into the early years. Many transactions that would mould her character occur before she was born.

Her parents both played important roles in the intellectual life of the time. William Godwin was a philosopher and political theorist, whose most important work is *An Enquiry Concerning the Principles of Political Justice* (1793). Godwin wrote novels as a popular means of elucidating his thought, the most durable being *Caleb Williams* (1794), which can still be read with interest and excitement. The influence of both these works on Godwin's daughter's writing is marked.

Mary Wollstonecraft wrote the first feminist tract, *A Vindication of the Rights of Woman* (1792). She came to the marriage with Godwin bringing little Fanny Imlay. Distracted by the failure of her love for Gilbert Imlay, Mary had tried to commit suicide by jumping into the Thames off Putney Bridge. Surviving to marry Godwin, she bore him a daughter, Mary, only to die ten days later.

Godwin remarried. His second wife, Mrs Mary Jane Clairmont, brought with her two children by her previous liaison, Charles and Jane. Jane later preferred to be known as Claire. She bore Byron an illegitimate child, Allegra. Fanny and Mary, four years old when

Godwin remarried, were further upset by the arrival of this new step-mother into their household. Alienation was no doubt increased when Godwin's new wife bore him a son. The five children crowding into one house increased Mary's feeling of isolation. Isolation is the refrain which sounds throughout her novels and short stories. Another constant refrain, that of complex familial relationships, derives from that confused childhood. Of the five children, no two could muster two parents in common, Charles and Jane excepted.

Mary grew to be an attractive woman. Her reserved manner hid a deep vein of feeling, baffled by her mother's death and her father's distance. The two kinds of coldness, one might say, are both embodied in her monster's being in a sense dead and also unloved. When Shelley arrived on the scene he received all her love, and Mary remained faithful to him long after his death, despite his frequent neglect of her.

> My dearest Mary, wherefore hast thou gone
> And left me in this dreary world alone?

So said Shelley. In fact, the reverse was true.

The product of two intellectuals, Mary Shelley was a blue-stocking, and through many years maintained an energetic reading programme, teaching herself several foreign languages. She had the good fortune to meet in childhood many of the celebrated intellectuals and men of letters of the time, Samuel Taylor Coleridge among them. Trelawny said of her that 'her head might be put upon the shoulders of a Philosopher'.

Percy Bysshe Shelley, poet and son of a baronet, was an emotional and narcissistic youth. Before his twenty-second birthday, the pair had eloped to France, taking Jane Clairmont—soon to be Claire—with them.

Europe! What freedom it must have represented to Mary, after her sixteen circumscribed years, and what brilliant companionship Shelley must have offered. The youthful travellers were among the first to enter France after the Napoleonic Wars, and a desolate place they found it, fields uncultivated, buildings and villages destroyed. On the way to Switzerland, Shelley wrote to invite his wife Harriet, now pregnant with Shelley's second child, to join the party. Before they reached Lake Lucerne, Mary knew that she also was pregnant.

Catastrophe followed the lovers. Mary's child, a daughter, was born after they returned to London and their debts. She was premature and died. A second child, William, scarcely fared better. In the summer of 1816, Shelley and Mary went to Switzerland again, taking along William and, inevitably, Claire Clairmont. They found accommodation at the Maison Chapuis, on the shores of Lake Geneva, next to the Villa Diodati, where Lord Byron was staying. Claire threw herself at Byron's head, and managed to encompass the rest of him. It was a creative time for them, with philosophy and learning pursued, as well as the more touted facets of the good life. It was here that Mary began to write *Frankenstein*. She was eighteen. Summer had too short a stay, and the party returned to England to face more trouble.

Mary's self-effacing half-sister, Fanny, committed suicide with an overdose of laudanum at the age of twenty two. The Shelley *ménage* had moved to the West Country. Claire still followed them, as the monster followed Frankenstein. She was now pregnant by Byron. Then news reached them that Shelley's wife Harriet had drowned herself in the Serpentine, when far advanced in pregnancy. Shelley and Mary married almost immediately.

The date of the marriage was 29 December 1816. Six and a half years later, in July 1822, Shelley drowned whilst sailing on the Ligurian Sea. By that time, the little boy, William, was dead, as was another child, Clara. Mary had also had a miscarriage. A further son, Percy Florence, was born. He alone of Mary's progeny survived to manhood. Even Claire's daughter by Byron, the little Allegra, died in Italy.

The rest of Mary Shelley's life is lived in the shadow of her first twenty-five years. After Byron died in Greece in 1824, both the great poets were gone. Mary remained ever faithful to the memory of her husband. She edited his poems and papers, and earned a living by her pen. *Frankenstein*, published in 1818, became immediately popular. She also wrote historical novels, such as *Perkin Warbeck* (1830), *Lodore* (1835) which enjoyed some success, travel journals, short stories, and a futuristic novel, *The Last Man* (1826) which, by its powerfully oppressive theme of world catastrophe, is classifiable as science fiction. Percy married. Her cold father, Godwin, died; Shelley's difficult father died. Finally, in 1851, the year of the Great Exhibition, Mary herself died, aged fifty-three.

This painful biography, as confused as any modern one, helps to explain why Mary Shelley's temperament was not a sanguine one. From it derives much of what we read in her two science fiction novels, *Frankenstein* and *The Last Man*. As do all novels, both owe a great deal to the literature that preceded them. Much is owed to experience. Critics are liable comfortably to ignore the latter to concentrate on the former.

The essence of the story of *Frankenstein* is familiar, if in distorted form, from many film, stage and TV versions; Victor Frankenstein constructs a creature from corpses and then endows it with life, after which it runs amok. The novel is more complex than this synopsis suggests.

Some of its complexities have recently been explored by Marilyn Butler in her exemplary edition of the novel (see Bibliography). Butler examines the work of scientists who were influential, in particular the *avant-garde* William Lawrence. Something of the disputes of the time regarding the role of mind, physical sciences, and the irrational, are preserved in *Frankenstein*'s three narrators, Walton, Victor, and the creature. In the same way, modern SF novels contain debates about the future of Artificial Intelligence, and whether AI will prove beneficial or otherwise.

Butler presents the 1818 text, with convincing arguments as to why it is to be preferred to the hitherto more popular 1831 text. The latter was toned down in many aspects, to make it more acceptable in a conformist age. Mary Shelley had to live by her pen, in a harsh society well depicted in William St Clair's biography (see Bibliography). Besides, that one surviving son of hers was to become a baronet . . .

Frankenstein: or, The Modern Prometheus begins with letters from Captain Walton to his sister. Walton is sailing in Arctic waters when he sees on the ice floes a sledge being driven by an enormous figure. The next day, the crew rescue a man from a similar sledge. It is Victor Frankenstein of Geneva. When he recovers, he tells Walton his tale. This account takes up the bulk of the book, to be rounded off by Walton again. Six chapters give the creature's own account of its life, especially of its education. If the style of the novel is discursive, Mary Shelley was following methods familiar to readers of Richardson and Sterne. It became unfashionable but—to readers of eccentric modern novels—is now increasingly sympathetic and accounts in part for the new-found popularity of the novel.

Most of the drama is set not in the seamy London Mary Shelley knew from her childhood, but amid the spectacular Alpine scenery she had visited with Shelley. The puissance of Frankenstein's creature gains greatly by its association with the elements—storm, cold, glaciers, desolation.

Interest has always centred on the monster and its creation. In the novel it has no name, being referred to as 'creature', 'daemon', or 'monster'. This accounts in part for the popular misusage by which the name Frankenstein has come to be transferred from the creator to the created—a mistake occurring first in Mary's lifetime. The roles of the two chief protagonists also become interchangeable. The essential SF core of the narrative is the experiment which goes wrong. This prescription is to be repeated later, many times, in *Amazing Stories* and elsewhere.

Victor Frankenstein's is a Faustian dream of unlimited power, but this Faust makes no supernatural pacts; he succeeds only when he throws away the fusty old reference books, outdated by the new natural philosophy, and gets to work on research in laboratories. Paracelsus out, Science in.

This is the new perception. This is the revolt of Shelley's generation. Kick out the old laws. Kick the Ottomans out of fair Greece. Get rid of those old spells. The new formulae of science, of a new age, have more power—even the power of life over death.

Mary Shelley in her Journals speaks of a tyrannical buried life she was forced to lead, 'an internal life quite different from the external one'. It is a revealing remark—and not an uncommon discomfort. For our hopes themselves come trailing a shadow side. And with the bold new experiments designed to change the world, a bill is always presented. Victor Frankenstein himself begins work with what are, on the surface, the best of motives. 'What glory would attend the discovery', he says in Chapter II, 'if I could banish disease from the human frame, and render man invulnerable to any but a violent death!'

But SF is not only hard science. Related to the first core is a second, also science-fictional, the tale of an experiment in political theory which relates to William Godwin's ideas. Frankenstein is horrified by his creation and abjures responsibility. Yet the monster, despite its ugliness, is gentle and intelligent, and tries to win its way into society. Society repulses it. Hence the monster's cry, 'I am malicious because I am miserable', a dramatic reversal of Christian thinking of the time.

The richness of the story's metaphorical content, coupled with the excellence of the prose, has tempted commentators to interpret the novel in various ways. *Frankenstein*'s subtitle, *The Modern Prometheus*, points to one level of meaning. Prometheus, according to Aeschylus in *Prometheus Bound*, brings fire from Heaven and bestows the gift on mankind; for this, Zeus has him chained to a rock in the Caucasus, where an eagle eats his viscera.[1] Another version of the legend, the one Mary Shelley had chiefly in mind, tells of Prometheus fashioning men out of mud and water. She seized on this aspect of the legend, whilst Byron and Shelley were writing *Prometheus* and *Prometheus Unbound* respectively. With an inspired transposition, she uses electricity as the divine fire.

By this understanding, with Frankenstein acting God, Frankenstein's monster becomes mankind itself, blundering about the world seeking knowledge and reassurance. The monster's intellectual quest has led David Ketterer, in *Frankenstein's Creation: The Book, The Monster and Human Reality* (University of Victoria, 1979), to state that 'basically *Frankenstein* is about the problematical nature of knowledge'. Though this interpretation is too radical, it reminds us usefully of the intellectual aspects of the work, and of Mary's understanding of the British philosophers, Locke, Berkeley and Hume.

Leonard Woolf, in *The Annotated Frankenstein*,[2] argues that *Frankenstein* should be regarded as 'psychological allegory'. This view is supported by David Ketterer, who thinks that therefore the novel cannot be science fiction. Godwin's *Caleb Williams* is also psychological, or at least political allegory; it is nevertheless regarded, for example by Julian Symons in his history of the detective novel, *Bloody Murder*,[3] as the first crime novel. Many good SF novels are psychological allegory as well as being science fiction. Algis Budry's *Who?* is an example.

By understanding the origins of 'real' science fiction, in which humanity seizes on new powers, we understand something of SF's function; hence the importance of the question. Not to regard *Frankenstein* but, say *The Time Machine* or even Gernsback's 1920's magazines as the first SF—as many did only a few years ago—is to underestimate the capabilities of the medium. Alternatively, to claim

1 One thinks here of the scene after Shelley's death, when Trelawny caused his corpse to be burnt on the shore, Byron and Leigh Hunt also being present. At the last possible moment, Trelawny ran forward and snatched Shelley's heart from the body.

2 Leonard Woolf, *The Annotated Frankenstein*, New York, Clarkson N. Potter Inc, 1977.

3 Julian Symons, *Bloody Murder*, London, Faber and Faber, 1972 (Harmondsworth, Penguin, 1974).

that *Gilgamesh* or Homer or the satirical Lucian of Samosata started it all is to claim that almost anything is SF.

Mary Shelley wanted her story to 'speak to the mysterious fears of our (i.e. humankind's) nature' . . . Is that not what SF still excellently does—or can do, for instance in Rob Holdstock's *Mythago Wood*?

No doubt the novel gave voice to Mary Shelley's own mysterious fears. What makes our flesh creep is not Boris Karloff or Christopher Lee in funny make-up, but the terror that there may be an enemy trapped within ourselves, waiting to leap out and betray us. This was the tyranny of Mary's inner life. It was also the tyranny inherent in another scientific experiment, written later in the century, Robert Louis Stevenson's *Dr Jekyll and Mr Hyde* (1886).

> [Jekyll] thought of Hyde, for all his energy of life, as of something not only hellish but inorganic. This was the shocking thing: . . . that what was dead, and had no shape, should unsurp the offices of life.

In his book, *In Frankenstein's Shadow* (OUP, 1987), Chris Baldick speaks of Stevenson's short novel as 'the clearest presentation of Victorian writers' concern with "the divided self" '. Mary Shelley's fear of further sexual reproduction is embodied on the one hand in Victor, while her rage and loneliness is embodied on the other hand in the creature. But the game is not as simple as that.

That the destructive monster stands for one side of Percy Bysshe Shelley's nature and the constructive Victor for the other is convincingly argued by another critic, Christopher Small, in *Ariel Like a Harpy*.[4] Mary's passion for Shelley, rather than blinding her, gave her terrifying insight. Mary Shelley herself, in her Introduction to the 1831 edition of her novel, means us to read it as a kind of metaphor when she says 'Invention . . . does not consist in creating out of void, but out of chaos; the materials must, in the first place, be afforded: it can give form to dark, shapeless substances, but it cannot bring into being substance itself'.

In referring to *Frankenstein* as a diseased creation myth (*Billion Year Spree*, 1973), I had in mind phrases with sexual connotations in the novel such as 'my workshop of filthy creation', used by Frankenstein of his secret work. Mary's experiences showed her life and death

---

4 Christopher Small, *Ariel Like a Harpy*, London, Gollancz, 1972.

closely intertwined. The genesis of her terrifying story came to her in a dream, in which she saw 'the hideous phantasm of a man stretched out, and then, on the working of some powerful engine, show signs of life, and stir with an uneasy half vital motion'. The words suggest both a distorted image of her mother dying—in those final restless moments which often tantalizingly suggest recovery rather than its opposite—and the stirrings of sexual intercourse. 'Powerful engine' is a term which serves in pornography as a synonym for penis.

The critic Ellen Moers, in 'Female Gothic: The Monster's Mother',[5] disposes of the question of how a girl still in her teens could hit on such a horrifying idea (though the authoress was herself the first to raise it). Most female writers of the eighteenth and nineteenth centuries were spinsters and virgins; Victorian taboos operated against writing about childbirth. Mary experienced the fear, guilt, depression and anxiety which attend childbirth, particularly in situations such as hers, unmarried, her consort a married man with children by another woman, beset by debt in a foreign place. Only a woman, only Mary Shelley, could have written *Frankenstein*. As Beard's girlfriend says, 'She was the only one of the lot of them who knew about life'.

It is commonly accepted that the average first novel relies for its material on personal experience. We do not deny other interpretations—for a metaphor has many interpretations—by stating that Mary sees herself as the monster. This is why we pity it. She too tried to win her way into society. By running away with Shelley, she sought acceptance through love. The move carried her further from society; she became a wanderer, an exile, like Byron, like Shelley, like Trelawny, and Claire Clairmont, who spent many years abroad. Her mother's death in childbirth must have caused her to feel that she, like the monster, had been born from the dead. Behind the monster's eloquence lies Mary Shelley's grief. Part of the continued appeal of the novel is the drama of a neglected child.

Upon this structure of one kind of reality, Mary built a further structure, one of the intellect. A fever for knowledge abounds; not only Frankenstein but the monster and Walton also, and the judicial processes throughout the book, are in a quest for knowledge of one kind and another. Interestingly, the novel contains few female characters (a departure from the Gothic mode with its soft, frightened heroines). Victor's espoused, Elizabeth, remains always a

5 In *Literary Women*, London, W. H. Allen, 1972.

distant figure. The monster, a product of guilty knowledge, threatens the world with evil progeny.

The monster is, of course, more interesting than Victor. He has the vitality of evil, like Satan in Milton's *Paradise Lost* before him and Quilp in Dickens's *The Old Curiosity Shop* after him, eloquent villains both. It is the monster that comes first to our minds, as it was the monster that came first to Mary Shelley's mind. The monster holds its appeal because it was created by science, or at least pseudo-science, rather than by any pacts with the devil, or by magic, like the Golem.

The point about discussing where science fiction begins is that it helps our understanding of the nature and function of SF. In France in pre-Revolution days, for instance, several books appeared with Enlightenment scenarios depicting a future where present trends were greatly developed, and where the whole world became a civilized extension of the Tuilleries. The best-known example is Sebastien Mercier's *L'An 2440*, set seven centuries ahead in time. The book was translated into several foreign languages.

Mercier writes in the utopian tradition; Mary Shelley does not. Here we see a division of function. Jules Verne was influenced by Mercier, and worked with 'actual possibilities of invention and discovery'. H. G. Wells was influenced by *Frankenstein*, and wrote what he called fantasies—the phrase set in quotes is Wells's, who added that he 'did not pretend to deal with possible things.' One can imagine Mary Shelley saying as much. With her, the impossible inner life found tongue.

As Muriel Spark says, Mary in her thinking seems at least fifty years ahead of her time.[6] She captured the Irrational, one of the delights and torments of our age. By dressing it in rational garb and letting it stalk the land, she unwittingly dealt a blow against the tradition to which Mercier was heir. Utopia is no place for irrationality.

Other arguments for the seminal qualities of Frankenstein are set out more fully in *Trillion Year Spree*. In sum, Victor Frankenstein is a modernist, consciously rejecting ancient fustian booklore in favour of modern science, kicking out father figures. His creation of life shows him further usurping maternal power, invading what was

6 Muriel Spark, *Child of Light: A Reassessment of Mary Wollstonecraft Shelley*, Hadleigh Bridge, Essex, Tower Bridge Publications, 1951 (revised and published as *Mary Shelley*, London, Constable, 1988).

previously God's province—the role medicine has played since Jenner's smallpox vaccine. Victor and his monster together function as the light and dark side of mankind, in a symbolism to become increasingly comprehensible after Mary Shelley's death.

As befitted an author writing after the Napoleonic Wars, when the Industrial Revolution was well under way, Mary Shelley deals, not merely with extrapolated development like Mercier before her, but with unexpected change—like Wells after her. Above all, Frankenstein stands as the figure of the scientist (though the word was not coined when Mary wrote), set apart from the rest of society, unable to control new forces he has brought into the world. The successor to Prometheus is Pandora. Excepting H. G. Wells, no other writer presents us with as many innovations as Mary Shelley.

In the year 1818, when *Frankenstein* was first published, news reached England of a terrible epidemic which had broken out in India. The inhabitants of the district concerned died or fled. The disease moved from Calcutta, its traditional capital, to march on Delhi and Bombay. It advanced beyond the confines of the sub-continent, and in 1821 crossed the Arabian Sea to cause such havoc that the bodies of the dead were too many to bury. It moved towards Tehran and Basra, and up the Tigris to Baghdad.

By 1822 it had spread by caravan to Southern Russia. Meanwhile, it engulfed Burma, Siam, and the Philippines. It entered the portals of the vast hunting grounds of China. Its name was Cholera.

After a lull came a second pandemic. The scourge appeared in Moscow. It moved along the Danube, infecting a quarter of a million people in Hungary alone within a three month period. Cracow fell to the invader, as did Warsaw and Riga.

As it travelled along the Baltic, it was still making its visitation in the Middle East. In Cairo and Alexandria 30,000 people died in a day. By 1831 cholera raged all over Europe. In the exceptional summer of that year, the disease crossed the North Sea to cause the famous Sunderland outbreak; from Sunderland it spread to London and elsewhere.

Plagues, epidemics of various kinds, have been a source of super-stitious and religious fear through the centuries. Plague is the hero of *The Last Man*. Mary Shelley's novel, when published in 1826, was topical, and scarcely more sensational than the facts.

Yet the Hogarth Press edition in 1985 was the first reprint in England of this important novel. Almost no-one had read it; histories of literature fail to mention it. After a slow beginning, it has all the magic of a tumbled landscape by J. M. W. Turner—a painter whom Mary Shelley admired, who died the year she did. Why such astounding neglect?

Indifference may be ascribed in part to male chauvinism, in part to the snobbishness of critics. Other factors working against her have been Mary Shelley's own self-effacing character, and the eclipsing fame of those surrounding her.

The tangle of relationships following William Godwin's second marriage forms a marked part of the first volume of *The Last Man*. Mary acquired a step-mother, step-brother and step-sister, and in due course a half-brother. Her confusion of mind was not helped by Godwin's neglect ('He never caressed me . . .'). Godwin became preoccupied with the publishing firm which he and his new wife, a good business-woman, were establishing. When Mary was ten, the *ménage* moved into Skinner Street, to live above the publishing shop. Skinner Street was close to Smithfield Market and Newgate Prison, an area then notorious for a variety of iniquity; the ominously named street had been so christened by reason of its relationship with the nearby market.

Mary Shelley had her escapes from Skinner Street—to a school in Ramsgate, to a friend of her father's near Dundee (then a seven-day sea voyage away). She remembered Scotland with affection; its wildness is recaptured in the early pages of *The Last Man*; but she would have felt too the chill of isolation which, experienced un-relievedly in childhood, frequently persists in adult life.

The landscapes of Scotland and Switzerland are put to good use in *The Last Man*: landscapes of chaos and grandeur. Mary's language, though it is the high-flown prose of Romantic sensibility, carries with it a modern apprehension that nature offers no refuge, being somehow implicated in disaster.

'Old towns are always dirty', said Claire Clairmont, dismissively cheerful. Mary Shelley and Claire had grown up in a time of war and destruction; for them, catastrophe formed part of the natural order. All of Mary Shelley's novels are to a large extent autobiographical; although *The Last Man* is a symbolist drama, its drama reflects suffering seen or endured. In many of its aspects, *The Last Man* is a transposition of reality, rather than pure fantasy.

During the eight years Mary and Shelley spent together, they were generally short of money, on the move and hungry. She was generally pregnant. But even the equable period of their relationship seemed to have fate against it. 1816 was known as 'the year without a summer'. Following the eruption of the volcano Tamboro in the East Indies, dust penetrated the stratosphere and deflected sunlight from the Earth. All over Europe, grain harvests and vintages were late. Rainfall was heavy. Weather anomalies were blamed for the typhus epidemics and that great cholera outbreak of 1818. The decade from 1810 to 1819—the decade in which Thackeray and Dickens were born—was the coldest in England since the 1690s. The phenomena in *The Last Man* appear less freakish when we recall the actual phenomena of Mary's lifetime.

Among these manifestations are a wind (Chapter V) raging for four months without cease. It is the occasion for one of Mary's finest apostrophes, written, no doubt, with Shelley's *Ode to the West Wind* in mind. Less scientifically, a black sun rises in the west and eclipses the 'parent of day', to the understandable terror of all who behold it. Such celestial effects were taken over wholesale by the painter of apocalypse, John Martin, whose water-colour, 'The Last Man', was painted only a few years after the novel was published.

Mary Shelley follows up her divine portents with speculations on human arrogance, in a passage which begins, 'What are we, the inhabitants of this globe, least among the many that people infinite space? Our minds embrace infinity; the visible mechanism of our being is subject to merest accident.' The inner voice is calling again, many miles from Mercier's utopianism.

The Last Man was published anonymously, as being 'by the author of *Frankenstein*'. Its reception was mainly cold. When the name of Shelley was mentioned in reviews, Shelley's father, tiresome old Sir Timothy, cut Mary's allowance.

Muriel Spark claims of *The Last Man* that it is not typical of anything written in the nineteenth century or earlier; nor can it be placed in any existing category. Nevertheless, it comes towards the end of a considerable series of romantic tales and poems about 'the last man' which probably commenced with *Le Dernier Homme* (1805) by Jean-Baptiste Cousin de Granville, where the world is brought to a close by secular, rather than religious, means. Byron's striking poem, *Darkness* (1816, 'the year without a summer'), must also have had its effect on Mary Shelley. Her novel, however, represents a culmination of this lineage, as *Frankenstein* does of the Gothic.

The twentieth century, engendering a fresh set of anxieties, released a fresh set of similar apocalypses—such as M. P. Shiel's *The Purple Cloud* (1901), in which the sole survivor of a poison gas roams the world setting fire to great cities. An American commentator, W. Warren Wagar, speaks of *The Last Man* as 'an event of high significance in the history of secular eschatology, and in the history of the secularization of Western consciousness itself'.[7]

The Last Man is set in the future, the late twenty-first century—a bold stroke for 1826; it contrasts elaborate schemes for the establishment of a utopia on Earth—or in England at least—with an unforeseen disaster which involves all mankind. Mankind's plans are disrupted by something unanticipated and hostile. It is a prescription which looks forward to H. G. Wells and the crowded SF publishers' lists of the present day.

Nevertheless, one sees Muriel Spark's difficulty, and one sees why *The Last Man* has been so long neglected. It is a non-Gothic. Terror is not its raison d'être. Like a concerto, it comes in three movements, and the movements are at odds with each other. The first movement is of great length, almost a social novel in itself; the second movement concerns the coming of the plague and the liberation of Constantinople by Lord Raymond; and the third is almost a travel diary alarmingly dominated by the mathematics of diminishing numbers. Also, Mary's prose, sinewy a decade earlier when she began to write *Frankenstein*, here runs a little to fat. A modern reader must accustom him- or herself to it.

To find one's way through *The Last Man*, it should be remembered that portraits of those Mary knew and loved best—almost all of them dead by 1826—are presented in thin disguises. The last man himself, Lionel Verney, is Mary herself. Shelley is Adrian, made Lord Protector of England, the legislator acknowledged. Byron becomes Lord Raymond, liberator of Constantinople. Others in the cast include the dead children such as Clara, and Claire Clairmont, although the resemblances are not always one-to-one. An assortment of relations and relationships harks back to the unhappy muddle of Mary's childhood. Still, one often wishes for more conversation and fewer descriptions, and altogether less rhetoric.

Mary enlivens the text with the occasional cameos. The astronomer, Merrival, who happily discusses the state of mankind 'six thousand years hence', while his wife and children starve, presents a less favourable aspect of Shelley. The Countess of Windsor (Mary was serendipitous in alighting on the name of Britain's future ruling

---

7 W. Warren Wagar, *Terminal Visions*, Bloomington, IN, Indiana University Press, 1982.

house) may represent the cantankerous father, Sir Timothy Shelley, who put so many obstacles in Mary's way.

The name of Raymond occurs in *Caleb Williams*, where Godwin's Raymond is a kind of eighteenth-century Robin Hood. In that novel, a 'malignant contagious distemper' carries off Mr Clare, the one good man, opening the gate to the endless injustice with which that novel concerns itself. Mary Shelley shows the influence of her father also in depicting England evolving peacefully from a monarchy into a republic; civil war threatens but is averted, thanks to the British aversion to violence, except in speech, and to 'the absence of the military'.

Nor does Shelley's voice go unheard, even from the early pages. When Adrian befriends Lionel, to bestow on the latter 'the treasures of his mind and fortune', this informal education recalls Mary's own, as well as that of the awakening of Frankenstein's monster's intellect.

Once the plague, 'this enemy to the human race', gets under way, the novel acquires tension. Here Mary Shelley shows a command of large movements, of political designs and human traits, particularly of forms of ambition, which only a good understanding of the world can encompass. Muriel Spark speaks of Mary's Platonism, especially in her reading of *The Republic*, as giving the novel 'a philosophical unity very rarely achieved in a work of so comprehensive a range'. We are better equipped than Mary's first readers to appreciate the comprehensiveness of the catastrophe.

As the multitudes of mankind are reduced to one, Lionel is revealed as the perennial outsider of no fixed spiritual address. As he begins, so he ends. Apart from the brief happiness of his marriage to Idris, he remains eternally alone. Mary Shelley's own story underlies her invention.

If some of the miseries of *The Last Man* flow from Mary's own harsh experience, so, paradoxically, does the note of tranquillity on which the novel ends. Solitude is not the worst of enemies. Mary Shelley always pined for Italy. During the time she was creating her novel, she was writing of England in a letter to Teresa Guiccioli, 'Happiness for me is not to be found here; nor forgetfulness of Troubles; I believe that in Rome, in the delightful life of my soul, far from woes, I would find again the shadow of pleasure' (*Letters*, Vol I). In the same year, she tells Leigh Hunt, 'I think of Italy as a version of Delight afar off'.

In Italy and Rome her story ends: calamity has given way to catharsis.

Frankenstein finishes on a sombre note, with the words 'darkness and distance'. *The Last Man* also concludes with distance; but here distance is coupled with light, the glorious light of the south, and of 'the spicy groves of the odorous islands of the far Indian ocean'. As long as life remains, there is light.

The novel was not the dominant literary form in the 1820s it was soon to become. Scott and Peacock were publishing, but the luminaries of the 1840s were still below the horizon. Gothic was going out of vogue.

It was a transitional period. Mary Shelley is a transitional novelist of stature, particularly when we consider a recent critical judgment that 'prose fiction and the travel account have evolved together, are heavily indebted to each other, and are often similar in both content and technique'.[8] This is perfectly exemplified in Mary Shelley's two best novels, *Frankenstein* and *The Last Man*. In both, travel and 'foreign parts' are vital components.

In *Mary Shelley*,[9] William Walling makes a point which incidentally relates *The Last Man* more closely still to the science-fictional temper. Remarking that solitude is a common topic of the period and by no means Mary's monopoly, Walling claims that by interweaving the themes of isolation and the end of civilization, she creates a prophetic account of modern industrial society, in which the creative personality becomes more and more alienated.

Tales and Stories by Mary Shelley were collected together by Richard Garnett and published in 1891. A more recent collection is noted below. Her stories are in the main conventional. Familial and amorous misunderstandings fill the foreground, armies gallop about in the background. The characters are high-born, their speeches high-flown. Tears are scalding, years long, sentiments either villainous or irreproachable, deaths copious, and conclusions not unusually full of well-mannered melancholy. The tales are written for keepsakes of their time. Here again, the game of detecting autobiographical traces can be played. One story, 'Transformation', sheds light on *Frankenstein*—but not much. We have to value Mary Shelley, as we do other authors, for her strongest work, not her

8 Percy G. Adams, *Travel Literature and the Evolution of the Novel*, Lexington, KY, University of Kentucky Press, 1984.

9 William Walling, *Mary Shelley*, Boston, MA, Twayne, 1972.

weakest; and her best has a strength still not widely enough appreciated.

In the course of eight years, between 1814 and 1822, Mary Shelley suffered miscarriages and bore four children, three of whom died during the period. She travelled hither and thither with her irresponsible husband, who probably enjoyed an affair with her closest friend, Claire. She had witnessed suicides and death all round her, culminating in Shelley's death. It was much for a sensitive and intellectual woman to endure. No wonder that Claire Clairmont wrote to her, some years after the fury and shouting died down, saying 'I think in certain things you are the most daring woman I ever knew' (quoted in Julian Marshall's *Life and Letters of Mary Wollstonecraft Shelley*, 1889).

Certainly in literature Mary Shelley was daring. She found new ways in which to clothe her powerful inward feelings.

II

New ideas in science are often followed up swiftly by science fictions which utilize or even examine them. The story may be successful even if the original idea is less so. The theory of 'continuous creation', so attractive in essence, posited by Fred Hoyle, had to give way to the Big Bang theory of creation. That theory is itself now being challenged.

Literary ideas are less subject to acid tests, more subject to fashion and changing taste.

To put forward a more personal view of *Frankenstein*, I would say that I seized upon this novel at the inception of *Billion Year Spree* because I needed to do something more than write a history of science fiction, and of the hundreds of thousands of books and stories I had read. I wished also to render SF more friendly towards its literary aspects. It is a battle needing to be fought; for still these days one sees reviewers and others use the adjective 'literary' pejoratively. SF is not separate from ordinary literature: merely apart. A means of distinguishing the best of it definitively from the writings of Herman Melville, Angela Carter, Franz Kafka, Gabriel Garcia Marquez, and Hermann Hesse has yet to be formulated.

As I have pointed out elsewhere, SF is not a literature of prediction, although some may see it in this light, although guesses may turn out to be proved accurate later. A scone, for all the currants in it, remains ineluctably a scone, not a currant. How many times have I been forced to say as much in television interviews? It makes no difference. Those who do not know SF well believe in the prediction theory. I am a literary sort of chap, and must fight my corner.

What SF can do well—it is what Wells does, and the precept is worth following—is take a new theory and dramatize it. James Lovelock's Galia hypothesis of the biomass of the planet conspiring towards its own survival conditions overtook me with excitement. Was it true? It deserved to be, so beautiful was it. It was adopted with Lovelock's agreement as one of the bases for my Helliconia novels of the 1980s.

My preference remains for the printed word, despite all that the movies, TV, and Nintendo can do. *Billion Year Spree* and its successor bear witness to that. There is a density to a page of text lacking even in radio (where you cannot turn back to check) and certainly in TV, where pictures so often get in the way of text; I like my coffee black, not served up as an ice cream.

Billion Year Spree proved an asset to many scholars. It gave them *carte blanche* not to have to study texts a million miles from the real thing unless they wished; they could narrow their sights on *Frankenstein* and all the amazements which have poured forth since. That proved to be good news.

The success of the volume meant that I was called upon to update it in the 1980s, when the field had greatly expanded and its parameters became even more blurred than previously. I could not manage the task without my colleague, David Wingrove, the most diligent collaborator a man could wish for. So we produced *Trillion Year Spree* in 1986, with the able editorial assistance of Malcolm Edwards, then at Gollancz. *Trillion Year Spree* won a Hugo. What follows is an account of the earlier ground-breaking volume, and some of its rivals.

But first, a story. The scene is the main convention hall of a science fiction convention, Lunacon, held in the crumbling Commodore Hotel, New York, in 1975. Famous critic, fan and collector, Sam Moskowitz, is holding forth from the platform. Fans are slouching around in the hall, sleeping, listening or necking. I am sitting towards the back of the hall, conversing with a learned and attractive lady beside me, or else gazing ahead, watching interestedly the way Moskowitz's lips move. In short, the usual hectic convention scene.

Fans who happen to be aware of my presence turn round occasionally to stare at me. I interpret these glances as the inescapable tributes of fame, and take care to look natural, though not undistinguished, and thoroughly absorbed in the speech.

Later, someone comes up to me and says, admiringly, 'Gee, you were real cool while Moskowitz was attacking you'.

That is how I gained my reputation for English *sang froid*. The acoustics in the hall were so appalling that I could not hear a word Moskowitz was saying against me. To them goes my gratitude, for my inadvertent coolness in the face of danger may well have saved me from a ravening lynch mob.

Few reviewers stood up in support of my arguments in *Billion Year Spree*. Mark Adlard in *Foundation* was one of them.[10] Yet it appears that some of my mildly ventured propositions have since been accepted.

Sam Moskowitz, of course, was pillorying me on account of heretical opinions in *BYS*. I did not gather that he said anything about my major capacity as a creative writer. One unfortunate effect of the success of *BYS*, from my point of view, is that my judgements are often quoted but my fiction rarely so, as though I had somehow, by discussing the literary mode in which I work, passed from mission to museum with no intermediate steps.

Such is the penalty one pays for modesty. I mentioned no single story or novel of mine in my text; it would have been bad form to do so. Lester del Rey, nothing if not derivative, repays the compliment by mentioning no single story or novel of mine in his text,[11] though to be sure, disproportionate space is devoted to del Rey's own activities.

This particular instance can perhaps be ascribed to jealousy. To scholarly responses we will attend later.

First, to rehearse and repolish some arguments advanced in *Billion Year Spree*, in particular the arguments about the origin of SF. On this important question hinge other matters, notably a question of function: what exactly SF does, and how it gains its best effects.

BYS was published in England and the US in 1973, the English edition appearing first, from Weidenfeld & Nicolson.

The book took three years to write. I had no financial support, and was assisted by no seat of learning. I favoured no clique. I used my

10 Mark Adlard, 'A Labour of Love', *Foundation*, 6.
11 Lester del Rey, *The World of Science Fiction*, New York, Garland Publishing, 1980.

own library. I consulted no one. Really, it was a bit of a gamble, since I have a wife and children to support by my writing. But there were two best sellers to fund the venture (*The Hand-Reared Boy* and *A Soldier Erect*). I looked both inward to the SF field itself and outward to the general reader, Samuel Johnson's and Virginia Woolf's common reader; I wished to argue against certain misconceptions which vexed me, and I hoped to demonstrate what those who did not read SF were missing.

There was no history of science fiction in existence. I wrote the sort of book which it might amuse and profit me to read.

Of the two initial problems facing me, I overcame the second to my satisfaction: how do you define SF, and what are its origins? Obviously the questions are related. My ponderous definition of SF has often been quoted, and for that I'm grateful, although I prefer my shorter snappier version, 'SF is about hubris clobbered by nemesis', which found its way into *The Penguin Dictionary of Modern Quotations*. The definition in *BYS* runs as follows:

> Science fiction is the search for a definition of man and his status in the universe which will stand in our advanced but confused state of knowledge (science), and is characteristi-cally cast in the Gothic or post-Gothic mould.

Not entirely satisfactory, like most definitions. It has the merit of including a consideration of form as well as content. On the whole, criticisms of this definition have been more effective than those directed at my proposals for the origins of the genre.[12]

It needs no great critical faculty to observe that most SF is not about 'a search for the definition of man'; it is about telling a story to please the reader—and in that it is no different from any other literature. Only when SF texts are piled together do we see a common restlessness about where mankind is heading through its own blind efforts. More questionable is that phrase about the Gothic mould.

I am not one hundred per cent sure about the phrase myself, but this much is clear: I got it from Leslie Fiedler. Fiedler writes the kind of criticism one can read with enjoyment, unlike most of the criticism which originates from within the orbit of SF academia.

---

12 An instance is 'The story', a scatty review of *BYS* in Robert Conquest's *The Abomination of Moab*, London, Maurice Temple Smith, 1979.

Fiedler has this to say of the Gothic mode, following on a discussion of Monk Lewis's *The Monk* of 1976:

> The major symbols of the gothic have been established, and the major meanings of the form made clear. In general, those symbols and meanings depend on an awareness of the spiritual; isolation of the individual in a society where all communal systems of value have collapsed or have been turned into meaningless clichés. There is a basic ambivalence to the attitude of the gothic writers to the alienation which they perceive. On the one hand, their fiction projects a fear of the solitude which is the price of freedom; and on the other hand, an almost hysterical attack on all institutions which might inhibit that freedom or mitigate the solitude it breeds. . . The primary meaning of the gothic romance, then lies in its substitution of terror for love as a central theme of fiction . . . *Epater la bourgeoisie*: this is the secret slogan of the tale of terror. (Leslie Fiedler, *Love and Death in the American Novel* (1960))

Spiritual isolation, alienation—these lie also at the heart of SF, like serpents in a basket.

Fiedler defines the sort of fiction that most of my admired contemporaries were writing. I saw in them, too, a reflection of my own responses to society which prompted me towards science fiction. The love of art and science I developed as a child was a rebellion against the smug bourgeois society in which I found myself. Art and Science were what *They* hated most. In this way, I reinforced the solitude I felt. This also: I merely wished to *épater* society, not overthrow it; the satirist needs his target.

This stinging function of SF was always apparent, from the days of Mary Shelley (*Frankenstein*, like its progenitor, *Caleb Williams*, contains more punitive litigators than punitive monsters within its pages), through H. G. Wells, and Campbell's *Astounding*, until the time when I sat down to write *BYS* in 1970. During the 1970s and 1980s, SF became widely popular, widely disseminated. Its sting has been removed. The awful victories of *The Lord of the Rings*, *Star Trek* and *Star Wars* have brought—well, not actually respectability, but Instant Whip formulas to SF. The product is blander. It has to be immediately acceptable to many palates, some of them prepubertal. Even the sentimentality of such as Spider and Jeanne Robinson's 'Stardance' is not considered too sickly sweet for consumption. As

Kurt Vonnegut ripened on the tree and fell with a thud to earth, so too did the nutritive content of SF.

The nutritive content has been fixed to suit mass taste. Nowadays the world, or solar system, or the universe, or the Lord Almighty, has to be saved by a group of four or five people which includes a Peter Pan figure, a girl of noble birth, and a moron, a Forrest Gump of some kind. The prescription thus incorporates an effigy for everyone to identify with. In the old days, we used to destroy the world, and it took only one mad scientist. SF was an act of defiance, a literature of subversion, not whimsy.

Notice Fiedler's comment on the basic ambivalence which gothic writers feel towards their alienation. Leaving aside Instant Whip SF, one can perceive an ambivalence in science fiction which goes deep—perhaps one should say an ambivalence which is the subject. The emphasis of this ambivalence has changed over the years. Gernsback's *Amazing* was decidedly technocratic in bias, and purported to demonstrate how the world's ills could be solved by increased applications of technology—a reasonable proposition, if a century late—yet large proportions of the fiction concerned experiments etc. which went terribly wrong. Hubris was continually clobbered by nemesis.

Another fundamental ambivalence is less towards technology than towards science itself. Even technology-oriented authors like Arthur C. Clarke show science superseded by or transcended by mysticism and religion; such surely is the meaning of his most famous short story, 'The Nine Billion Names of God'. It is not science but the fulfilment of religion which brings about the termination of the Universe. The world ends not with a bang but a vesper.

Another ambivalence is the attitude of writers and fans to SF itself. They declare it publicly to be far superior to any possible 'mimetic' fiction; yet privately they laugh about it, revel in the worst examples of the art, and boast of how little SF they read.

SF is a function of the Gothic or post-Gothic. So, for that matter, are the novels of Peter Straub, and they also—in such examples as the tantalizingly named *Ghost Story*—bestraddle customary definitions of the ghost stories and mainstream literature.

What I wish I had altered was the final word of my definition, to have said not 'mould' but 'mode'.

One of the difficulties of defining SF springs from the fact that it is not a genre as such, just as the absurd category 'Non-fiction' is not a

genre. Taking my cue from Rosemary Jackson,[13] I suggest that
our problems in the area of definition will be lightened if we
think of SF as a mode. Jackson says, 'It is perhaps more helpful
to define the fantastic as a literary mode rather than a genre, and
to place it between the opposite modes of the marvellous and the
mimetic'.

This may not help with the question of to what extent SF is a
department of fantasy; 'fantasy' as a literary term, like 'classical' and
'romantic', has come through usage to be defaced; but it helps us to
appreciate SF as the obverse of the realistic mode, and to see that SF
can itself assume various generic forms. There is, for instance, a fairly
well-defined category of 'disaster SF' and this in itself can be sub-
divided into cautionary disasters (like *1984*) and into what I have
termed 'cosy catastrophes' (such as *The Day of the Triffids*), in which
the hero ends with the power and the girl, and is personally better off
than he was at the beginning. No form which includes more than
one genre can itself be a genre.

The relevant dictionary definition of 'mode' is 'A way or manner
in which something takes place; a method of procedure', and 'A
manner or state of being of a thing'.

While my critics argued, as well they might, with the *BYS* definition
of SF, they rarely advanced a more convincing alternative. The same
must be said for the response to my proposal for a great SF progenitor.

My search for ancestors went back no further in time than
Frankenstein. The wide acceptance of this proposal by academics may
have been prompted by relief—a sensible relief occasioned by their
therefore not having to teach *Gilgamesh*, Dante and Otis Adelbert
Kline to their classes.

One sees that this argument of origins can never be definitively
settled, for conflicting genres have contributed to the modern mode.
But it is an argument worth pursuing, just as palaeontologists and
others pick over the so far insoluble question of the early origins of
mankind.

When first claiming for *Frankenstein* a pre-eminent role, I intended

13 Rosemary Jackson, *Fantasy: The Literature of Subversion*, London,
Routledge Chapman and Hall, 1981 (Routledge paperback 1990).

to put forward an argument, not an avowed truth. In particular, I wished to present a counter-argument to those two entrenched views which claimed either that SF was as ancient as literature itself or that 'it all began with Gernsback'. Some commentators managed to hold both assumptions at the same time. No names, no pack drill.

Claims for the pre-eminence of *Frankenstein* had been advanced before I wrote—rather long before, in one case. Rosalie Glynn Grylls' *Mary Shelley: A Biography* (1938) is sympathetic to the author, less sympathetic to her most distinguished book. Grylls does, however, say in one of her appendices that it 'is the first of the Scientific Romances that have culminated in our day in the work of Mr H. G. Wells'. This claim is advanced because of its 'erection of a super-structure of fantasy on a foundation of circumstantial "scientific" fact'. These remarks are made only in passing. Grylls finds the novel 'badly dated'.

Desmond King-Hele is both a scientist and a literary man, best known in the latter category for books on Shelley and Erasmus Darwin. In his *Shelley: His Thought and Work*, he speaks of *Franken-stein* as standing 'in a unique position half-way between the Gothic novel and the Wellsian scientific romance'. In his *Erasmus Darwin* (1963), King-Hele is more positive, saying—with reference to Darwin as mentioned in the preface to *Frankenstein*—that 'Darwin stands as a father-figure over this first and most famous work of science fiction'.

Having got this far, however, the case has to be argued out at some length.

If we claim as SF anything which includes a departure from the natural order, or which exhibits Darko Suvin's cognitive estrange-ment, we gather to ourselves a great body of disparate material, so disparate that it renders the term 'SF' meaningless and the material impossible to study in any effective way.

Beyond this argument of necessity is a philosophical objection to lumping together, say, Plato, Lucian, Paltock, Swift, Poul Anderson and Terry Pratchett. Although sophisticated analysis may reveal what these writers have in common, the sensible reader will be alienated; he will remain aware that the cultural differences are greater than any unifying thread of wonder, speculation, or what-ever.

As Darko Suvin puts it, if such books as Hardy's *Two on a Tower* and

Wilkie Collins's *The Moonstone* are SF just like Wells's *The Invisible Man*, then in fact there is no such thing as SF.[14]

That there is a kind of tradition of the fantastic is undeniable, but it does not admit to easy study, possibly because many of the popular texts are missing, as we might imagine that much popular SF (the magazines of the 1940s, for example) would be missing, were it not for a few devoted individuals who defied a general contemporary neglect. Equally, the writers in this tradition had a nose for their predecessors, and generally reveal themselves as familiar with their writings—though to be familiar with was not always the same as to understand. Writers are impatient creatures and take only what they need; thus, H. G. Wells can say that Frankenstein 'used some jiggery pokery magic to animate his artificial monster', whereas this is precisely what Frankenstein does not do.

The argument that SF began with Gernsback hardly needs refuting any more; I will detain no one with the obvious counter-arguments. Yet when I wrote *BYS*, the refutation was necessary, and I had some fun with that old phrase about Gernsback being 'the father of SF'. Edgar Allan Poe has received the same accolade. This quest for father-figures reached what we hope was its nadir when, in the same year *BYS* was published, Isaac Asimov wrote one of his Introductions, entitled 'The Father of Science Fiction', and nominated John W. Campbell for that role.[15] It was a relief to be able to appoint a mother-figure instead. A relief? An intellectual *coup d'etat*!

This appointment appeals to female and feminist critics, making SF—for a long while regarded as a male preserve—more open to them. Their scholarship is becoming an increased contribution to the field—and perhaps beyond. One indication of this effect occurs in the latest Frankenstein film, *Mary Shelley's Frankenstein*, directed by Kenneth Branagh. Hitherto, the poor creature has been born in a dry Spartan manner upon a slab, the method immortalized in the song, *The Monster Mash*, where

> suddenly, to my surprise,
> My monster from his slab began to rise . . .

14 Darko Suvin, *The Metamorphoses of Science Fiction: On the Poetics and History of a Literary Genre*, New Haven, CT, Yale University Press, 1979.

15 In *Astounding: John W. Campbell Memorial Anthology*, ed. Harry Harrison, New York, Random House, 1973.

In Branagh's film, amino acids are injected into the creature's feet and it is born in—or tipped out of—a copper bath full of amniotic fluid, in a striking approximation of a real birth. Child and father (Robert de Niro and Kenneth Branagh) splash together nakedly in the gushing waters. This may not have happened in the book, but it certainly does in the sub-text.

The seminal point about *Frankenstein* is that its central character makes a deliberate decision. He succeeds in creating life only when he throws away dusty old authorities and turns to modern experiments in the laboratory. One of Victor Frankenstein's two professors scoffs at his reading such ancients as Paracelsus, Agrippa and Albertus Magnus—'These fancies, which you have imbibed, are a thousand years old!'—while the other professor is even more scathing: the ancients 'promised impossibilities and performed nothing'.

Frankenstein rejects alchemy and magic and turns to scientific research. Only then does he get results. Wells was absolutely mistaken in his remarks about 'jiggery-pokery magic'; it is jiggery-pokery magic which Frankenstein rejects.

This is qualitatively different from being carried to the moon accidentally by migratory geese, or being shipwrecked on Lilliput, or summoning up the devil, or creating life out of spit and mud. Victor Frankenstein makes a rational decision: he operates on the world, rather than vice versa; and the reader is taken by plausible steps from the normal world we know to an unfamiliar one where monsters roam and the retributions of hubris are played out on a terrifying scale.

I say that the reader is taken by plausible steps. In fact, the interwoven processes of the *Frankenstein* narrative are better described by Suvin—'the ever-narrowing imaginative vortex . . .' etc. (*ibid.*)

To bring about the desired initial suspension of disbelief, Mary Shelley employs a writerly subterfuge which has since become the stock-in-trade of many SF writers. Wells imitated her method some decades later, to good effect. She appeals to scientific evidence for the veracity of her tale.

It is no accident that Mary Shelley's introduction to the anonymous 1818 edition of the novel begins with a reference to one of the most respected scientific minds of her day, Dr Erasmus Darwin. Darwin, grandfather of Charles Darwin, and early propagandist of evolutionary theory, was referred to by S. T. Coleridge as 'the most original-minded man in Europe'. The opening words of the Introduction are 'The event on which this fiction is founded has been supposed, by Dr Darwin, and some of the psychological writers of Germany, as not of impossible occurrence'. Thus Mary Shelley makes it clear that the first aspect of her novel which she wishes to stress is the scientific-speculative one.

This is the most revolutionary departure of *Frankenstein*. This is the one which separates it most markedly from any preceding Gothic novel (another factor being the absence of simpering heroines). We must not ignore a further novelty. The monster in his isolation operates as a criticism of society, as later does Wells's *The Invisible Man* and the central figure in Vonnegut's *Galapagos*. When the monster cries 'I am malicious because I am miserable', this atheistic note echoes the central blasphemy of Frankenstein's diseased creation. SF was to become a refuge for anti-religious and anti-establishment thinking, and some criticism of society is present in most successive SF, save in the trivial examples of Instant Whip.

In his edition of *Frankenstein*, Leonard Woolf argues that the novel should not be considered as SF, but rather as 'psychological allegory'.[16] This is like arguing that *Red Dust* is not SF because it is about terraforming. There is no reason why both books should not support both functions. The strength of SF is that it is not a pure stream.

David Ketterer, who has written perceptively about Mary Shelley's novel,[17] agrees with Woolf, while saying that the concerns of *Frankenstein* might more broadly be described as 'philosophical, alchemical, and transcendental, than psychological or scientific'. Ketterer also argues that *Frankenstein* cannot be described as SF.[18]

Arguments against *Frankenstein* being SF at all rest on very uncertain ground. Not only is there Mary Shelley's own intention, as expressed in her Introduction, but her sub-title points to where she believes its centre to lie; she is bringing up-to-date the myth of Prometheus. Her fire comes down from heaven. It was an inspiration—and one that Universal Studios would later make much of—to utilize the newly captive electricity as that promethean fire. Later

16 Leonard Woolf, ed., *The Annotated Frankenstein*, New York, Clarkson N. Potter Inc., 1977.

17 David Ketterer, *Frankenstein's Creation: The Book, The Monster, and Human Reality*, Victoria, BC, University of Victoria, 1979.

18 David Ketterer, 'Frankenstein in Wolf's Clothing', in *Science Fiction Studies*, 18, July 1979.

generations of writers, with neither more nor less regard for scientific accuracy, would use 'the power of the atom' with which to energize their perceptions of change. Nowadays, telepathic superpowers get by under the name of SF and cyberpunk passes for prophesy.

The argument against *Frankenstein*'s being the first novel of SF could be more convincingly launched on other grounds, historiological ones. The more any subject is studied, the further back its roots are seen to go. This is true, for instance, of the Renaissance, or the Romantic movement. So perhaps the quest for the First SF Novel, like the first flower of spring, is chimerical. But the period where we should expect to look for such a blossoming is during the Industrial Revolution, and perhaps just after the Napoleonic Wars, when changes accelerated by industry and war have begun to bite, with the resultant sense of isolation of the individual from and in society. This sense of isolation is a hallmark of Romanticism, displayed in the opening paragraph of that milestone of Romanticism, Jean-Jacques Rousseau's *Confessions*: 'I feel my heart and I know men. I am not like others whom I have seen; I dare believe that I am not made like anyone else alive'.

This is the region of *Frankenstein*. Mary Shelley found an objective correlative for the cold intellectual currents of her day. It has maintained, and even implemented, its power to our day.

We need to resist a temptation to classify rigidly, thinking to achieve intellectual clarity by so doing. There is no contradiction involved in regarding this remarkable transitional novel as a Gothic story, as one of the great horror stories of the English language, and as the progenitor of modern SF.[19]

Nobody seeks to argue that *Frankenstein* is not a horror story. The influence of the movies has greatly persuaded us to concentrate on the horror aspect. Yet the movies have always cheapened Mary Shelley's theme. The creature is usually turned into a dotty bogeyman, allowed only to grunt, grunt and destroy. It is presented as alien to humanity, not an extension of it.

Mary Shelley depicts the creature as alienated from society. Just when we have learned to fear the creature and loathe its appearance,

19 For an impressive and up-to-date confirmation of Mary Shelley's interest in science, see the long introduction by Marilyn Butler to her edition of *Frankenstein, The 1818 Text*, London, Pickering and Chatto, 1993.

she shows us the reality of the case. This is no monster. It is a lost soul. Above all things, it wishes to reverence its absent creator.

Every good Frankenstein-watcher has his own opinions about the monster. It is the French Revolution, says Suvin. It is Percy Bysshe Shelley, says Christopher Small. It is an hermaphrodite, says William Veeder. It and Victor are two different modes of one consciousness says Mary K. Patterson Thornburg.[20] I have come to believe that the stricken creature is Mary herself, that she found in the monster a striking objective correlative for her misfortunes at birth. Later in her career, in her other SF novel, she projects herself as Verney, the Last Man in a world of death wandering alone without a soulmate.

The novel is firmly anti-alchemy. The science is not very clear—impossible, if you like—but it is science as perfectly distinct from alchemy, although Mary was writing some years before the word 'scientist' was coined. As for the philosophical and transcendental qualities, they arise from the central science-fictional posit, just as they do in Arthur Clarke's *Childhood's End*, and rule the novel out of the SF stakes no more than does Woolf's psychological element.

If I were rewriting *BYS* now, I should qualify *Frankenstein*'s pre-eminence by allowing more discussion of the utopianists of eighteenth-century France, and such works of the Enlightenment as Sebastien Mercier's *The Year 2440* (1770).[21] The hero of this work wakes up seven centuries in the future, to a world of scientific and moral advance. But between such examples and later ones come the guillotines of the French Revolution, to deliver a blow to pure utopianism from which it has not recovered. The prevailing tone was to be set, at least in the Anglo-American camp, by the glooms of Gothic-Romanticism. As Bruce Sterling says, the colour of SF is *noir*.

I began by saying that the question of function was involved with the question of origin. To regard SF as co-existent with literature since

20 Studies by these three authors are: Christopher Small, *Ariel Like a Harpy: Shelley, Mary and Frankenstein*, London, Gollancz, 1972; William Veeder, *Mary Shelley and Frankenstein: The Fate of Androgyny*, Chicago, Chicago University Press, 1986; and Mary K. Patterson Thornburg, *The Monster in the Mirror: Gender and the Sentimental/Gothic Myth in Frankenstein*, Ann Arbor, MI, UMI Research Publications, 1987.

21 Discussed in 'Since the Enlightenment', in Brian Aldiss, *This World and Nearer Ones*, London, Weidenfeld & Nicolson, 1979.

Homer is to bestow on it no function not also operative in literature; which contradicts the experience of most of us who enjoy both literature and SF.

To regard SF as 'all starting with Gernsback' is to impoverish it to an unfair degree. SF then becomes a kind of gadget fiction, where every story more than ten years old is hailed as a 'Classic', and reputations can be made by rewriting one's previous story ad infinitum. SF may be a microcosm, but it is larger than a back yard.

To speak practically, one has to consider how best to introduce historical SF to new readers or students. Should one confront them with Homer's *Odyssey*, Mercier's *Year 2440*, Mary Shelley's *Frankenstein*, or the wretched crust of Gernsback's *Ralph 124C41+*? I trust that the answer is obvious.

It was a passage in *BYS* concerning Hugo Gernsback which most offended readers. This, it appears, was what Sam Moskowitz was attacking me for at the Lunacon. Later, the enthusiast David Kyle took me to task for saying that Hugo Gernsback was arguably one of the worst disasters ever to hit the SF field. Well, admittedly I stated the case strongly in order to be heard above the sound of choristers praising Old Uncle Hugo, but there was truth in what I said. Ten years later, I would parse the remark: worse disasters have struck since, notably commercial exploitation.

Kyle's *Pictorial History of Science Fiction* (1981), scores slightly better than Lester del Rey's. It actually manages to mention the title of one of my novels, *Barefoot in the Head* ('extravagant if not incomprehensible'). The gain is offset by a veiled threat. The last time anyone said such rough things about Gernsback, we are told, 'was at the 1952 Chicago con; a fan named Chester A. Polk was sent to hospital and Claude Degler, head of the Cosmic Circle, drove Don Rogers out of fandom for good'.

Alexei Panshin, reviewing *BYS* in *F&SF*, also threatened to have me drummed out of the regiment.

Fans like Kyle have had to watch SF taken out of their hands, when once they must have thought it was in their pockets. Well, chums, it belongs to Big Business now, so we're all losers. The media have taken over—and First Fandom is preferable to the Fourth Estate.

More ambivalent is the attitude of general critics of the field. There's a feel of punches being pulled. Tom Clareson, in 'Towards a

History of Science Fiction',[22] evades the issue entirely, with a bland paragraph on *Frankenstein* which follows on a reference to Asimov's *The Gods Themselves*. In James Gunn's history of SF,[23] he gives *BYS* a more than friendly nod, but cannot resist delivering the familiar litany of defunct magazines, backed by displays of gaudy covers. Like del Rey, Gunn names none of my fiction; like del Rey he lumps me in with the New Wave, though obviously without malice. In his later four-volumed critical anthology,[24] Gunn—always honest and pain-staking—becomes more venturesome; he is a 'safe' scholar moving slowly to a more individual, and creative, position.

Clareson and Gunn, like Kyle and Moskowitz, may be regarded honourably as old-timers in the field. Robert Scholes and Eric S. Rabkin, one gathers, are relative newcomers—as their 'thinking person's guide to the genre' demonstrates.[25] This means they cannot reel off litanies of dead stories in dead magazines. It also means they adopt *Frankenstein* as the progenitor of the species. Hooray! No matter they don't acknowledge where exactly they derived the idea from. They are genial about *BYS*, and mention in passing that I have written fiction, though of all my novels only *Barefoot in the Head* is named. More laziness! Perhaps someone somewhere taught it once. Charles Platt, are you blushing?

All the critical books I have mentioned are quirky, including my own. I am less conscious of quirks in two recent encyclopaedic works, Neil Barron's *Anatomy of Wonder: Science Fiction*[26] and the John Clute, Peter Nicholls *Encyclopedia of SF*,[27] both of which seek to be dispassionate in judgement. Both take cognizance of the range of my work over the last twenty-five years, short stories as well as novels, for which I am grateful.

Clute's *Encyclopaedia* is more bulky than *The Oxford Companion to English Literature*. It is a fact worthy of consideration.

22 In Marshall Tymn, ed., *The Science Fiction Reference Book*, San Bernardino, CA, Borgo Press, 1981.

23 James Gunn, *Alternate Worlds*, Englewood Cliffs, NJ, Prentice Hall, 1975.

24 James Gunn, *The Road to Science Fiction*, 4 volumes, New York, New English Library, Mentor, 1977–81.

25 Robert Scholes and Eric S. Rabkin, *Science Fiction: History, Science, Vision*, London, Oxford University Press, 1977.

26 New York, Bowker, 1976, Fourth Edition, 1995.

27 London, Orbit, Second Edition, 1993. Editors, John Clute & Peter Nicholls.

On the whole *Billion Year Spree* has entered the blood stream. I have gained fewer black marks for it than for my defence of the New Wave writers in England during the 1960s, when I fought for their right to express themselves in their own way rather than in someone else's. Despite the attempts of persons like del Rey to lump me in with the New Wave, I flourished before it arrived, and continue still to do. That experience taught me how conservative readers of SF are, for all their talk about The Literature of Change. But perhaps the study of SF, virtually non-existent when I began *BYS*, has brought in a more liberal race of academics; one hopes it is so.

This also must be said. I know, am friendly with, or at least have met, almost all the living writers and critics mentioned in this article. Such is part of the social life of science fiction writers, nor would one have it otherwise. David Kyle I have known since the 1950s—a man who would not set the head of the Cosmic Circle on to me unless I really deserved it. This gregariousness, reinforced by such SF institutions as conventions and fanzines, with their informal critical attitudes, forms a kind of concealed context within which—or against which—most SF writers still exist, long after the collapse of Gernsback's SF League.

Samuel Delany has pointed to this concealed context, urging formal critics to take note of it.[28] Certainly, I was aware of it when writing *BYS*, even if I missed it at Lunacon, when it became solid flesh in the form of Sam Moskowitz. My brief here has been to talk of adverse responses to *BYS*. So I have not talked about the praise it has received in many quarters, outside and inside the SF field. I intended the book to be enjoyed, and rejoiced when it and the Aldiss/ Wingrove successor gave enjoyment.

BYS concluded by forecasting a great increase in academic involvement in science fiction. That involvement has developed rapidly, as all can testify. Watching from the sidelines, I see some of the difficulties from which academics suffer.

Humanities departments are under threat in times of recession, in a way that science departments—though themselves not without difficulties—are not. In self-defence, academics in humanities posts write their papers in a form of language which imitates the jargon of their colleagues in the harder sciences. The result is frequently an

28 Samuel R. Delany, 'Reflections on Historical Models of Modern English Language Science Fiction', *Science Fiction Studies*, Vol. 7, Pt. 2, July 1980, reprinted in *Starboard Wine*, 1984.

inviolable form of gobbledegook. An example of what I mean is taken almost randomly from a respected critical journal:

> The most serious difficulty with the genre concept comes from the fact that the existence of a particular genre structure (variant) in a given epoch is usually accompanied by literary consciousness of writers, critics, and readers who recognize this structure as different from the synchronic structures of other genres. This intersubjective recognition, depending as it does on the general level of education and culture, on the familiarity of the reading public with traditional and modern literatures, and on the state of criticism in the epoch, is of course, often arbitrary.

While not entirely resisting attempts at divination, these two sentences seem to say little, and say it in an ugly way remote from the graces of our language as she is spoken. A defence mechanism is in operation. To speak plainly is to risk being taken for a fool. Difficulty must be seen to operate in the texts, or else there may be difficulty with grants in the future. SF criticism, being new, is particularly vulnerable to the administrative chopper.

Beneath the tortured language, what is said rarely carries malice. At least not openly. Our boat is still new and not properly tested: it must not be rocked. Thus criticism and its object have come full circle since the eighteenth century. Then, judgements were expressed with clarity and style, and were often designed to wound:

> Cibber, write all your verses upon glasses;
> So that we may not use them for our ——.

Bibliography

Betty T. Bennett, ed., *The Letters of Mary Wollstonecraft Shelley*, Baltimore, MD, Johns Hopkins Press, 3 vols, 1980–1988.

Betty T. Bennett & Charles E. Robinson, eds., *The Mary Shelley Reader*, Baltimore, MD, Johns Hopkins Press (Softshell Books), 1990.

Paula R. Feldman & Diana Scott-Kilvert, eds., *The Journals of Mary Shelley 1814–1844*, Oxford, Oxford University Press, 2 vols, 1987.

Robert Gittings & Jo Manton, *Claire Clairmont and the Shelleys 1798–1879*, Oxford, Oxford University Press, 1992.

George Levine & U. C. Knoepflmacher, eds., *The Endurance of 'Frankenstein'. Essays on Mary Shelley's Novel*, Berkeley, CA, University of California Press, 1979.

Charles E. Robinson, ed., *Mary Shelley: Collected Tales and Stories*, Baltimore, MD, Johns Hopkins Press (Softshell Books), 1990.

Mary Shelley, New Introduction by Brian Aldiss, *The Last Man*, London, The Hogarth Press, 1985.

William St Clair, *The Godwins and the Shelleys. The Biography of a Family*, New York, W. W. Norton & Co., 1989.

Mary Wollstonecraft, *Letters Written during a Short Residence in Sweden, Norway and Denmark*, Fontwell, Centaur Press, 1970. Or as *A Short Residence in Sweden, Norway & Denmark*, Harmondsworth, Penguin Classics, 1987.

Mary Wollstonecraft Shelley, edited with introduction and notes by Marilyn Butler, *Frankenstein: or, The Modern Prometheus. The 1818 Text*, London, William Pickering, 1993.

STURGEON: THE CRUELTY OF THE GODS

What a battering we took in those first years of reading science fiction! What a pounding and pummelling with the extraordinary, with the extravagant, with the extra-mural! What a sexless time we had of it in those big spaceships thundering through the American void towards planets where just to take one breath—well, I can remember when you simply opened the airlock door and *sniffed* to see that the air was okay . . . And if it wasn't okay, obviously anything could happen, shape-changing being the least of it.

The problems we faced on those planets! The awful creatures we encountered! Not that things were much better on Earth. Even before nuclear war was invented, ruined cities abounded. Plagues were always breaking out, ants were mutating, madmen gabbling strait-jacketed in mental wards proved to be sole possessors of the awful Truth about Earth . . .

Sometimes, terrible new and ingenious threats were just round the corner, awaiting their moment to burst forth. A twisted millionaire with a power complex was breeding a new species, little creatures who could survive any manner of disaster he brought down on them. And the little creatures were planning to escape and strike back. As a boy, you could not help wondering, awed, what manner of man could dream up such a story. He must be a marvel. Why, there was magic even in his name—Theodore Sturgeon . . .

There it was, perpetually cropping up attached to the stories I most admired. Sturgeon: quite an ordinary Anglo-American word among exotics like A. E. Van Vogt, Isaac Asimov, Heinlein, Simak and Kuttner. Yet—spiky, finny, odd. And it was not his original name. Theodore Hamilton Sturgeon was born Edward Hamilton Waldo, to the usual boring, undeserving parents. That was on Staten Island, the year the First World War ended.

So there were two of him, as there are of many a good writer. A bright side, a dark side—much like our old SF image of Mercury, remember, so much more interesting than banal reality. He had a mercurial temperament.

The bright side was the side everybody loved. There was something so damned nice, charming, open, empathic and elusive about Ted that women flocked to him. Men too. Maybe he was at the mercy of his own fey sexuality. If so, he was quizzical about it, as about everything. One of his more cutesy titles put it admirably: 'If All Men Were Brothers, Would you Let One Marry Your Sister?'. Not if it was Sturgeon, said a too-witty friend.

He played his guitar. He sang. He shone. He spoke of his philosophy of love. Ted honestly brought people happiness. If he was funny, it was a genuine humour which sprang from seeing the world aslant. A true SF talent. Everyone recognized his strange quality— 'Faunlike', some nut dubbed it; faunlike he certainly looked. Inexplicable, really.

Unsympathetic father, unsatisfactory adolescence. Funny jobs, and 'Ether Breather' out in *Astounding* in 1939. So to an even funnier job, science fiction writer. It's flirting with disaster. I could not believe those early stories: curious subject matter, bizarre revolutions, glowing style. And about sexuality. You could hardly believe your luck when one of Ted's stories went singing through your head.

'It', with Cartier illustrations, in *Unknown*. Terrifying. 'Derm Fool'. Madness. The magnificent 'Microcosmic God', read and re-read. 'Killdozer', appearing after a long silence. There were to be other silences. 'Baby is Three': again in the sense of utter incredibility with complete conviction, zinging across a reader's synapses. By a miracle, the blown up version, *More Than Human*, was no disappointment either. This was Sturgeon's caviar dish. Better even than *Venus Plus X* with its outré sexuality in a hermaphrodite utopia.

As for those silences. Something sank Sturgeon. His amazing early success, his popularity with fans and stardom at conventions—they told against the writer. Success is a vampire. In the midst of life we are in definite trouble. They say Sturgeon was the first author in the field ever to sign a six-book contract. A six-book contract was a rare mark of distinction, like being crucified. A mark of extinction. Ted was no stakhanovite and the deal did for him; he was reduced to writing a novelization of a schlock TV series, *Voyage to the Bottom of the Sea*, to fulfil his norms.

At one time he was reduced further to writing TV plot scripts for

Hollywood. He lived in motels or trailers, between marriages, between lives. Those who read *The Dreaming Jewels* or *Venus Plus X* or the story collections forget that writing is secretly a heavy load, an endless battle against the disappointments which come from within as well as without—and reputation is a heavier load. Ted was fighting his way back to the light when night came on.

About Ted's dark side.

Well, he wrote that memorable novel, *Some of Your Blood*, about this crazy psychotic who goes for drinking menstrual discharge. Actually, it does not taste as bad as Ted made out. That was his bid to escape the inescapable adulation.

Here's one small human thing he did. He and I, with James Gunn, were conducting the writer's workshop at the Third Conference of the Fantastic at Boca Raton, Florida.

Our would-be writers circulated their effusions around the table for everyone's comment. One would-be was a plump, pallid, unhappy lady. Her story was a fantasy about a guy who tried three times to commit suicide, only to be blocked each time by a green monster from Hell who wanted him to keep on suffering. Sounds promising, but the treatment was hopeless.

Dumb comments around the table. I grew impatient with their unreality. When the story reached me, I asked the lady right out, 'Have you ever tried to commit suicide?'

Unexpected response. She stared at me in shock. Then she burst into a hailstorm of tears, collapsing onto the table. 'Three times', she cried. Everyone looked fit to faint.

'It's nothing to be ashamed of', I said. 'I've tried it too.'

'So have I', said Sturgeon calmly.

He needn't have come in like that. He just did it bravely, unostentatiously, to support me, to support her, to support everyone. And there certainly was a lot of misery and disappointment in Ted's life, for all the affection he generated. Yet he remained kind, loving, giving. (The lady is improving by the way. We kept in touch. That's another story.)

If that does not strike you as a positive story, I'm sorry. I'm not knocking suicide, either. Everyone should try it at least once.

Ted was a real guy, not an idol, an effigy, as some try to paint him. He was brilliant, so he suffered. I know beyond doubt that he would be pleased to see me set down some of the bad times he had. He was not one to edit things out. Otherwise he would have been a less powerful writer.

There are troves of lovely Sturgeon tales (as in the collection labelled *E Pluribus Unum*), like 'Bianca's Hands', which a new generation would delight in. He wrote well, if sometimes overlushly. In many ways, Ted was the direct opposite of the big technophile names of his generation, like Doc Smith, Poul Anderson, Robert Heinlein et al. His gaze was more closely fixed on people. For that we honoured him, and still honour him. Good for him, that he never ended up in that prick's junkyard where they pay you a million dollars' advance for some crud that no sane man wants to read.

Ted died early in May 1985 in Oregon, of pneumonia and other complications. Now he consorts with Sophocles, Phil Dick, and the author of the *Kama Sutra*. He had returned from a holiday in Hawaii, taken in the hopes he might recover his health there. That holiday, incidentally, was paid for by another SF writer—one who often gets publicity for the wrong things. Thank God, there are still some good guys left. We are also duly grateful for the one just departed.

Of course, Sturgeon had his faults, but at his best his turn of phrase, his twist of mind, should have made him a widely admired name in American letters. A story like 'When You're Smiling', which appeared in *Galaxy* in the 1950s, is beautiful and brutal, spiked with psychological understanding. It's the old conundrum, posed every day to those of us who love SF: why doesn't everyone recognize its sterling virtues?

So Ted slowly went into eclipse—not that that is not often the fate also of better-known writers. He showed up at one of Harry Harrison's Dublin conferences in the late 1970s with a charming lady in tow. He addressed me in these words, 'Hey, Brian, you and I are the best ever SF writers, why don't we get together and write the best ever novel? Why don't I come back to your place for a coupla months, settle in and work with you?'

A hundred reasons for saying no leapt immediately to mind.

Now there's a Sturgeon Project,[1] aiming at returning all of Sturgeon's stories to print. In 1993, the project published *Argyll*, an eighty-page booklet. It is Ted's tragic story of his relationship with his step-father. Samuel R. Delany, in a well meaning afterword, compared *Argyll* with Kafka's *Letter to His Father*. That's a mistake. Kafka's profound document adds to our understanding of human nature. Whereas Ted Sturgeon's piece, though of great interest, is just a self-

---

1 For more information, write to The Sturgeon Project, c/o Paul Williams, Box 611, Glen Ellen, CA 95442, USA.

pitying account of a man's cruelty to a small boy, a persecution of the almost helpless.

At least it tells us where 'Microcosmic God' came from.

THE DOWNWARD JOURNEY
Orwell's *1984*

> 'There is a word in Newspeak', said Syme, 'I don't know whether you know it: *duckspeak*, to quack like a duck. It is one of those interesting words that have two contradictory meanings. Applied to an opponent, it is abuse; applied to someone you agree with, it is praise.'

Neologisms such as *duckspeak* and slogans like WAR IS PEACE provide dramatic signposts in the landscape of George Orwell's *1984*, and direct our attention towards the oppositions and paradoxes of which it is constructed. The whole novel charts an example of enantiodromia, that is, the inevitable turning of one thing into its opposite; its strategy is to anatomize Winston Smith's progression from hatred to the time—dramatically achieved in that resounding last sentence of the text—when he comes to love Big Brother.

In this mirror effect, left has become right, right left. I shall deal here with some of the ways in which Orwell mirrors life.

One major mirror effect is proclaimed in the very title, for *Nineteen Eighty-Four* is itself a piece of wordplay, the year 1984 being a mirror image, at least as far as the last two digits are concerned, of the year in which Orwell was writing the novel, 1948.

The novel itself is full of similar oppositions. Winston Smith's barrack-like flat is contrasted with the love-nest over the antique shop. The elaboration and importance of his work at the Ministry is contrasted with its triviality. The astronomical number of boots manufactured on paper by the state is contrasted with the fact that half the population of Oceania goes barefoot. When O'Brien holds up four fingers, Smith sees five, in the final obscene triumph of doublethink.

It is a profoundly disturbing view of life: everything depends on words and what goes on in the head. External reality no longer exists, at least as far as the Party is concerned. *1984* might have been written by Bishop Berkeley.

There is another hierarchy of oppositions, the ones which most grasp our attention because they are mirror images of assumptions we make in the everyday world. We do not believe that IGNOR-ANCE IS STRENGTH or that FREEDOM IS SLAVERY—although the novel shows clearly how these things can be. We believe that peace is the norm and war is the exception, unlike the rulers of Oceania. Nor do we readily accept that political confessions, extracted under duress, are true.

All these oppositions, which are word-orientated, are paraded in order to unsettle us. If the novel's title is 'merely' wordplay, then we are entitled to ask to what extent Orwell was actually trying to predict the future, or to what extent he was simply deploying 'the future' as a metaphor for his present; in other words, using the future for yet another mirror effect.

In many of its aspects, *1984* captures accurately daily existence in World War II for the civilian population. Reading Orwell's sordid future, we relive the tawdry past.

Here are the run down conditions under which people in England, Germany, and elsewhere actually lived, here are the occasional bombs falling, the spirit of camaraderie, and the souped up hatred of a common enemy. The rationing, the propaganda, the life lived in shelters, the cigarettes which must be kept horizontal so that their tobacco does not spill out, the shortage of razor blades, the recourse to cheap gin: these are details of common experience in the 1940s, gathered together for maximum artistic effect. At the same time, on a more personal level, Smith's work at the Ministry of Truth reflects Orwell's work at the BBC in Broadcasting House.

In such aspects, Orwell used a general present. It is the general present which provides the furniture of the novel.

More deeply part of the centrality of the book are some of Orwell's own obsessions. The familiar Orwellian squalor is in evidence throughout. The woman poking out a drain in *The Road to Wigan Pier* reappears as Mrs Parsons with her drain problem, and so on. Such matters are in evidence even in Orwell's first novel, *Keep the Aspidis-tra Flying*, and a preoccupation with illness and personal decay infect the novel—hardly surprising, in view of Orwell's deteriorating health. He died only a few months after *1984* was published and proclaimed. In the final scenes, when Smith and Julia meet for the last time, it is age as well as torture which has ruined them: 'her thickened, stiffened body was no longer recognisable from behind'.

But this is a novel operating beyond the compass of the ordinary realist novel. Being a political novel—that rare thing, an English political novel—it has more dimensions to it than the physical. Its principal preoccupation is with betrayal, betrayal through words. In this respect, it is a sibling of *Animal Farm*. ALL ANIMALS ARE EQUAL BUT SOME ANIMALS ARE MORE EQUAL THAN OTHERS is a step, or rather a long stride, towards *duckspeak*, and the betrayal of the deepest intentions of a revolution. Winston Smith, right from the start, is not only a secret enemy of the Party he serves. He also betrays himself by his enjoyment of the work he does for it. 'Smith's greatest pleasure in life was his work'—and his work is bound up with words, distorting the truth by falsifying old records even when those records are themselves already fake.

Orwell's deployment of the philosophical entanglements inherent in words and phrases is masterly. He was early in life fascinated by G. K. Chesterton's unparalleled talent for paradox. *1984* may owe something to Chesterton's future-fantasy, *The Napoleon of Notting Hill*; it certainly extends its paradoxes. One example must suffice. When Smith asks O'Brien if Big Brother exists 'in the same way as I exist', O'Brien answers immediately, 'You do not exist'. Here the paradox is that no paradox exists, for, in Newspeak terms, Smith has become an unperson and indeed does not exist.

Nor is it too fanciful to imagine that Orwell believed that his novel would falsify the future. Certainly, that seems to have been one of its effects. Fear is a great hypnotizer, and some people are prepared to believe that we live in an actual Orwellian vision of the future, in that world whose image is a boot stamping on a human face forever. In a literal sense, of course, this is totally untrue. We still live in a world worth defending. War and peace are still distinguishable states of mind. (And in *1984* at least one atomic bomb has been dropped on Airstrip One; that has not happened in our real world.)

The West may, like decadent Byzantium apeing the manners of its besiegers, ultimately betray itself from within to the enemy without. But we still live in a community where diverse opinion is tolerated, where individual salvation may be found, where TV sets have an Off button, and where we are not subject to that prevailing Chestertonian paradox which subjugates Orwell's proles: 'Until they become conscious they will never rebel, and until they have rebelled they cannot become conscious.'

To see *1984* as a nest of paradoxes is not to denigrate its power. Indeed, it may be in part to admit that to attempt to chronicle the future using the past tense is itself a paradox, one committed unwittingly every time a science fiction writer puts pen to paper. But *1984* is a more humorous novel than is generally acknowledged, though admittedly the humour is decidedly *noir*. In that respect, it bears a resemblance to Franz Kafka's work, about which learned commentators have rightly expended much serious thought. (Learned commentators are correct in regarding humour as subversive.) Yet when Kafka read extracts from *Der Prozess* to Max Brod and friends, they all laughed heartily, and Kafka often could not continue for tears of laughter. But Kafka and Orwell both acknowledged Dickens among their masters of grim humour.

To Orwell's own paradoxes, time has added another. For many years during the Cold War, Orwell's phrase 'Big Brother is watching you' was popular. It referred, of course, to all those TV cameras which were never switched off, keeping the population of Airstrip One under surveillance.

But as social life became nastier, rougher, during the 1980s, as the murder count rose in New York, London and elsewhere, the public in their malls and supermarkets began to beg for more cameras to be installed everywhere. They begged for more surveillance. They wanted to be watched. In an age when we no longer believe in the attention of an omni-present God, even the cold eye of the camera is welcome.

When I first became interested in Orwell's play with paradox and mirror image, I conceived the idea that the plot of *1984* is much like that of an A. E. van Vogt science-fantasy novel, in which one man alone has a vision of the truth, sets out to overturn the world, and finally manages to do so ('Asylum' is one such example). Orwell took a great interest in trash literature. This interest manifests itself in *1984* in the passages where Smith, as part of his work, invents a story about a fictitious character called Comrade Ogilvy. 'At the age of three, Comrade Ogilvy had refused all toys except a drum, a submachine gun, and a model helicopter . . . At nineteen, he had designed a hand-grenade which . . . at its first trial, had killed thirty-one Eurasian prisoners in one burst . . .' This clearly is a kind of science fiction story at whose absurdity we are meant to laugh.

In pursuit of the van Vogt connection, I once took the opportunity of asking Orwell's widow, Sonia, if Orwell had read much pulp science fiction (it existed at that period only in pulp magazine form).

Had he ever read any A. E. van Vogt, with plots centering on world-wide conspiracy?

Her answers, like so many answers life gives us, were enigmatic. She thought he had read some science fiction. She did not know the name of van Vogt.

About H. G. Wells Orwell was much better informed. He expressed his delight more than once in Wells's scientific romances, even going so far as to claim that 'thinking people who were born about the beginning of the century are in some sense Wells's own creation'. But he disagreed strongly with Wells as political sooth-sayer, and in particular with Wells's views concerning a world state, of which he said, 'Much of what Wells has argued and worked for is physically there in Nazi Germany'.

Shortly after World War I, Wells rebuked Winston Churchill for speaking of the Bolsheviks as if they were a different order of being. Orwell argued that Churchill was more realistic and that he was right and Wells wrong. With totalitarianism, a new order of men had come into the world, perverting science for their own ends. *1984* is the history of that new order. O'Brien and the Party members are Orwell's ghoulish mirror image of Wells's Samurai in *A Modern Utopia*, while at the same time representing the new totalitarianism rising to threaten the post-war world. The debt to Wells is unavoidable; he was the man who had created the future as a forum for debate on present ends and means at the turn of the century.

We can now see the answer to our question. Was Orwell trying to predict the future or was he using the notion of the future as a mirror for his present? Of course the answer is ambiguous. Most of the novel mirrors the past (' "The past is more important", agreed O'Brien gravely'), including the tradition of constructing utopias, but this is built about a core of futurism, that core in which Orwell conjures up the spectre of England under a totalitarian regime, a regime in which science is at the service of a new brutality, and in which the world is locked into a kind of dreadful unity through the war that is peace. The future and its polemics are given reality by the employment of the furniture of the past.

As with many novels, *1984* mirrors the author's own life and the books to which he is indebted. What is different about *1984* is that it utilizes the most powerful lever available to science fiction; it places the events it depicts ahead of us, and so to be yet experienced, instead of behind us in the past, and so safely out of the way.

In Orwell's world, the very word 'freedom' has been banished. Whereas in our world, words like 'freedom' and 'democracy' are bandied about in everyday use on all sides. But has freedom in fact been banished for the fictitious inhabitants of Airstrip One? In order to maintain a boot stamping on the human face forever, the owner of the boot must suffer as well as the owner of the face. The price of loss of freedom is eternal vigilance.

There are few rewards for the Party faithful except power. Power is seen as an end in itself. The real, undeclared aim of the Party is, we are told, to remove all the pleasure from the sexual act. This startling but negative aim, which Orwell does not consistently pursue, reflects the negativity of power; it is doubtful whether Big Brother actually exists, while higher up officials like O'Brien are merely inquisitors with some new, some ancient, tortures at their command. Orwell can imagine rats but not Stalin.

Power, like money, is useless in itself. There has to be something to spend it on. It is true that 'purges and vaporizations' are a part of the mechanism of the Party's regime of government, but this is scarcely enough to satisfy a Party member. Puritanism is all they get. Orwell himself was possibly dissatisfied with this arrangement. When Smith gets to O'Brien's flat, we see that it is not as austere as all that. There is wallpaper on the walls, the floors are carpeted, the telescreen can be switched off, the butler pours wine from a decanter, and there are good cigarettes in a silver box. Not sybaritic, exactly; more the sort of thing to which typical Old Etonians (Orwell was an untypical example) could be said to be accustomed.

Even in these elegant surroundings, O'Brien is discovered still working. The proles he helps to oppress enjoy greater freedom.

For the proles in their seedy bits of decaying London there are trashy newspapers, astrology, films 'oozing with sex', pornography, rubbishy novels, booze, sport and gambling. These are all in plentiful supply. Orwell shows his traditional mixture of despisal and envy of the working classes; Smith's attitude is very much that of Gordan Comstock in *Keep the Aspidistra Flying*, written thirteen years earlier. Gordan 'wanted to sink down, down into the muck where the money does not rule'. The proles are free from worries, only the proles have double beds, and no one cares if there are bed bugs. Smith manages to reach that place mentioned longingly by Gordan: 'down, down, into some dreadful sub-world that as yet he could only imagine'. Orwell did finally imagine it, in his most extraordinary novel, and that repeated 'down, down' shows how far the journey was.

One can see how George Orwell enjoyed writing *1984* for its own sake. I believe the prophetic element to be only part of its attraction, and in any case the prophesy was apotropaic, intended to warn. Thus, the more it succeeded in conveying its warning, the less likely was its picture of the future to become reality. Its success is that it fails to paint a true portrait of the true 1984. However grim we may hold our 1984 to be, it is not Orwell's grimness. We perhaps owe Orwell some gratitude that his widely influential *1984* is not our 1984.

Some commentators have claimed as a weakness the fact that the dialectic of the novel is all with the Party, with O'Brien, with the Thought Police, and that nothing positive is offered by the way of opposition. Such comments show a misreading of the book. In the long line of utopianists, Orwell has an honourable place.

H. G. Wells perceived that for a utopia to exist in a period of rapid communications it had to be world-wide; and for 1905, before the First World War, this was an acute perception. By the late 1940s, after a second World War, Orwell saw that a countervailing paradox was required. His way to happiness on Earth lies in the subversive message which Julia slips Smith in the corridor, a note saying merely I LOVE YOU. And utopia, far from being worldwide, has shrunk to a shabby little room over a shop, with a willing girl, a double bed, and plenty of privacy.

Thus have our expectations diminished over the century.

Such a utopia needs no dialectic. Its strength is precisely that it does not require words. For the true enemy in *1984* is ultimately words themselves, those treacherous words that will serve any vile purpose to which they are put. Even Julia's message has a taint to it, since its three words hold the most important one in common with that other well known three-worder, the much-feared Ministry of Love: indeed in Smith's case, one leads almost directly to the other.

In place of words came objects, and the inarticulate life of proledom, personified in the old washerwoman singing under the lovers' window as she hangs out her washing. It is a distinctly nostalgic substitution. As Smith says, referring to a paperweight he has bought, a piece of coral embedded in glass, 'If the past survives anywhere, it's a few solid objects with no words attached to them, like that lump of glass there'. Words are the allies of doublethink.

In a television broadcast made over the Christmas period, 1982, the novelist Anthony Burgess claimed to have read *1984* thirty times. He said of it that it was one of those rare books which tells us what we need to know, which informs us of what reality is.

Like all of Orwell's novels, with the brilliant exception of *Animal Farm*, *1984* is not a masterpiece judged purely as novel. Judged as a vehicle for putting over what Orwell wished to tell us, for conveying that pungent mixture of squalor, nostalgia, disillusion and analysis of betrayal, it is brilliant.

Although *1984* does not on the surface hold up a mirror to our 1984, I believe that Burgess was right on a more inward plane. In 1948, that drab year best never relived, the novel seemed indeed to be a prediction of the future, exact in each realistic detail. Read in the year of its title, it turned disconcertingly into a secret history of all our lives. For we have lived in a parallel world of political bullying and hypocrisy, of wars and totalitarianism, of cultural revolutions and anti-cultural movements, of blind hedonism and wild-eyed shortage. Even if these things have not overcome us, they have marked us. Our shadows—to use the word in a Jungian sense—have conspired with the Thought Police and the Party. What has happened to us here is, in O'Brien's words, forever.

We see the novel's transformation through time: from a prophecy of the future to a parable of our worldly existence, 1948–1984.

It will be interesting to see what becomes of Orwell's novel now that the year 1984 is over and concentration on it has died away. It would be pleasant to believe that *Animal Farm* would be more generally read and recognized, for it remains *the* book on revolution and revolution's betrayal and one of the seminal fables of our century.

My personal feeling is that *1984* will continue to be read and loved by ordinary people; and this for a good reason. Though we prefer to overlook the fact, many aspects of *1984* closely correspond to the lives of those 'ordinary people'. For most, life is a battle against poverty, shortages, inadequate housing, ill health. They too experience betrayals which may prove fatal. They too come to experience in their own anatomy—and without needing words—what Julia experienced, a thickened stiffened body, unrecognizable from behind. They too are manipulated by uncaring governments.

In one film version of *1984*, the ending showed Smith and Julia reunited, clinging happily to each other, unchanged by their ordeal. We have a contempt of that sort of thing. Not only is such nonsense untrue to Orwell's novel: it is unfortunately untrue to most people's experience.

What we value most about Orwell's work is not its prophecy or even its polemics, but rather the way it faithfully mirrors the experience of the majority of the people.

PEEP

~~~~~~

When James Blish was yielding finally in the battle against cancer which he had fought for many years, my wife and I went to visit him in the ominously named Battle Hospital in Reading, England.

He lay in bed in a towelling robe, dark, bitter, lightweight—intense against the pallid room. As ever, he radiated great mental energy. Books were piled all over the place, by the bedside, on the bed. Oswald Spengler's *Decline of the West* lay open, face down, on the blankets.

Dear Blish! What tenacity of life and intellect! I thought of that incident in Battle Hospital when reading *The Quincunx of Time* once again. *Quincunx* is a rare thing, true SF with a scientific basis—the sort of story that readers have always been saying isn't written any more. And it is something more than that. It is, in a way, gadget fiction; central to it is a marvellous gadget, the Dirac transmitter—but the Dirac leads to deep metaphysical water, into which Blish plunges with glee.

The science chiefly involved is mathematics, proverbially the queen of the sciences. New dimensions of time are opened in the novel; a more complex math has been achieved in the future, in which time is subsumed as an extra spatial dimension. Hence *Quincunx*'s world-lines. Hence, too, one of its most famous passages, when one of the characters who has been listening to the transmitter declares:

> I've heard the commander of a world-line cruiser, travelling from 8873 to 8704 along the world-line of the planet Heth-shepa, which circles a star on the rim of NGC 4725, call for help across eleven million light years . . .

The characters who overhear this extraordinary communication are perplexed, as well they might be. They work out the problem, the solution to which is neat and exciting. Their perplexity springs from the fact that they are looking into a future where different number-worlds from ours prevail. It's wonderful but also logical: *there is not, and there cannot be, numbers as such*. The line in italics is not mine but Spengler's. He put it in italics too.

Spengler amplified his statement by saying, 'There are several number worlds as there are several Cultures. We find an Indian, an Arabian, a Classical, a Western type of mathematical thought and, corresponding with each, a type of number—each type fundamentally peculiar and unique, an expression of a particular world-feeling . . .'

Whether or not Blish derived some of his ideas direct from Spengler, we cannot now determine. In this case, it seems likely.

A different cultural base would naturally make the future difficult for us to comprehend, and vice versa. The future will no more understand our compulsion to stock-pile enough nuclear weapons to destroy the world several times over than we understand why the Egyptians built the pyramids.

'You'll know the future, but not what it means', says one of the characters in *Quincunx*. 'The farther into the future you travel with the machine, the more incomprehensible the messages become . . .'

One of the many original features of this novel is that it does actually concern the future. Most science fiction, if it is not fantasy, is about some extension of the present which only by agreement do we call 'the future'. It catches our attention because we see it in the mirror of the present day. Blish was after something different. *Quincunx* is like few other fictions, and does not resemble closely anything else Blish wrote.

Another strange feature is the fact that the story is about a galactic empire, although this does not appear to be the case at first. (I anthologized it under its original title, 'Beep', in my two-volume *Galactic Empires* (Avon Books, 1979). Blish solves the vital question of how communications could be maintained over vast distances. The strange thing about Blish's galactic empire is that it is a utopia. This we have never heard before. Things always go wrong in galactic empires, as we know. In Blish's empire, things go obstinately right. Instant communication has brought perfect communion.

The long short story 'Beep' has been only slightly expanded to make *Quincunx*. Most of the expansion is in the nature of philosophical exploration of the theme, and includes a portrait of Captain Weinbaum as seen through an extra dimension: 'a foot thick, two feet wide, five feet five inches in height, and five hundred and eighty-six trillion, five hundred and sixty-nine billion, six hundred million miles in duration'.

Blish in his introduction makes a typically prickly defence of his book, quoting a critic's comment that it is 'not redundant with physical action'. That may be so. But 'Beep' achieved immediate popularity, and has proved unforgettable. There is no rule which says that science fiction has to be packed with action. Better a tale of real imagination and ingenuity—like this one.

One of the most ingenious features of the original story lay hidden in its title, 'Beep'. 'Beep' contains a wealth of meaning just like the beep in the story. Noise is information in disguise, Blish tells us. To ram the notion home, he has two people in disguise, plus a popular song, also disguised. And free will disguised as rigid determinism.

We are not taken into the galactic empire. All we are allowed is a *peep*, because we are stuck here in the present, without benefit of Dirac transmitters. But that peep, like the beep, contains infinite worlds, once you consider it.

Quincunx is really a clever bag of tricks. No wonder readers loved it. Its story-line is shaped in an odd spiral, the world-line of which whirls you into a fiery heart of speculation, then out again.

I just wish Blish in his introduction had taken the opportunity to explain his new title, since that task now devolves on me.

The title refers to the five-dimensional framework within which the affairs of the story are conducted. A quincunx is an arrangement of five objects at four corners with one in the centre, in the figure of a lozenge or other rectangle. The structure of the story leads us to believe that Blish may have visualized his small cast of characters set out in some such quincuncial fashion:

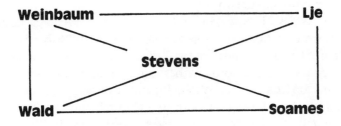

This figure lines up the males on the left and the women on the right, with the indeterminate figure of J. Selby Stevens in the middle to represent the vanishing fifth dimension.

Blish seized upon the idea of a mystical all-pervasive quincunx from Sir Thomas Browne's curious work, *The Garden of Cyrus, or the Quincuncial Lozenge* (1658). Cyrus the Great, the founder of the Persian Empire, restored the Hanging Gardens of Babylon, planting out saplings in lozenge configurations. Our word 'Paradise' comes from the Persian word for garden, and *Quincunx* depicts a kind of paradise, where sins and crimes are easily forgiven and young lovers have guardian angels—in the shape of Event Police—watching over them.

Browne's tract is a discourse upon all the manifestations of quincunxes in nature, in mankind, on earth, and in the heavens. According to Browne, it is an all-pervasive sign, although little commented upon. This, of course, fits in with Blish's conception of the world-lines and the math behind them. Despite all of which, I still think that 'Beep' is the better title.

But Blish liked such archaic systems of knowledge as Browne's, and his books are choked with their fossils. We both had a passion for Browne's writings, though I lack Blish's ferocious appetite for archaic systems. Also by his bedside, that last time we saw him in Battle Hospital, lay a copy of Samuel Taylor Coleridge's *Biographia Literaria*. Coleridge described this book as 'sketches of my literary life', but it consists mainly of discussions of Wordsworth's poetry and the philosophy of Kant, Schelling, and the German philosophers. I had a vision of Blish about to enter the complex realm of Coleridge's thought. He seemed too frail to traverse those gusty corridors of metaphysics. Here was one more ramshackle structure of thought, tempting him in. But Time, with which he wrestled in *Quincunx* and the other works, had run out.

When James Blish and his stalwart wife Judy received visitors in their Harpsden home during the last stages of Blish's illness, he would not be able to speak at first. In any case, he was not a man all found it easy to feel at home with, though his intimate friends had no problems on that score. When he had drunk a neat tumbler of whisky, he would liven up, and then would begin to talk. He spoke impersonally for the most part, eyes darkly gleaming in his skull; perhaps he could talk about opera, to which he listened on LPs. The operas of Richard Strauss especially appealed to him. He made dry jokes as he went along, creaking with mirth. He had great admirations, great hatreds.

At one time, when our mutual friend, Harry Harrison, was also present, Blish was going on at some length about Wagner's *Ring des Nibelungen*, on which he was an enthusiastic authority.

Harry grew impatient at last.

'Come on, Jim', he said 'it's only a bunch of krauts singing'.

At which Blish broke off into tremendous fits of laughter.

All Blish's novels repay reading and re-reading. He was never one of the most popular writers in our field, although his *Cities in Flight* series received great acclaim, and certainly *A Case of Conscience*—which won a Hugo Award—became popular even beyond the confines of SF. Perhaps it is because most of his books are 'not redundant with physical action' that he has otherwise been less widely enjoyed. He is, however, one of the most original of writers, and *The Quincunx of Time* one of his most original books.

He would have been delighted to see this new edition.

Time has gone by since the above was written. Books do not get reprinted as once they did, as the babble of voices grows higher. Jim Blish's name is no longer greatly remembered.

I remember him. He died during a heatwave, on 30 July 1975, which happened to be the day I finished writing *The Malacia Tapestry*. It fell to my wife and me to find a burial place for Jim in Oxford. His last wish was to be buried in an Oxford college—he who was the graduate of an American college. It proved no longer possible to be buried in a college, unless one was perhaps a principal: the sacred but limited ground is choked with bones of earlier scholars.

'They lie three deep', one sexton reported to me, leaning on his divining rod.

We found Jim a resting place finally, in the overgrown St Cross cemetery. He lies within sight of the walls of Magdalen, not too far from where Maurice Bowra is buried, and another story-teller, Kenneth Grahame, author of *Wind in the Willows*. I often pass the cemetery when going through Oxford, and think of my old friend, whose imagination travelled beyond the limits of our universe. R.I.P.

CULTURE
Is it Worth Losing Your Balls For?

The learned papers on the SF of Kingsley Amis—even with titles like *Revisionary Right-Wing Hermeneutics*—have been few. I cannot compete in that area. However, some reflections might be set down with a view to reminding readers of an author, remarkable in his own right, who also took a great and amiable interest in SF over a number of years. During that period he produced two novels which should be better known to all those seriously interested in SF.

Since *New Maps of Hell* was published as long ago as 1960, we perhaps need reminding how widely influential it was. It was witty and knowledgeable, cocking a snook at the establishment, and served to silence many ill-informed critics. Indeed, it contributed to the slow upward climb ('if that's what it is', I hear some say) of SF into respectability.

With that respectability, Amis and his friend Robert Conquest were soon to quarrel. Their argument was that SF was best within narrow compass under John W. Campbell's jurisdiction, that the so called *avante-garde* experiments merely replayed much work of a similar disastrous kind done in the 1920s, and that respectability inevitably meant forsaking a previously unembarrassed muse.

On another front, Amis was conducting a war against educationalists, at a time when educational establishments were opening their doors to more students—and, Amis argued, thereby diluting quality. His slogan was, 'More means less'.

In view of what has been happening since, we can see that if this slogan is applied to the SF field, Amis is probably right. Certainly the SF short story—the jewel in the crown of 1940s and 1950s SF—has suffered of late, when it is half-way financially profitable to write SF. (Once upon a time, so the legend goes, you wrote because . . . well, because it was SF, not because it paid.)

However, whatever Amis's doubts, he wrote a few SF stories,

'Something Strange' being published in *The Spectator* in 1960, and broadcast on the BBC Third Programme. It bears a family resemblance to my story 'Outside'. He also edited the *Spectrum* anthologies with Robert Conquest, and reviewed SF for many years in *The Observer*—a post later taken over less sympathetically by his son, Martin Amis.

I had an early suspicion regarding Amis's reading tastes. After the still explosively funny *Lucky Jim* he wrote *That Uncertain Feeling* (1955). Both novels were filmed, the latter as *Only Two can Play*, with Peter Sellers as Lewis, the awful Welsh librarian. (Amis himself appears in the film, hopping nimbly off a double decker bus.)

In *That Uncertain Feeling*, Amis came out of the closet. Whatever faults Lewis may have, in the way of boozing and chasing skirt, he is redeemed by his addiction to *Astounding Science Fiction*. *Astounding* gets two mentions in Chapter Five and one in Chapter Eight. It was about this time that Amis and I first met, to discover how well-versed we were in *The Worlds of Nul-A*.

Amis's two SF novels are elegant exercises in their particular subgenres. *Russian Hide-and-Seek* (1980) is cautionary: 'If this goes on . . .' *The Alteration* (1976) is an impeccable alternative world.

Incidentally, we observe that when a noted humorist like Amis turns to SF, he becomes rather serious. *The Alteration*, indeed, centres round the topic of whether a young chorister, Hubert Anvil, should have his testicles removed. The scene is an England which has never renounced Catholicism.

At the end of the drama, contemplating its effects, the American Ambassador to Britain says, 'When I think of the immensity of the chance . . .' Ambassador van den Haag looks down in pity at Hubert Anvil in his hospital bed. He is unable to finish his sentence. Words have failed him.

But that unfinished sentence contains, in a way, the whole substance of the story. Are we to believe that what happens to Hubert is simply malign chance—or could it be the action of a malign God? Accident? Design? Are we reading in *The Alteration* a further instalment of Kingsley Amis's depiction of the triumph of the forces of evil, continued from *The Anti-Death League* and *The Green Man*? There's no reason to imagine otherwise.

The Alteration ranks in the succession of Ward Moore's *Bring the Jubilee* (1953) and Philip K. Dick's *The Man in the High Castle* (1962). Amis's novel also has something in common with Harry Harrison's *Tunnel Through the Deeps* (1972); both novels depict the United States

in globally subsidiary roles. Amis's New England is Dutch-domin-
ated and rather full of 'Red Indians', while Harrison's America
remains a British colony, in which George Washington ranks as a
traitor. Harrison receives honourable mention in Amis's novel: 'the
great Harrison' is the engineer who has built the railway line
between Coverley and Rome, on which Hubert travels in the Eternal
City Rapid.

Both Amis's and Harrison's novels feature early industrial forms of
transport. Against Harrison's coal-powered airplanes, Amis offers
giant dirigibles, the 'Edgar Alan Poe' being over one thousand feet
long, as the only form of aerial transport. But the jovial tone of
Harrison's alternative world is a far cry from Amis's grim presenti-
ment of what in *New Maps of Hell* he dubs a 'counterfeit world'.

Amis's major alteration is to display a religion-ruled present very
different from what passes as the real one. The England in which his
story is set is dominated by the Vatican in Rome. The power of the
Catholic Church stretches round the world, as far as Hanoi and
Nagasaki. Only the Republic of New England is Protestant. It is to
New England that Shakespeare has fled—to die in exile. The main
enemy of Christendom is the Ottoman Empire; and the Turks get as
far as entering Brussels.

Critics have argued about whether the novel is an attack on
Catholicism, or on religion in general or, more generally, on a super-
power mentality (rather a safe wicket, you might say, in the 1970s).
The Church stands in here for the role played by the conquering
Russians in *Russian Hide-and-Seek*; both prelates and commissars,
professing creeds in which they have no belief, represent thuggish
oppression. Talents as non-diverse as Beria and Himmler have found
refuge in the cloth. A delicate distaste for empty rituals salts both
novels. Amis's universal church has come into being because intelligence and creativity have been beaten down.

His great alterations hinge on a number of historic factors—Martin
Luther, instead of being a prime mover in the Reformation, became
Pope Germanius I; Henry VIII never got his divorce; the Spanish
Armada was not defeated; and so on. Four centuries of near-peace
have resulted, in which the powers that be have gradually tightened
their grip.

It's small wonder the American ambassador finds that words fail
him when in England. Under the dispensation which he hates,
words have lost their value. As one of the plotting clerics puts it, 'In
our world a man does what he's told, goes where he's sent, answers

what he's asked'. Even singing becomes another perversion of the voice.

When the story opens, the might of the Church is about to be exercised on the crotch of a ten-year-old choir boy, Hubert Anvil.

Hubert is singing in the choir at the laying-to-rest of King Stephen III of England. It's a great ceremonial occasion, held in the Cathedral Basilica of Coverley, a magnificent place built by Christopher Wren. There's irony even here: Coverley, we learn, is Cowley. In our reality, Cowley, a suburb of Oxford, is far from being the home of sanctity. It is the home of one of Britain's main car manufacturers. But private cars don't exist in Hubert's day and age—though there is a hint that Coverley will revert to type.

What does exist is a seemingly decent holy calm over all, in which the arts have a revered place. We might think, to begin with, that this quiet world was a pleasant enough place in which to live. However, Amis follows the general rule in these matters; the tenor of alternative world stories is generally consolatory. We realize as we read that accidents of history—such as the Reformation?—have landed us in a better world than might have been the case (though undoubtedly the writers take pleasure in constructing their reactionary worlds—else why bother?).

So behind the holy calm lies force, behind the present, smothering tradition, behind the arts, cold calculation. Before Hubert Anvil, a decision. Hubert's beautiful voice will break in a short while. The decision hardly rests in his hands, but in the hands of the manipulative clergy. There is a need for that wonderful high voice of Hubert's to be preserved. Women may not sing in the churches of Rome. And there is a way by which his voice can be preserved: by a little alteration. He can become rich and famous—but also despised; or he can remain whole, probably obscure, and experience sexual love.

The action aspect of the novel involves Hubert's attempts to comprehend his predicament and escape from it. Soon enough, he is on the run and being hunted.

And so begins a tug of war, with interesting characters ranged on both sides.

For preserving Hubert's creative powers as a composer, along with his testicles, are Margaret Anvil, Hubert's mother, and Father Matthew Lyall, the Anvil family chaplain; unexpected support comes from the American ambassador, who happens to have a pretty daughter of Hubert's age. Those who are determined that Hubert should have the operation as soon as possible include Abbot

Peter Thynne, Father Dilke (reminiscent of Trollope's character Obadiah Slope), Tobias Anvil, Hubert's coldly pious father, and the dead weight of custom. At every step, the cruelty is masked by piety.

When Hubert's alteration appears to be a foregone conclusion, he is taken to Rome on the Rapid by his father. There they are granted an audience with Pope John XXIV. The Pope, an Englishman (a Yorkshireman), is the most amusing character in a book where humour is generally subdued into irony and satire. After their audience, Tobias and Hubert meet with two ageing castrati, Mirabilis and Viaventosa. Viaventosa breaks down and begs Tobias not to consent to the operation on his son. Otherwise the boy will become the pitiful creature he (Viaventosa) is.

Once away from their company, Tobias falls on his knees, clutches Hubert and begs his son to comfort him. Almost to himself he says, 'Where am I now to find the strength to endure what will be done to this child of mine?' Such devouring selfishness and hypocrisy finds a strong place in the novel, as it does in the later *Russian Hide-and-Seek*. It seems that if absolute power corrupts, hypocrisy is one of its chief pimps.

Even more fervently hypocritical is Abbot Thynne, who schemes to have the altered Hubert glorifying his own church and sing in Coverley, not Rome. It is Thynne who prays to God regarding Hubert to 'bring it about in Thine own way that he forsake the path of rebellion . . .' Does God directly answer this prayer? On that score Amis leaves every reader to decide for himself. Although God does not put in a personal appearance in *The Alteration* (as he does to scarifying effect in Amis's horror novel, *The Green Man*), He certainly makes his presence felt. He is, after all, the head of the Church—or at least its absentee landlord.

In the midst of his troubles, Hubert has one consolation. He and his friends in the choir school read science fiction, a forbidden kind of gutter literature. He buys his SF from Ned, a stable boy whom Hubert, to his confusion, sees copulating with a country girl.

Considering the ecclesiastical suspicion of science, it is hardly surprising to find that the term 'SF' is unknown. Hubert and friends read 'TR'—Time Romance—and 'CW'—Counterfeit World. The boys in their dormitory are reading Philip K. Dick's *The Man in the High Castle*. This delicate tribute reveals that of course Dick's novel in Hubert's world is not quite the same as the version we know and love . . .

One of Hubert's friends, Decuman, scoffs, saying that TRs always contain flying machines. But by the end of the book we learn that the Smith brothers in America have achieved flight in a winged machine travelling at a speed of ninety miles an hour (thus saying something about the predictive qualities of SF).

Part-concealed throughout Amis's novel lie various references to other works of science fiction: John Wyndham's *The Kraken Wakes*, Keith Roberts' *Pavanne*, and Anthony Burgess's *The Wanting Seed*. In similar vein, for this is a feature of the game-playing of alternative worlds, one can find references to Ian Fleming's 'Father Bond' stories. We learn that Percy Shelley, 'a minor versifier', lived to commit both arson and suicide. Mozart lived to a ripe old age. G. B. Tiepolo has taken the place of Michelangelo, who committed suicide, prompted by Luther's philistinism. And so on.

Despite the background of art and music, many of the characters are as indifferent to arts as they are to science. The Pope shrouds his apartment in the Castel Alto with plain hangings, so that he is spared the sight of fine marbles and the Tiepolo 'Creation' on the ceiling. I have always regarded this as a particular blasphemy. My own alternative world, *The Malacia Tapestry*, published in the same year as Amis's novel, is based on an interpretation of Tiepolo's magical etchings.

This contempt by the powerful for the finer things of life is more heavily emphasized in *Russian Hide-and-Seek*. In the later novel, Shakespeare is decisively rejected by the English—just as here he is excommunicated. Not only words but their sensible orderings have failed. His two novels, so unlike in other ways, dramatize Amis's feelings of distaste for the way the world was going, as he saw it, in the 1970s, and a fear of the latent evil in men—of which Hubert's alteration is a small but significantly betraying detail.

Culture is precious—but is it worth losing your balls for?

The central motif of *Russian Hide-and-Seek* is a time-honoured one in SF terms: invasion. Britain, owing to its lack of vigilance, has been taken over by the Russians, and is now a satellite of the Soviet Union. This seems to place the book in the dire warning category of *The Battle of Dorking* and *When the Kissing had to Stop*. In 1980, the question carried a freight of topicality.

But matters are less simple than that. It is part of Amis's cunning that he does not show us the invasion of the island. Like an Ibsen play, a lot of history has flowed under the bridge before the curtain goes up. We are confronted with a Britain fifty years after the coup.

And we are to find that the English have lost both balls and culture.

The opening is magisterial. A grand English country house is surrounded by pasturage. The son, Alexander, an ensign in the Guards, is vexing his family, and indeed everyone else. The mother worries about flowers and dinner arrangements. We might be embarking on a leisurely nineteenth-century novel. The one blemish to the rural picture seems to be the hundreds of tree stumps which disfigure the grounds of the mansion. That, and the family name, Petrovsky.

What we at first may assume to be threatened is in fact absolutely overwhelmed. There is no way to undo fifty years of history. This is an England no longer England. It is now the EDR, Soviet-occupied.

There is nothing futuristic about the EDR. It has been reduced to an imitation of pre-revolutionary Russia. It's a world of stately country homes with a vengeance, with the English as servants. Parties are thrown, dances are held, and dashing young fellers ride about on horseback. This reversion follows the somewhat similar patterns the victorious Nazis impose on Europe in Sarban's *The Sound of His Horn*, which once appeared with an admiring introduction by Kingsley Amis.

The novel is one of fine surfaces and corrupt interiors. Here is another large house. White-coated servants move about, supplying drink and food. Tennis is in progress on two courts. A small orchestra is playing old-fashioned waltzes. Everything is supposedly done in high style.

But:

> No one thought, no one saw that the clothes of the guests were badly cut from poor materials . . . that the women's coiffures were messy and the men's fingernails dirty, that the surfaces of the courts were uneven and inadequately raked, that the servants' white coats had not been properly washed, or that the pavement where the couples danced needed sweeping . . . No one thought any of that because no one had ever known any different.

Ignoring the fact that this is rather obtrusive authorial comment, we see embodied here the fine surface/corrupt interior principle on which the novel hinges. To everything there is another aspect.

Alexander Petrovsky starts like a Henry Fielding hero, young and spirited. He makes a fine impression on readers—and on Commissioner Mets, the power in the land. He impresses Mets by addressing him in good English, the language of the conquered. Alexander has gone to some pains to learn a few useful phrases and to pronounce them properly. 'But his vocabulary had remained small and his ability to carry on a conversation smaller still.' Alexander bullies his subordinates. His sexual appetites are gross, and scarcely satisfied when he encounters Mrs Korotchenko, who likes being trampled on before the sexual act, and introduces her twelve-year-old daughter Dasha to join her lusty variety of fun. They perform in a kind of sexual gymnasium.

If the occupying force is shown as corrupt under its polished veneer, the English are no better. The good ones were killed off in the invasion and the Pacification. Those left are mainly a pack of docile tipplers, devoid of morale and culture, living in a kind of rustic sub-world. It is a dystopia quite as convincing and discomfiting as Orwell's urban warrens.

To parallel this total loss of English qualities, the occupying force has lost all belief in its motivating creed, Marxism, which died out about 2020.

A Moscow-generated New Cultural Policy, 'Group 31', plans to restore England to the English.

Group 31 wish to get Alexander involved. He is willing enough. To be a revolutionary is a great romantic pose which panders to his narcissism. He is callously prepared to assassinate his liberal father, if need be.

Unexpected deaths follow, yet the underground theme proves less exciting than it should be. What is more interesting, perhaps because more unusual, is the attempt, prompted by Moscow, to launch a performance of a once banned Shakespeare play, *Romeo and Juliet*. The play is to be the climax of a festival in which English culture is handed back to the English.

The Russians do not and cannot care for the past they have obliterated. Nor do the English care—except for a few over fifties, who scarcely count. It is true that they refer to their conquerors as The Shits, but this is a fossil appellation, almost without malice. By such small authentic notes, the originality of the novel declares itself.

An audience is somehow raked up to attend the great event. The music recital is moderately successful. It includes works by 'Dowland, Purcell, Sullivan, Elgar, the composer of "Ta-ra-ra-boom-de-ay", Noel Coward, Duke Ellington (taken to have been an English nobleman of some sort), Britten and John Lennon.' But with *Romeo and Juliet* it is different.

Alexander has a drink at the Marshal Stalin in St John's Street before attending the theatre. The play about the death of innocence—although it has been cut to an hour in order not to tax people's patience too greatly—is a disaster. There is a near riot, the theatre is set on fire, and Alexander decides not to rescue the girl playing Juliet.

In scenes of ghastly comedy, Shakespeare's island race rejects its old culture and religion when they are offered. It prefers to queue quietly for food—a typical meal being cabbage soup, belly of pork with boiled beets (since there's now a third fresh-meat day in a week), and stewed windfalls. Or it will booze at the Marshall Grechko (to become The Jolly Englishman under the New Cultural Policy).

Once a culture ceases to be common coinage, it has gone forever. It is a grim warning, one which elevates the novel far above the jingoistic military warning, Be Prepared! Sadness rather than jingoism is the imprint of these pages.

Alternative histories and worlds represent curious byways of science fiction, seeming usually to have more affinity with history than science. Such is the case with the novels cited here. Often this is because their authors stand rather apart from the mainstream of science fiction. Such can be said of Robert Harris, for instance, author of *Fatherland*, in which Nazi Germany, having won World War II, is about to celebrate Hitler's seventieth birthday.

The exceptions to this rule are, of course, Philip Dick and Harry Harrison, both life-long practitioners of the art. Amis is not an exception. Despite his life-long interest in SF, and his anthologies, his reputation lies elsewhere, as a major comic novelist. There is almost a sense in which alternative histories are prolonged poker-faced jokes—as is the case with the classic *Bring the Jubilee*, by Ward Moore, in which an accident changes the history of the United States.

Like Ward Moore's novel, *Russian Hide-and-Seek* presents us with military or militaristic situations. No joke is intended, just as its serious and unusual cultural theme is no cause for laughter.

Fittingly, the usual Amis humour is, in *Russian Hide-and-Seek*, suffused into a permeating irony. Detail is piled on disconcerting detail—each unexpected but just—like the young English woman girlishly longing to get to Moscow (an echo of Chekhov here), until the whole disastrous tapestry of a lost England hangs before us.

All that we value has been swept away. Culture is irrelevant. Nihilism prevails.

Those who know Amis, or perhaps have read only his *Memoirs*, will recognize his powers as an anecdotalist. One of his stories well illustrates the theme of his novels.

Amis was invited in the early 1980s to dine with the Prime Minister, together with other illuminati at 10 Downing Street. It happened to be the very day on which Hutchinson published *Russian Hide-and-Seek*, so Amis took along a copy of the novel, inscribed to Mrs Thatcher. She asked him what it was about.

Amis replied, 'Well, in a way it's about a future Britain under Russian occupation'. It was a typically modest Amis answer. And what was Margaret Thatcher's response?

'Huh! Can't you do any better than that? Get yourself another crystal ball.' As Amis says in his memoirs, an answer both unfair and unanswerable.

Now we know what those with power over us think about SF. They share an uninquiring ignorance of intellectual literary circles. And they know as much about culture as the occupying Russians.

WELLS AND THE LEOPARD LADY

Lecture delivered at the International Wells Symposium

~~~~~~

H. G. Wells's *Men Like Gods* begins with Mr Barnstaple driving along what Wells calls 'the Wonderful Road', and entering Utopia. Barnstaple and his party meet with a leopard which is benevolently inclined. By this symbol, Wells shows us the nature of an earthly paradise; the lion lying down with the lamb, etc. Dante on his journey to the Inferno first meets a leopard as a sign of great mysterious change ahead.

Large cats, leopards, cheetahs, panthers, and other furry carnivores, play a fairly active role in the Wellsian pantheon, generally linked with Wells's perennial impulse to escape from the mundane world. While presenting these carnivores as tame and amiable, he also depicts himself, as he often says, as a carnivore. This policy of reversal operates in many of his books, including one or two of the neglected ones I mean to discuss.

But the theme of my talk is really the strangest reversal of all: the fact that despite his enormous success, which it would be impossible for any author nowadays to rival, there was a part of Wells, and a vital part, which no amount of success could ever appease, and which he was continually trying to suffocate under more work.

If our opinion of Wells is to be revised, then it is first necessary to confront the Himalaya of Wells studies: that long career punctuated so conspicuously by the ascent of literary heights and the decline into political shallows. The Wells, in other words, with that marvellous sense of fun, the Great General of Dreamland, to use his own description, who became the hollow apostle of world order, who exchanged the cloak of imagination for the tin helmet of instruction—as the Chinese say. Wells was a dear and honest man;

he would not mind, I hope, our looking into this puzzling question. For he has become, rather unexpectedly, not the great prophet whom earlier generations saw, but the brilliant if eccentric writer who—almost by his own decision—went off the gold standard.

Wells had a career problem. He rose from the unprivileged classes to a position of great privilege where he was free to travel round the world talking to Stalin and Franklin D. Roosevelt. This rise—this escape—one of Wells's numerous wonderful escapes—challenged his early identification with 'the little man'. *The Food of the Gods* (1903) is almost a parable of this dilemma. The novel starts on the side of the little men and ends up on the side of the big, the Gods. Such reversals manifest themselves in numerous ways in Wells's life and thought.

Let me remind you of one of Wells's most famous reversals, which occurs in *The War of the Worlds*. Wells cleverly delays his description of an invading Martian until well into his story—in fact until Chapter 2 of Book II. And then the creatures are revealed as horrible enough to shock anyone. Not only do they exist by sucking the blood of living things—like those monsters of which Bram Stoker had written only a year earlier—but they never sleep. And—mounting horror—they are 'absolutely without sex'.

These are, nevertheless, no alien creatures. Wells continues, remorselessly, 'It is quite credible that the Martians may be descended from beings not unlike ourselves, by a gradual development of brains and hands . . . at the expense of the rest of the body'.

It is an evolutionary point Wells is making. Eighty years later, it may sound fairly conventional; that was not the case originally. Not only was Wells one of the first writers to use evolutionary themes directly in his work, but he was here using them against the grain of his generation's perception of the meaning of evolution. Whereas many interpreted evolution as a biological mechanism which had carried man to the top of the tree, Wells understood Darwin better; indeed, no English writer has shown a surer grasp of the scientific challenges of the modern age. *War of the Worlds* demonstrates that the continuous process of evolution was as likely to work against mankind as for. If we continued as we were doing, there was no known way in which we could prevent ourselves becoming, in effect, Martians. The Eloi and Morlocks, you remember, had already pointed that moral, with different emphasis.

Embedded in Wells's first scientific romance are many of the themes—not only the evolutionary one—which he would develop in the course of his next 120-odd books. The idea of utopia is there. The Eloi live in a kind of utopia. Present too is the dream of a perfect garden, which always haunted Wells. Perhaps when he visited his absconding mother, Sarah, at Up Park, where she worked as house-keeper, he saw something like a perfect garden, a place without stress. And his father had been a gardener.

Here is the descriptive passage from *The Time Machine*:

> After all, the sanitation and the agriculture of today are still in the rudimentary stage. The science of our time has attacked but a little department of the field of human disease, but, even so, it spreads its operations very steadily and persistently. Our agriculture and horticulture destroy a weed just here and there and cultivate perhaps a score or so of wholesome plants, leaving the greater number to fight out a balance as they can. We improve our favourite plants and animals—and how few they are—gradually by selective breeding: now a new and better peach, now a seedless grape, now a sweeter and larger flower, now a more convenient breed of cattle. We improve them gradually, because Nature, too, is shy and slow in our clumsy hands. Some day all this will be better organized, and still better. That is the drift of the current in spite of the eddies. The whole world will be intelligent, educated, and co-operating: things will move faster and faster towards the subjugation of Nature. In the end, wisely and carefully we shall readjust the balance of animal and vegetable life to suit our human needs.

In summary, Wells says, 'There were no hedges, no signs of proprie-tary rights, no evidence of agriculture; the whole earth had become a garden.' It's clever comment, wedding the evolutionary with the social.

The gardens reappear. Meanwhile, there was all of mankind to be reformed.

The promising thing about mankind, as Wells perceived, is its mutability. Yet that mutability is also perceived as threatening.

If we had prognathous jaws only two million years ago, why not grossly over-developed crania two million years from now? The leopards and the big cats are different. They were plain leopards two million years ago, not a spot different, and will presumably continue to be leopards two million years from now—unless we exterminate them next year. So the big cats in Wells's books are free not merely in

the ordinary sense in which big playful pussies always mean liberty,
but in the way they appear to be apart from that dreadful evolutionary machine which so inspired and alarmed Wells.

This link between big cats and freedom appears in one of Wells's
best-known and most poignant short stories, 'The Door in the Wall'.
You recall that when Wallace the narrator was between five and six,
that crucial age, he came upon the door somewhere in Kensington—
that magical door through which he went to pass into 'Immortal
realities', and, throughout the rest of his life, was never again able to
enter.

> Wallace found himself in a garden. 'You see', he said, with
> the doubtful inflection of a man who pauses at incredible
> things, 'there were two great panthers there . . . Yes, spotted
> panthers. And I was not afraid. There was a long wide path
> with marble-edged flower borders on either side, and these
> two huge velvety beasts were playing there with a ball. One
> looked and came towards me, a little curious as it seemed. It
> came right up to me, rubbed its soft round ear very gently
> against the small hand I held out, and purred. It was, I tell
> you, an enchanted garden.'

Well, there are many enchanted gardens in fantasy writing, just as
the symbol of the country house appears over and over in English
fiction. None so poignant though as this one of Wells's. If you
wonder why there is no big cat in that first garden, in *The Time
Machine*, well, of course, there is: that enigmatic cat, The Sphinx.

Exactly how Wells felt is stated simply in *In the Days of the Comet*,
when Leadford's mother is dying. ' "Heaven", she said to me one
day. "Heaven is a garden." '

The leopard in *Men Like Gods* also stands as a sort of sentinel to the
magic which is to follow. It is about to allow itself to be stroked, when
it sneezes and bounds away, and the cattle don't stir a muscle as it
runs past them. That's another reversal of the natural order.

Later we learn more about this particular leopard. Like others of
its kind, it has sworn off meat. 'The larger carnivora, combed
and cleaned, reduced to a milk dietary, emasculated in spirit, and
altogether de-catted, were pets and ornaments in Utopia.' In this
Utopia, so we hear, 'the dog had given up barking'. Wells was always
dubious about dogs. They brought dirt into the house, and disease
with the dirt. Perhaps that dreadful late-Victorian London had given
him an especial loathing of dogs and horses, whose mess was

everywhere to be seen. They certainly aren't allowed in *A Modern Utopia*:

> It is only reluctantly that I allow myself to be drawn from my secret musings into a discussion of Utopian pets.
>
> I try to explain that a phase in the world's development is inevitable when a systematic world-wide attempt will be made to destroy for ever a great number of contagious and infectious diseases, and that this will involve, for a time at any rate, a stringent suppression of the free movement of familiar animals. Utopian houses, streets, and drains will be planned to make rats, mice, and such-like house-parasites impossible: the race of cats and dogs—providing as it does, living fastnesses to which such diseases as plague, influenzas, catarrh and the like, can retreat to sally forth again—must pass for a time out of freedom, and the filth made by horses and the other brutes of the highway vanish from the face of the Earth.

No wonder the horsey classes objected to Wells. All the same, there is a whiff of crankiness about his attitude to pets. Science would vote against him now, claiming that pets are good for psychic health, stroking them helps people get over heart attacks, and so on.

Of course, all utopias fear dirt. I've yet to read of a utopia where dogs were encouraged. Maybe in dog utopias there are no men.

The utopia in *Men Like Gods* is also likened to a garden. We read of 'the weeding and cultivation of the kingdom of nature by mankind'. Nowadays, as in so many other things, we would not trust ourselves with that same confidence to do a good job. The cultivation of Brazilian rainforest into timber is not an encouraging example.

In *The Shape of Things to Come* we find more gardens, termed 'enclosures and reservations', in which specially interesting floras and faunas flourish. 'Undreamt-of fruits and blossoms may be summoned out of non-existence.' Here sex is directly linked to big cats. The Puritanical Tyranny, in suppressing sex, thought they had 'imprisoned a tiger that would otherwise consume all'. It was not so. Under the more relaxed dispensation following the Tyranny, people could now go naked and love as they like—the old Wells aspiration. 'Instead of a tiger appeared a harmless, quiet, unobtrusive, and not unpleasing pussy-cat, which declined to be any way noticeable.' As early as *The Time Machine*, free love-making is a feature of utopia, without emotional attachment.

Sex and big cats. Also sex and childhood. Consider a passing remark in that large rambling volume, *The Shape of Things to Come* which yokes such matters with the idea of utopia.

> One must draw upon the naive materials of one's own childhood to conceive, however remotely, the status of mind of those rare spirits who looked first towards human brotherhood. One must consider the life of some animal, one's dog, one's cheetah or one's pony, to realize the bounded, definite existence of a human being in the early civilizations.

One's *cheetah* indeed!

These strands of sexuality, utopia and escape play a large role in Wells's work, both before and after that Himalaya in his career. Even 'one's cheetah' turns up again. *The Research Magnificent* features the peculiar relationship between Mr Benham and a beautiful woman called Amanda, whom he marries. Amanda, to him, is 'a spotless leopard', while he, to her, is 'Cheetah, big beast at heart'. So they address each other. The terms are transposed from real life. In Wells's long involvement with Rebecca West, she, to him, was 'Panther', while he, to her, was 'Jaguar'. They escaped into an animal world.

Not that there is a one-to-one relationship between the fictitious Amanda and Rebecca West. For after Benham and Amanda are married, he starts staying away from her, to her disgust, and Amanda shrinks into a Jane Wells role. Wells liked his freedom, and it is his voice we hear when Mr Benham says, evasively, to Amanda, 'We should meet upon our ways as the great carnivores do'. He then proceeds to trot round the world, overlooking the fact that jaguars occupy only narrow stretches of territory.

All this metaphorical use of cats—of which Wells was avowedly fond—and gardens and utopian innocence is immediately accessible to the imagination. The nature of a metaphor is not so much that it should be exact as that it should illuminate with a mysterious glow. That mysterious glow is certainly present in early Wells, and accounts for much of his abiding popularity. But something got in the way of the glow, and that something manifested itself as politics.

We are here to re-evaluate Wells. My contribution would be to say, in part, that Wells is interesting when he talks about people, or social conditions, or science, or those possible worlds of his science fiction; but he was, or has become, terribly boring when he goes on about politics, as, after the mid-twenties, he increasingly does.

Remember the Open Conspiracy? The Life Aristocratic? The Voluntary Nobility? The World Brain? The New World Order? Such ideas are now lifeless. We salute the endeavours and intellect of the man who conceived them; but it is as well to face the fact that Wells was no political seer, and there is nothing that turns to dust as promptly as yesterday's politics.

Those reversals of which Wells was so fond in his fiction were carried into his life. He turned from a creative writer into a sort of political journalist. Why did he do it? What drove him away from the literary to the ceaseless activity represented by *The Work, Wealth and Happiness of Mankind*?

I will mention one more leopard in Wells's life and then drop the subject. That leopard leads us into what was next to come in the way of reversals. This time it is a Leopard Man, the famous one who appears in *The Island of Dr Moreau*. Rendered half-human by Moreau's vivisection, the Leopard Man escapes and Prendick tracks it across the island, discovering it at last 'crouched together in the smallest possible compass', regarding Prendick over its shoulder. Then comes a passage I still find moving:

> It may seem a strange contradiction in me—I cannot explain the fact—but now, seeing the creature there in a perfectly animal attitude, with the light gleaming in its eyes, and its imperfectly human face distorted with terror, I realized again the fact of its humanity. In another moment other of its pursuers would see it, and it would be overpowered and captured, to experience once more the horrible tortures of the enclosure. Abruptly, I slipped out my revolver, aimed between his terror-struck eyes, and fired.

The beast in the human, the human in the beast—it's a powerful theme, and one which seems in Wells's case to owe as much to inner emotion as to evolutionary understanding. At the end of *Island*, when Prendick gets back to civilization, he cannot lose his horror of the ordinary people round him, scrutinizing them for signs of the beast, convinced that they will presently begin to revert—an interesting passage derived from Swift's *Gulliver's Travels*.

Wells has presented us with many striking images, of which this one I have quoted is not the least. To me, this coining of images is one of the true marks of imaginative genius, greater than the creation of plot or character. But as Wells grew older, the ability to coin images grew fainter. From the image—enigmatic, disturbing, beautifying—

he turned instead to elucidation, the image's opposite. It was another reversal. He set his considerable talents to educating and enlightening the world, stating, in his autobiography, 'At bottom I am grimly and desperately educational'. That was his mid-thirties, when the urge to pontificate was taking over, when he became shut in a schoolroom of his own making, far from the sportive leopards of his youth.

That remarkable short story, 'The Door in the Wall', written when Wells was almost forty, is precognitive in showing what became of his early vision. Wallace, the central character, spends his life searching for that door leading to the garden where the panthers and the beautiful lady were. In later middle age, Wallace comes across it again. In fact, he comes across it three times in a year, that door which goes into 'a beauty beyond dreaming', and does not enter it. He's too busy with worldly affairs. He's a politician now, and has no time . . .

The reason Wells has never been properly accepted into the pantheon of English letters—or some would say 'pantechnicon'—is mainly a squalid class reason, and has nothing to do with the fact that his original soaring imaginative genius eventually fell, like Icarus, back to Earth.

Those of us who love Wells and his books have sought in the past to defend him by claiming that he was successful first as an artist and later as propagandist. This is approximately the view of Bernard Bergonzi in his book *The Early H. G. Wells*.[1] Bergonzi says, 'Wells ceased to be an artist in his longer scientific romances after the publication of *The First Men in the Moon* in 1901'. So persuasive is Bergonzi's book that many of us have gone along with the reasoning. Any considerable revision of Wells must take into account Bergonzi's arguments.

All the same, the minor amendment I have to offer is based largely on what I see as Wells's second gambit to outwit the death of inspiration—second, I mean, to increasing doses of political speculation which fill his books. The second gambit is the policy of reversal, to which I have referred.

Even his role of educator is a role reversal. He had been the educated. To education he owed his escape from drapers, ignominy, and boots. The great leap of his life was from taught to teacher.

Teachers are forced into cycles of repetition to get the message to

1 Manchester, Manchester University Press, 1961.

sink in. Wells's books work rather like that at times. The little man of earlier books, Hoopdriver, Kipps, Mr Polly, Mr Lewisham, are recycled as powerful figures, at times only semi-human: Ostrog, Mr Parham, Rud Whitlow in *The Holy Terror*, and the grand Lunar.

With reversal went repetition. Other commentators have pointed out that the New Woman appears in more than one Wells novel. Ann Veronica has many sisters, not least Christina Alberta, and the charming Fanny Smith in *The Dream*. I don't find this cause for complaint. Nor can we complain that so many of the books chase that idea of human betterment; this is grandeur rather than narrowness. What we are justified in complaining about is that so many of those plans for the future reveal an almost wilful lack of understanding of mankind's nature. It was Orwell who said that most of Mr Wells's plans for the future had been realized in the Third Reich.

A fresh look at Wells's canon, however, reveals some unexpected pleasures. I have recently had the chance to defend in print *In the Days of the Comet* (1906), not as a science fiction novel, which it only marginally is, but as one of Wells's prime Condition of England novels—the phrase is Disraeli's. It is a reversal, demonstrating how *A Modern Utopia* might come about, while providing as abrasive a picture of Edwardian England as *Tono-Bungay*; while in time it stands sandwiched between the two.

I would like to cite a paragraph from *In the Days of the Comet*, to serve as a reminder of how brilliantly Wells could recreate life in the days before he decided instead to theorize about it.

This is the passage where the humbly born Leadford is about to leave home forever, and to desert his mother as Wells's mother later deserted him:

> After our midday dinner—it was a potato-pie, mostly potato with some scraps of cabbage and bacon—I put on my overcoat and got it [my watch] out of the house while my mother was in the scullery at the back. A scullery in the old world was, in the case of such houses as ours, a damp, unsavoury, mainly subterranean region behind the dark living-room kitchen, that was rendered more than typically dirty in our cases by the fact that into it the coal-cellar, a yawning pit of black uncleanness, opened, and diffused small crunchable particles about the uneven brick floor. It was the region of the 'washing-up', that greasy, damp function that followed every meal; its atmosphere had ever a

cooling steaminess and the memory of boiled cabbage, and
the sooty black stains where saucepan or kettle had been put
down for a minute, scraps of potato-peel caught by the
strainer of the escape-pipe, and rags of a quite indescribable
horribleness of acquisition, called 'dish-clouts', rise in my
memory at the name. The altar of this place was the 'sink', a
tank of stone, revolting to a refined touch, grease-filmed and
unpleasant to see, and above this was a tap of cold water, so
arranged that when the water descended it splashed and
wetted whoever had turned it on. This tap was our water
supply. And in such a place you must fancy a little old
woman, rather incompetent and very gentle, a soul of
unselfishness and sacrifice, in dirty clothes, all come from
their original colours to a common dusty dark grey, in worn,
ill-fitting boots, with hands distorted by ill use, and untidy
greying hair—my mother. In the winter her hands would be
'chapped', and she would have a cough. And while she
washes up I go out, to sell my overcoat and watch in order
that I may desert her.

Everything comes beautifully together: the hatred of bad social
conditions, the mixed feelings for the old woman, the sense that one
can only get out and go on. It's magnificent.

Later, in the mid-1920s, when, on the Bergonzi scale, Wells
should be quite past it, we have a couple of novels which form
reversals of an interesting kind. *Christina Alberta's Father* is about a
man who believes himself to be the Sumerian Sargon the First, King
of Kings. The present of the novel becomes Sargon's future. In *The
Dream*, Sarnac is a man of the future who relives a life in the
Edwardian present. Both these novels are highly readable, and *The
Dream* is excellent—overlooked, apparently, because Wells failed to
give it a noticeable title. The comedy and descriptions of low-life are
in the best Kippsian manner. These novels date from 1924 and 1925,
when Wells was under considerable mental stress. Indeed, *Christina
Alberta's Father* strikes a new note. A theme of insanity is introduced
for the first time, and the scenes in the mental institution are vivid.

Where Sarnac dreams himself back into an ordinary life, the low
Mr Preemby in *Christina Alberta's Father* imagines himself to be lord
and protector of the whole world. It is a role Wells was clearly taking
on himself.

There's much in Wells which reminds us of the productive French genius, Honoré de Balzac. Balzac wrote to a friend in 1820, saying, 'Before long, I shall possess the secret of that mysterious power. I shall compel all men to obey me and all women to love me.' He also said, 'My only and immense desires, to be famous and to be loved'. He achieved both, and killed himself by overwork. Fame and love together were not enough to quench that void within him which was the fruit of his mother's rejection and coldness to him. Wells is a similar case. His high and demanding productivity—*The Outline of History*, for instance, written in a year of 'fanatical toil'—his de-romanticized sexual activity, which continued into his seventies, point to an underlying anxiety and unhappiness.

Some commentators—among them the Mackenzies, I think—ascribe this to Wells's feeling of pique against the middle class, to whom he had once been made to feel inferior. No doubt class enters into the matter, as it does into most English departments. But something buried deeper fed on Wells, that unassuageable void which a derelicting mother sometimes imposes on her children. Sarah Wells, H. G.'s mother, did her best, but she left her husband and kicked Bertie, then almost fourteen, into the wide world, to fend for himself—or rather, into the narrow world behind the draper's counter—the same age at which another utopian, Aldous Huxley, lost his mother. The Mackenzies say that Wells bitterly resented this rejection, and we see that bitterness fermenting in his life.

His one escape from the draper's counter was through education. No wonder that in later days he saw life as a race between education and catastrophe. So it had been for him. But he had made another reversal, into a solipsistic universe, where what was true for him as a youth became true for the whole world.

This turning away from the literary world to quasi-political involvement still seems curious, and curiously unfruitful. Yet an explanation for it appears in the best book on creativity ever written, which explores the vagaries of the creative spirit. In his work, *The Dynamics of Creation*,[2] Anthony Storr says:

> The inability to stop working, to enjoy holidays, to allow time for relaxation or personal relationships, is often found among intensely ambitious men. In psychiatric practice, it is more often found among politicians and financiers than among artists . . . Politicians often arrange life so that they are busily engaged all the time they are awake . . . Political

2 London, Secker and Warburg, 1972.

life is an ideal one for men who need to be ceaselessly occupied, who are driven to seek power by an inner insecurity, and who substitute extroverted activity for the self-knowledge which comes from cultivating personal relationships . . . Creative production can be a particularly effective method of protecting the self from the threat of an underlying depression.

We look on Wells with admiration. We also should spare him some sympathy. He who had so much drive was greatly driven. We have a right to be sad when his wonderful early sense of fun dies.

Wells reverts to animal metaphors to describe his state of mind. He is 'a creature trying to find its way out of a prison into which it has fallen'. Indeed, his life seems unsettled and unsatisfying, despite his encounters with the wonderful Moura Budbergs of this world, despite his escapes to the South of France, and the various households he maintained in England and France.

No wonder he dreamed of panthers and pleasant gardens. Big cats are symbols of a guiltless promiscuity. Wells worked hard at that activity, but there was no way in which the door in the wall would ever open again. Such doors have a time-lock on them.

THE ADJECTIVES OF ERICH ZANN
A Tale of Horror

In my lifetime, I have read only one story by H. P. Lovecraft. Yet that story I remember well, if only because I came upon it shortly after my twin brother committed suicide.

Somehow, talk of Lovecraft implies hushed talk of the past—awful attics or seedy cellars in which dreadful things lurk, waiting to emerge from long ago or far away, or both. From what I have heard, it is useless for anyone in the Lovecraftian universe to struggle. Lift a finger, and evil forces will come busting in. It was with compulsion greater than myself that I decided I must—whether I liked it or not—read once more that special story of his which has remained with me throughout so many years.

So, bearing a flambeau, I climb the stairs to a dusty attic where my precious few books are kept. On the way, I ponder the kindly if damp spirit of Lovecraft. This was the man who once declared, in words to be echoed by HAL in the movie *2001* almost half a century later, 'Existence seems of little value and I wish it might be terminated'.

Remembrance told me how L. Sprague de Camp, in his 1975 biography of Lovecraft, had quoted the master as announcing that mankind were 'wolves, hyenas, swine, fools, and madmen'. What sort of wisdom might we not expect from a man who had torn thus aside the tissue of lies behind which we hide our frailties? Even as I reached the chill attic, pulling my shawl more securely round my shoulders, I was aware of fear welling up inside me in a cascade of adjectives.

There on an upper shelf . . . I reach out . . . ah!, got it! That aged black book, from which I blow the dust. I open its pages with trembling fingers.

No, no, it's not the Necronomicon, Cthulhu be praised! It's a volume entitled *Modern Tales of Horror*, selected by Dashiell Hammett. The volume was published in London in 1932, by Victor Gollancz.

A precocious lad, I was seven when I bought it. For many years, it was my favourite book—favourite because it scared the life out of me. Also precious to me because at that age I was trying to become on good terms with my mother, and discovered that she was not averse to a good horror story. So I read aloud to her in our scullery while she did the ironing.

Two stories in the Hammett collection I read her over and over. They were Paul Suter's 'Beyond the Door' and Michael Joyce's 'Perchance to Dream'. (Thirty years later, I included that marvellous latter story in my *Best Fantasy Stories*, published by Faber & Faber.) We both trembled, my mother and I, in those long cosy peacetime afternoons. As long as she kept ironing and I kept reading, she never said another word about sending me off to an orphanage.

One story in the Hammett collection made us scream. It was 'The Music of Erich Zann', written by H. P. Lovecraft. We screamed with laughter. After all these years, it's hard to see why we found it so funny; of course, it was a nervous time for us: the police were still investigating. The very name of Erich Zann broke us up. Then again, Zann, the crazy old musician, played a viol. Come on, guys, viola is serious. Violin is serious. *Viol* is FUNNY! Sounds like VILE, right?

This is my dictionary's definition of a viol: 'held between the knees when played'. You imagine someone playing a kind of violin, gripping it with his knees . . . I was also reading funnies to my mother, to keep her amiable, like Saki and Stephen Leacock. You remember Leacock's 'My Financial Career'? That broke us up. I thought she would have one of her fits. Lovecraft's story is a kind of 'My Musical Career'. I know that what I am saying will offend the devout, and that it just goes to show I was a hopeless neurotic aged seven, but that's how it was. That's what Zann did up in that peaked garret. Anyone for masturbation fantasies?

How was Zann's playing on this instrument of his? Fantastic, delirious, hysterical, is the answer. Okay, but later? Oh, later, the frantic playing became a blind mechanical unrecognizable orgy, is the answer. And what was Zann doing while he played? He was dripping with an uncanny perspiration and twisted like a monkey, is the answer. You see, he was playing a *wild Hungarian dance*. Hence the uncanny perspiration. Are all Hungarian dances like that? Hope not, is the answer.

Something broke the glass and came in through the window while Zann was in this state. We never figured out what actually came in, apart from the blackness—though it's true blackness screamed with shocking music. The Hungarians at it again, we supposed. Mother loved that bit. Perhaps she was thinking that my so-called father might be going to break in and attack us again. The idea certainly entered my mind. There was an hysterical edge to our laughter. Even as I read, I was dripping with uncanny perspiration.

It's all so long ago. We were living in New England then. How foolish we were, how innocent, how—unread!

Even now, grey-haired and no longer quite so neurotic, I still see how whole sentences in that wonderful story must have struck those two 1930s idiots as funny. 'My liking for him did not grow.' 'I had a curious desire to look out of that window, over the wall and down the unseen slope at the glittering roofs and spires which must lie outspread there.' Well, all I can say is that when we looked out of our kitchen window we gazed down unseen slopes onto a banana yard.

To top it all, poor old Erich Zann was dumb and deaf. We had no idea of political correctness in our house. We were Presbyterians. We found deafness funny, particularly in a musician. (Beethoven was not on our curriculum.) Funny too, we thought in our perverted way, was the fate that overcame the old deaf wistful shabby grotesque strange satyrlike distorted nearly bald—with what youthful zeal I shouted out the adjectives!—viol-player. There's the divinely hilarious moment when the unnamed hero feels 'strange currents of wind' and clutches Zann's ice-cold stiffened unbreathing face, whose bulging eyes bulged uselessly into the void. I could hardly get the words out. Mother burnt a pair of pink bloomers with the iron.

Jesus, how we laughed. How silly I was at seven. Didn't know a bit of good hokum when I saw it . . .

JEKYLL

~~~~~~

All the characters in Stevenson's story are isolated males: Mr Utterson, the lawyer; his friend and distant relation, Mr Enfield; Poole, the servant; and, of course, Dr Jekyll himself. They live separately in a city, the loneliest place. Jekyll himself foresees this isolation increasing in the future, when men become scarcely human, but rather 'incongruous and independent denizens'. In the story, London masquerades as Stevenson's native Edinburgh. All told, it's a good setting for horror.

The horror is of a markedly cerebral kind. There are no monstrous creatures going about the world, as in *Frankenstein* or *Dracula*. Of course there is Hyde. But Hyde is a projection of Jekyll. This is why the story still interests us: *Dr Jekyll and Mr Hyde* is a pre-Jungian fable, a vivid illustration of the Shadow side of a decent man, that aspect— vigorously suppressed by the religious and 'unco' guid' of Victorian Calvinist Scotland—of our natures whose presence we all have to acknowledge. The aspect which, as Jekyll says of his drug, shakes 'the very fortress of identity'.

The fable concerns the shattering of this fortress. This is the point. The drug Jekyll takes is not the instrument of Hyde's coming into being. The drug is merely a neutral means of transmission. In Jekyll's words, 'The drug had no discriminating action; it was neither diabolical nor divine; but it shook the doors of the prison house of my disposition'.

With these powerful words, Jekyll admits that had he undertaken his experiment in a nobler spirit, he might have released from within himself 'an angel instead of a fiend'. How remarkably this reflection of the 1880s recalls comments on LSD experiments of the 1950s!

The best part of the novella—it's scarcely a novel—resides in the final section, in Jekyll's statement. It's wonderful, a *tour de force*, although at the same time rather bloodless. Hyde's sins are no more than alluded to. This is more a sermon than a horror tale. Here again, the future is prefigured. The drug cannot be correctly administered, or its effects controlled; we are reminded of L-dopa in Oliver Sachs's remarkable story *Awakenings*, where any dose proved too little or too much.

Here is Stevenson's moral imagination speaking, fleshing out what started as a dream (as did Mary Shelley's *Frankenstein*). 'It fell out with me, as it falls with so vast a majority of my fellows, that I chose the better part and was found wanting in the strength to keep to it.' This is the Calvinist speaking, trying to hold to a rigid morality which the world was to cast aside in another generation or so, letting loose the Hyde of the First World War, 1914–1918.

Like the other two nineteenth-century novels of terror already referred to, *Dr Jekyll and Mr Hyde* has frequently been filmed. To my mind, all film versions of *Frankenstein* and *Dracula* are crude and almost parodic versions of the novels themselves.

Such is not the case with film versions of *Dr Jekyll*. The horror, as I've said, is too cerebral, too bloodless, for the movies. Injustice must be seen to be done. We have to be shown Frederick March or Spencer Tracy, or whoever it is, consorting with prostitutes, wielding the stick, being cruel. We have to see the beaker foam, with its deadly but seductive brew, to watch the terrible transformation, whiskers and all, take place . . . To witness what is at first willed become involuntary.

I believe Stevenson, the old Teller of Tales, would be pleased that Hollywood reached towards something darker and more disturbing than *Treasure Island*.

ONE HUMP OR TWO

Lecture given at the IAFA Conference of the Fantastic

I have come to few conclusions regarding national differences in British and American fantasy. The longer you look at the two animals the vaguer seem the distinctions. If you observe the dromedary or Arabian camel and the Bactrian camel—the only two sorts of camel on the planet—you immediately see the distinction we all know from childhood: the former has one hump, the latter two. But if you look at all other animals in the zoo, you don't find anything else resembling a camel. Not even their relations, the llamas. The similarities are overwhelmingly greater than the differences.

Here we have these two camels, the US and the UK variety of fantasy. Here you have this panel reduced to counting humps.

Perhaps because of my early reading—my very early reading, when books still contained pictures—I regard fantasy, as distinct from SF, as having a spiritual, or perhaps I mean a religious, or perhaps I mean a metaphysical side. This regard comes from the area whence all memories spring, the personal deeps, compounded of old forgotten stories told and read, alchemic woodcuts, and perhaps a surly reproduction of Dante Gabriel Rossetti's *doppelganger* drawing, *How They Met Themselves*, with lovers deep in the forest, transfixed. Perhaps too the interchange of light and shade above one's cot—who knows?

If forced to it for the purposes of this forum, I'd say that this spiritual aspect is largely absent in American fantasy and at least flickeringly present in the English stuff. Why should this be? Possibly for a simple reason: the English stuff is so much older, has a much more ancient lineage (though I don't forget that lineage also became, because of our shared language, a shared American lineage two centuries ago; were it otherwise—were you all Greek speakers, say—I'd not be here arguing the toss). Did the 1980s yield in the US anything so powerful—so full of ancient power—as Robert Hold-stock's wonderful *Mythago Wood*? The past activates fantasy, as the future SF.

I've never seen a reference, even in *Trillion Year Spree*, to the fourteenth-century poem, written in Middle English, entitled 'St Erkenwald'. The poem is probably by the unknown author of *Sir Gawain and the Green Knight*. In the seventh century, the saint Erkenwald, as the poem tells, rebuilt St Paul's cathedral in London on what had been a pagan site. Digging in the foundations, the workers come across an impressive sarcophagus on which are carved arcane sentences.

> Wise men with wide foreheads, wondering in that pit
> Struggled without success to string them into words.

They lever up the lid of the coffin and find there a body nobly clad. The body is as fresh as if it were alive, with red lips and so on. After a prayer, St Erkenwald speaks to the corpse and rouses it, raises it from the dead, or at least from limbo. Unlike Lazarus, who keeps quiet about what happened to him, this revenant is talkative. He was a judge who has remained in limbo for almost eight hundred years. Having been born before Christ, he cannot enter Heaven, for all his good works. He's a heathen. A point of Christian doctrine is being raised.

As Erkenwald blesses the judge in the name of the Father, his tears fall on the sufferer, who is thereby baptized. With joy, the heathen relates how his soul is released, to fly to Heaven.

> With that he stopped speaking and said no more.
> But suddenly his sweet face sank in and vanished,
> And all the beauty of his body blackened like mould,
> As foetid as fungus that flies up in powder![1]

We seem to perceive here the precursor of a number of themes, from the Seven Sleepers of Ephesus, mentioned in Gibbon,[2] through to those two nineteenth-century monoliths of corrupt resurrection, *Frankenstein* and *Dracula*, passing on the way all the eerie vaults which lie in wait for the heroines of such Gothic works as Mrs Ann Radcliffe's *The Mysteries Of Udolpho*.

One might also mention here ghost stories, a very English genre.

1 Trans. Brian Stone, *The Owl and the Nightingale*, Penguin Books, 1971.
2 Edward Gibbon, *The History of the Decline and Fall of the Roman Empire*, 1773, Chapter XXXIII.

Ghosts always appeared dressed—wearing something, armour, archaic costume, a winding sheet. In the poem, Erkenwald's heathen similarly has the power to preserve his clothes intact. A peculiar power.

All this could hardly be called a tradition, but it does represent a line of thought. Perhaps it's part and parcel of a consciousness of the buried past which is peculiarly British. In the USA, there was no buried past until yesterday; T. H. O'Sullivan was there to photograph the Battle of Gettysberg. You don't share Europe's secrecy. That's why Hollywood's in California, USA, not say, Paris, France. We have Stonehenge; you have Scientology. When you began to turn to scientific disciplines to uncover the forgotten story of the nomads who entered by way of the Bering Straits bridge, to fill this continent and its southern counterpart thousands of years ago, you created a new past—a future, as it were, with a sell-by date long expired.

Yet your past lacks a domestic touch, that intimacy with the past as dwelling in the next room behind the wardrobe, which is one essential of many British fantasies. Alan Garner's work, for example, in *Red Shift* or *The Owl Service*, where ancient Celtic remains lie within sight of Jodrell Bank.

There isn't and can't be the equivalent of this kind of fantasy in the USA. The house is, of course, a dominant symbol in fiction from last century on, a common symbol all over the Western world. But houses evidently signify different things in the US and the UK.

Consider, for instance, the comparative scarcity of houses in the US, where 64% of the population own their own houses. The figure in England is about the same. With a population only four times larger than the UK and a land area about 3,000 times greater, the US plainly has comparatively fewer houses. Scarcity breeds suspicion. When our houses—our homes (that very English English word)— are haunted, we continue to live in them, quite often cherishing our ghost, giving it pet names. In the US, if we are to believe the evidence of the movies, from the celebrated Usher abode onwards, houses burst apart with evil. They provide no sanctuary. There's little amity in Amityville, is there? Fantasy after fantasy shows houses going up in flames. Even in realist fantasies such as the movie *Fatal Attraction*, the home provides no secure place: the enemy worms her way in, supernaturally able to glide through phone, apartment and country house, into that *sanctum sanctorum*, the bathroom . . .

Having said all this, I have almost persuaded myself that there is a difference between the fantasy of the two countries. I've been talking only of subject matter and approach. Had we discussed style, we would have found more differences. But really it's a matter of camels and humps again.

And, of course, the two animals have mated. The moment of coupling occurred in the 1960s, with the publication of Tolkien in the States. In England Tolkien's *The Lord of The Rings* caused little stir. We're long on genius, short on enthusiasm. It was here in the States that he was taken up on the most extraordinary scale. From then on, there was no respite. From then on, fantasy was to gain over SF. From then on, it was but a giant step forward for womankind to the Age of Le Guin and Earthsea and Anne McCaffrey and her dragons.

Now, fantasy and the elder gods rule supreme, like groundelder over-running a neglected estate.

> Tis an unweeded garden,
> That grows to seed; things rank and gross in nature
> Possess it merely.

There's so much imitation, so much derivation, so much commercialism, who can be bothered to judge? Discernment is lost. At last, all fantasy is the same. The successors of Thomas Covenant roam through lands resembling the lands of the Belgariad.

Et voilà—at last, what we've all been longing for! The result of this industrious miscegenation? A monstrosity with three humps! Yours, mine, ours.

KAFKA'S SISTER

> 'How cold it is in the exploding world'
> *Julia and the Bazooka*

When Franz Kafka wrote his famous letter to his father, one of his accusations was that his father did not keep the commandments he imposed on his son. Hence, said Kafka, his world had become divided into three parts.

In the first world, he felt himself a slave. The second world was a world of power, remote from him. The third was where everyone else lived happily and free from orders. Kafka's lifelong guilt feelings arose from his oppressive sense of these divisions, brought about by his father's transgressions. Kafka, in the words of one of his editors, Erich Heller, had 'an irresistible tendency to fall apart', contained only by his writing. Writing was his way of survival.

The parallels with the writer calling herself Anna Kavan are strong. Her quarrel was with a mother who would not keep her own commandments. Like Kafka, Kavan seems as a child always to have felt herself in the wrong; and this feeling, as she reached adult years, also matured, into the prevailing sense that somehow her existence was unjustified, insubstantial. Like Kafka, she suffered in her struggle to come to terms with other people, and with herself.

'It is as if I were made of stone, as if I were my own tombstone', complains Kafka in his diary for 1910.

'What exactly is it that's wrong with me? What is the thing about me that people can never take?', asks the narrator in Kavan's wartime story, 'Glorious Boys'.

'And where am I to find a little warmth in this?', asks the narrator in 'My Madness', as she becomes her own tribunal.

Implicitly, these and similar questions are asked in story after story. The 'I' character, a mirror image of Kavan, always expresses the same gamut of anxiety. The search is on, for something lost in childhood to be found in adult life. Insidious as a serpent comes the fear of others, the fear of relationships, but, most destructively, the fear of the self with its inadequacies, the first of Kafka's three dreaded divisions.

'Once and for all, I've declared myself against life and people, on the side of otherness and indifference, isolation, the mineral beauty of the nonhuman world'—so says a character in 'High in the Mountains', speaking in the voice of alienation.

'All we see of the mentally ill', says Carl Jung, 'regarding them from the outside, is their tragic destruction, rarely the life of that side of the psyche which is turned away from us.' Kavan shows us the hidden side, and it has its beauty, as it struggles to make sense of an illogical world. Extracts similar to the ones quoted above can be taken almost at random from Kavan's writings, showing her alienation, her madness.

Yet, as her friend Raymond Marriott warns us, she was in many ways an ordinary and pleasant creative person, chic, generally fun to be with. The fiction remains at least at arm's length from the facts of her life. Writers have many reasons for using a persona not entirely congruent with their own natures, for fact is more complex than fiction. What rises from the printed page is part of an elaborate game of hide-and-seek which a writer plays, perhaps unconsciously, not necessarily with the reader but with herself or himself. Kavan is dextrous in the use of symbols, and symbols are easily mistaken for the real thing.

Although she often looked outwards with a shrewd and witty eye—'the church clock is calling the hour again in its dull voice', as she says in 'My Madness', and we have all heard that particular chime—all roads lead back, like the strands of a web, to the spider of her self-obsession.

Yet hers is not a fiction of claustrophobia. The prose is too fine-spun for that. Her longing for abstraction takes refuge in its symbols: Madness, Ice, China—as one should say Trial, Castle, America. Her narcissism flew to another universe, ethereal and 'on the side of otherness'. Hence Kavan's great attraction, that she sees beyond the personal to an impersonal infinity. She is not a victim but a creator, not a mad thing but a winged thing.

Her literary evolution is of remarkable interest. Born somewhere at the turn of the century (the imprecision is necessary, for she would never reveal her age), she was then plain Helen Edmonds. That did not satisfy her. A divine discontent was on the move in her.

The chilly sexuality in the novel *Let Me Alone*, in its very title, perhaps conveys something of what was happening to Helen Edmonds. In that novel, Anna is the protagonist, taken to the East against her wish. Findlay, Anna's lover, finally holds her in his arms. The night of the country now called Sri Lanka is about them. 'For the moment, she was open to him.' Yet they do nothing; not so much as a kiss is exchanged. The isolation is unbridgeable. 'They were in different worlds.'

That seems to have been a lifelong problem, not merely for the fictional Anna but also for the real one.

After the ineffectual encounter with Findlay, Anna is raped by her husband, Matthew. She suffers atrociously, yet her spirit remains cold; 'nor did he ever become real to her'.

The sense of unreality, perhaps the heart of symbolism, was a lifelong problem. And here indeed the fictional character—as a vampire is supposed to take over the living—becomes imposed upon the form of the author.

A contemporary reader of *Let Me Alone* feels a shock when the irreconcilable Matthew and Anna are introduced at an up-country club in Burma as 'Mr and Mrs Kavan'. The very words seem ill-assorted. But *Let Me Alone* was first published in 1930, and the author's name on the title page given as Helen Ferguson.

Helen Ferguson evidently felt that she had defined herself in the character of Anna, who so courts yet fears isolation. Shortly there-after, her own marriage failing, she encountered the writings of Franz Kafka, and changed her name by deed poll to that of the character she had invented, Anna Kavan. Art inundated nature.

This change of name, so full of masochism and pride, followed a period in a mental hospital, the period brilliantly defined in 'My Madness'. It represented a transformation, the crossing of a frontier away from the real. Anna Kavan had converted herself, as writers sometimes do, but rarely so deliberately. From now on, the realm of fantasy commanded her, and she it.

The discontinuity of personality is reflected in the discontinuities of Kavan's prose. The prose is always lucid, without latinate con-structions, without long words or literary allusions; the complexity lies in what is omitted. Often the discontinuities are nothing short of terrifying, as for instance in some of the stories in the collection *Julia and the Bazooka*, made soon after Kavan's death. That is to say, they may terrify the reader, although to the 'I' character they are merely the stuff of life. Living somewhere on an unnamed continent, you may find friends turn into tigers.

Much of the strength of the laconically entitled story, 'A Visit', in that same collection, derives from the proffered discontinuity of its opening sentence: 'One hot night a leopard came into my room and lay down on the bed beside me'. We are at once in the unknown territory of the Douanier Rousseau, where communication between human and animal happens as punctually as the full moon.

'A Visit' dispels the notion that Anna Kavan's writings are merely depressing. Such is not the case; and the luminosity of even the dark pieces gives light enough. In her sudden transitions of mood and feeling we see the kinship with Kafka, and perhaps even something of that concealed humour which was Charles Dickens's gift to Kafka.

Many people are surprised to learn that when Kafka first read extracts from *The Trial* to Max Brod and their circle of friends, he could sometimes hardly continue for laughter. Similarly, Chekhov was first played outside his own country for tragedy, not comedy. Kavan's reputation is at present for gloom, madness and paranoia. Not undeservedly. Yet the whisper of mocking laughter is often to be heard, even in the sybilline 'Sleep Has His House'.

Kavan in person, too, did not always project her shadowed side. In conversation with her English publisher, Peter Owen—it's to be doubted if there would be an Anna Kavan without a Peter Owen—I said something of this kind, having enjoyed her friendly company. Owen agreed. It took a while to see through the camouflage of normality; or perhaps, human nature being so diverse, one should rather say that the camouflage of tortured romanticism concealed much that was no more or less than normal. In either event, Anna was of smart, cheerful appearance. She enjoyed male company.

Neither in her appearance nor her behaviour did she reveal her incurable heroin addiction. As Peter Owen admits, it was a while before the fact of that addiction dawned on him.

When I met her, towards the end of her life, I too knew nothing of the heroin. By then, she had been on the habit for some thirty years. Heroin was her accomplice, her truce with reality. I saw only another dedication: to literature, and to that I responded.

Raymond Marriott, another long-term friend of Anna's, emphasizes her worldly, everyday side, reminding us that she was a good gardener, an excellent painter, and a skilled designer of small houses.

*   *   *

Anna was friendly and welcoming, in the small house of her own design in Hillgate Street, in the Kensington district of London. I had selected *Ice* as the best science fiction novel of 1967, less from any firm conviction that it was science fiction, or from a desire to dismay rivals, than to draw attention to a splendid piece of writing which might have been overlooked in the face of more noisy claimants for public attention. We talked in the ordinary way of two strangers wanting to get to know each other, and I gave her a novel of mine which, I felt, also operated in the same regions of otherness as *Ice*.

Anna had some complaint about Cyril Connolly, the editor of *Horizon*, for whom she had worked in the war years. He could have been more supportive of her with regard to her own writing, she felt. It was the sort of remark anyone might make. She longed to have a reputation, and thought that perhaps my attention marked a new start; she liked the idea of being regarded as a science fiction writer. It sounded modern. One sees in her work the sort of modernism—love of cars and speed and so on, not to mention the 'fast set'—which surfaces in Aldous Huxley's novels.

Little financial reward had followed from the publication of her novels and stories. She was reduced to selling some paintings (of which the house seemed still full), including a Graham Sutherland she had liked; and there was the tiresome business of designing houses or their interiors for other people.

No doubt her eye for design was sharp. She showed me over her house, walking with a stick. I supposed her to be in her late sixties. Her home was cunning and discreet, garden and house interlocked. It would have been no great matter for a leopard to enter her bedroom. Exotic plants grew everywhere, indoors and out, and mirrors basked mistily among paintings. A pleasant place in which to exist, with a flavour of the admired Henri Rousseau about it.

I offered to do something about American publication for *Ice*, since she had no agent. I sent a copy of the novel to Lawrence P. Ashmead, then my publisher at Doubleday. Larry was—is—a fine and understanding editor, but it took him some while to work through the Doubleday machine.

Finally, he sent me a letter saying that Doubleday accepted *Ice*. Anna had just died. She died of heart disease on 6 December 1968; I read of her death in the obituary columns of *The Times*. It was not suicide. Only a week earlier, I had received a letter from her which concluded with the words, 'Sorry this is such a disjointed note. I really don't feel human at present'. The ice was closing in fast.

Doubleday's hardcover edition was followed in the States by a funny little Popular Library (New York) paperback edition, which proclaimed on its cover, 'Sci-Fi at its Best'. Of course, *Ice* is not sci-fi, and only marginally science fiction, existing as it does in that fertile area—increasingly fertile as the century diminishes—where unreality prevails and life strategies are not those of the false everyday world we have constructed between ourselves and what Kavan calls 'no-times'.

'Reality had always been something of an unknown quality to me', she says at the start of *Ice*.

If one plays the game of categories, then Anna Kavan ranks as a symbolist, one of the few English symbolists. It is a rare breed, which is perhaps why she has found no protagonist to speak up for her. A slightly coterie publisher published and nourished her. She formed no alliances with other authors. Her name does not appear in *The Oxford Companion to English Literature*. Symbolism is not a part of the solid English mainstream of writing. We prefer our fictional protagonists to turn into successes or failures, rather than leopards.

The characters in *Ice* are designedly symbolic and nameless. The girl, the hero, the warden. The countries through which they travel are anonymous. Their decisions are makeshift, their actions almost random, their circumstances as arbitrary as the advance of the ice. Their world is ramshackle, and under sentence of death. In such a situation, war attains a positive value: 'By making war we asserted the fact that we were alive and opposed the icy death creeping over the globe'.

The maddened military activity, the nameless nations, everything contributes to a sense of doom. Yet all is lively, mobile, even joyous after a fashion, since catastrophe for such affectless people is just a way of life. The response to catastrophe can only be indifference. 'Once prominent states had simply dropped out of existence.' States of mind also.

This vertiginous sense is counterpointed by the business of personal disintegration. 'Something in her demanded victimization and terror, so she corrupted my dreams, led me into dark places I had no wish to explore. It was no longer clear to me which of us was the victim. Perhaps we were victims of one another.'

Ice lures us to the heart of Kavan's writing, and to the peak of her achievement, where personal concerns become universalized.

That relationship with Kafka. What are we to make of it? 'Helen Ferguson's' instinct to ally herself with the Czech writer was a true one. Kafka is clearly her literary and spiritual mentor. Both were self-torturers, both aspired to dissolve themselves into literature. 'I have no literary interests, but am made of literature', said Kafka. Their own personalities, deprived of self-respect through nature or more probably nurture (overweening fathers and mothers), sought an established basis in a projected writing self; the writing self became what could be cherished.

In comparison with Kafka, Kavan is a watercolourist. Yet direct comparison is unfair; Kafka remains one of the great dark beacons of twentieth-century literature. She still offers her original torments, and we do not forget that she was a painter as well as a writer, her canvasses also offering wry comment on her state of mind. Headless creatures hug one another, becoming one body. One head out-Januses Janus, its three heads perhaps girl, hero, warden, the watcher. And there was also the life of the drug addict, that decades-long communion with otherness. By the end, Kavan had created herself even more decidedly than her literary mentor. Hers is the honourable position of Kafka's sister.

Anna Kavan is at present that uncomfortable thing awaiting final judgement, a cult figure. Her situation is as ambiguous as she could desire.

Indications are that her reputation may belatedly spread further. At the University of Tulsa, her newly discovered journals and diaries are being edited for publication. A biography has appeared.[1] Kavan's friend, Rhys Davies, wrote a novelized version of her life, *The Honeysuckle Girl*, which it would be good to have reprinted.

Yet perhaps she would perversely become hostile to the world's acclaim. It would not bring back the lost hours or the lost Sutherland. In one of her stories, 'A Summer Evening', she yearns towards a final grand gesture of alienation.

> 'I can never go back to the living world unless I am changed completely . . . If this whole structure could be transmuted into something hard, cold, untouchable, unaffected by any emotion . . . then and then only, indifferent to isolation and independent of time, I might endure the world.
>
> '. . . Inexhaustible and impervious, I would stride all over the world, seeing everything, knowing everything, needing

1 David Callard, *The Case of Anna Kavan*, London, Peter Owen, 1992.

nothing and nobody . . . finally leaving earth and the last
human being behind me and turning away to the most
remote galaxies and the unimaginable reaches of infinite
space.'

CAMPBELL'S SOUP

Setting nostalgia aside, what was achieved by *Astounding Science Fiction* under the editorship of John Wood Campbell? Campbell edited this famous magazine from May 1938, when he took full charge, until he died in July 1971, at the age of sixty-one. It was a long tenure. Many of us still think of those years, particularly the magazine's rich decades of the 1940s and 1950s, as 'Campbell's years'.

The situation must be faced, that the stories in which we gloried in our youth become tarnished on a disillusioned re-reading, many years later. The revelations in the stories are now part of our world-outlook; that they have become incorporated in, have formed, our way of life is a tribute to their earlier power.

It is hard to define exactly what gives a story or novel perennial appeal. We're dealing here with the fragile, things not designed to last, and sometimes written in desperation for four cents a word.

One reason why science fiction is so little regarded is because it is often ahead of its time, and therefore unpalatable to the general or even the literary reader. By 'ahead of its time' we mean mainly forward-looking in interests.

To take a random example: James H. Schmitz's story 'Grandpa' was published in Campbell's magazine in the mid-1950s. It is a story of symbiosis on an alien planet. A human being, Cord, is using a kind of giant perambulating lily pad to navigate round a bay. They call this raft 'Grandpa'. But Grandpa buds and starts doing sinister and unexpected things, like heading out to the open sea, to the cold Zlanti Deep. A symbiote, the Yellowhead, has joined Grandpa and taken control of it. This is the dilemma from which Cord must extricate himself and his three companions.

It was a wonderful story. I went about for months muttering to myself that thrilling name, 'The Zlanti Deep'—resonant synonym for the Unknown.

What was new to me at the time was the story's sustained

botanical aspect, although *ASF* writers and readers had long been interested in ideas of symbiosis. Researchers more skilled than I could trace this theme through the years. Also, 'Grandpa' was about ecology, some years before Herbert's *Dune* appeared.

Well, forty years on, ecology has become one of the buzz words of the age. What one perceives, on going back to Schmitz's clever story now, is that it belongs in a rather dated category: the resourceful human on an alien planet who solves a little puzzle with good old American know-how and a gun. In fact, its structure derives from the men's adventure tales of the Clayton pulps, where *Astounding Stories of Super-Science* was born in 1930.

A generation has gone by since Schmitz wrote. Even the vast Zlanti Deep has been drained and cities are built upon the reclaimed land. Times change.

So, if the *ASF* stories have passed their sell-by date, why is Campbell's magazine, rightly, so prized today? The answer must be that it was *ASF* itself which was the great work of dedication, the work of art. No, not quite a work of art: the spectrum was too narrow. No spirituality at one end, no eroticism at the other. What produced the excitement, the intellectual stimulation, was the whole ambience of the magazine, the variety of every issue, and, of course, that mixture of madness and sanity which is at the heart of SF.

It was a rich soup. Campbell's *Astounding* (later *Analog*) nourished a generation of minds—and not only in the USA. We honour it still, although times have changed.

The theme of Albert Berger's recent book, *The Magic That Works*, with its sub-title, 'John W. Campbell and the American Response to Technology',[1] concerns precisely those things, Campbell's *ASF* and the changes which overtook Campbell, though Berger's main concerns are more technological than literary.[2]

When the going was good, 'Campbell's editorial judgment was functioning as a creative force to resolve many of the contradictory impulses that go into the making of science fiction'. This perceptive

1 In the Milford Series: *Popular Writers of Today*, vol. 46, San Bernardino, CA, Borgo Press, 1993.

2 Berger is the author, with Mike Ashley, of the excellent article on *ASF/ Analog* in that indispensable work of reference, edited by Marshall B. Tymn and Mike Ashley, *Science Fiction, Fantasy and Weird Fiction Magazines*, Westport, CT, Greenwood, 1985.

remark lies at the heart of Berger's comprehensive discussion of Campbellian SF—arguably the most formidable body of popular magazine-writing ever. And formidable because of the capacious, argumentative character of its editor.

He brought together a group of writers who grew and developed with the magazine. Their names are well-known: Heinlein, Asimov, Clarke, van Vogt, Blish, Sturgeon, E. E. Smith, Poul Anderson, and some whose names are now less well-remembered, such as Eric Frank Russell, E. B. Cole and William Tenn. Most of them owed a great deal to their editor. James Blish always swore—with generous exaggeration—that his entire 'Oakie' series (*Cities in Flight*) sprang from a four-page letter Campbell wrote him.

Those of us who read *ASF* throughout the early years of Campbell's reign, which coincide very roughly with the war in Europe, into the first years of the Cold War, will never forget the intense excitement Campbell generated. The time came when one felt it would be impossible for new readers to join in, so—and this was the joy of it—in-bred and self-referential was the whole blue-print of fictional discussion.

But Berger's book is not exactly about the stories or the authors—or indeed about Campbell himself. It probes the ideas and ideology which Campbell espoused, as measured against society's changing attitudes. Berger lays out in intellectual terms what Campbell's readers perceived in a more visceral way: that gradually *ASF* came to seem dated, stuffy, conservative. To imagine less. To preach more—at a time when sermons were increasingly the prerogative of Joan Baez. The cutting edge of *ASF*'s invention grew blunt. Gimlets gave way to Anvils. The soup had gone sour. The wits seemed sharper over at *Galaxy*. Of Smiths, not E. E., but Cordwainer.

By the time the all-conquering *Dune* arrived in *ASF* ('Dune World', 1963–64), it came overloaded with too-familiar Campbellian topics, especially parapsychology. As for Arrakis—that sandy wilderness seemed to owe a little too much to Doughty's *Arabia Deserta* . . . and Doughty wrote better . . . Herbert's ecology was timely, but his feuding feudal barons appeared a shade *passé* to the new breed of writer then delightedly discovering the present.

But for years the going previously had been good indeed. Berger epitomizes those years as a 'mixture of ebullience and fear', which seems about right. The universe was a hostile place, choked with cold equations. For a young readership, many of whom were involved in a war becoming increasingly science-fictional (ending in the long-predicted atom bomb), the landscape of *ASF* varied pleasurably between the low-lying swamps of the All-too-likely (Cleve Cartmill) and the high mesas of the Unlikely, as pioneered by Doc Smith and A. E. van Vogt.

This landscape was underlaid by the rock strata of John Campbell's mind and opinions. A short article cannot attempt to disentangle Berger's long well-reasoned chapters, but basically his argument, from which it seems hard to dissent, is this: that scientist-heroes and lone inventors became phased out, in *ASF* as in real life. The 'nuts-and-bolts' aspect of SF too was phased out, in favour of greater science, 'the magic that works'—the vastly expanded powers of human minds.

In the real world, the old nuts-and-bolts age of *Popular Mechanics* was fading, giving place to the electronic age. Marshall McLuhan was at large in the land. The Pill and the transistor, those tiny revolutionaries, were at work. No corresponding expansion of human mental power took place. Even Flower Power had only a short period in the sun. Our minds are as miniaturized now as they were when Hugo Gernsback cut his first rivet. Indeed, there's a case to be argued that our citizens are even less well educated today than yesterday; half of them still reckon the Sun goes round the Earth. Psionics did not happen, for all Campbell's insistence, for all the neighing of his hobby horse through the mouths of derivative authors. Now we're pinning our hopes on AI instead—another doomed craze, due for the Zlanti Deep.

As Berger rightly says, Campbell was a shaper of SF's intellectual history: he woke writers up to the importance of their theme. After his success with the atomic bomb predictions, he thirsted for more success over and above the narrow outcast world of *ASF*. In 1950 came L. Ron Hubbard's *Dianetics*—launched in *ASF*'s pages. It proved one step backward for mankind; I suspect many people regard SF as a similar quack religion. Increased authoritarianism, too, became unfashionable in the more liberal 1960s. Lively debate sprang from the freer speech which Campbell's successor, Ben Bova, brought to *ASF* later.

The audience which Campbell addressed was changing. It became richer, as did America. A fair percentage of scientists worked for the very research institutions Campbell attacked. That held true even for those who had been drawn to super-science. This was Campbell's increasing dilemma. Young Edisons and Fords now served as anonymous cogs in R & D. In the final book of *Dune*, Leto Atreides evolves into a god. It's the true destiny of a Campbellian hero. But by then the 1960s had come and gone. Campbell was dead. And his old readers were gainfully employed in Bell Labs and elsewhere. Even space wore a faded air.

SF, in fact, did not shoot out into the universe, as we all expected in the fifties. Instead, it took a dive into little boxes—Nintendos, computers and computer games.

Inevitably, Berger's book has an element of tragedy about it, since it chronicles a literary decline. Nostalgia is not its objective, as it was in Alva Rogers's *A Requiem For 'Astounding'* (1964). Instead, Berger presents a grasp of sociological movements which would please Hari Seldon. The argument is that Campbell fossilized, while society—fortunately—continued to change. The same process overtook H. G. Wells. No man's mental grasp is infinite. Even Campbell's.

Perhaps it is disappointing not to have a closer examination of the contents of *ASF* when the going was good, or to read a fuller account of how, in person, Campbell could be both humorous and courteous. This sort of tough-minded and illuminating study reminds us of the pleasure we had when we were just clever enough to misunderstand van Vogt.

If Berger has chosen not to celebrate the time 'when the going was good', he certainly knows all about 'the contradictory impulses that shape science fiction', where visionary meets crank. It's a fine contribution to the history of SF.

SOME EARLY MEN IN
THE MOON

~~~~~~

When the spacecraft Apollo 11 landed on the Moon in July of 1969,
and Armstrong and Aldrin walked upon that ancient surface, a new
era was widely believed to have begun. As is generally the case, the
opening of one era marked the closure of another. In a new
mythology, Apollo slew Diana, and signalled an end to centuries of
pleasurable speculation about life on the Moon.

Two centuries before the Apollo landings, a Florentine artist,
Filipo Morghen, of whom little is known, produced a series of nine
engravings and a frontispiece, showing 'Life on the Moon'. Or rather
his idea of life on the Moon. A rather Florentine moon.

The engravings are great fun. They mark an interesting moment in
the history of such speculations. As examples of mid-eighteenth-
century imaginings of lunar life, they show the first incursions of
science into pure fancy. Fancy and science can supplement each
other, to the benefit of both.

Plutarch, in the first century AD, considered the question of
whether the Moon was inhabited. In his *De Facie in Orbe* ('The Face
in the Moon', which Kepler translated from Greek into Latin) he
concludes that demons inhabit our sister world; the violent ones are
sometimes exiled from the Moon to Earth. This idea was taken up
some centuries later by A. E. van Vogt, in *Asylum*.

It would hardly be worth raising the question of the Moon's
habitability if the answer were to be in the negative. We need our
fun. The Moon has been the most powerful of symbols over the ages:
as it has drawn the ocean's tides about the Earth, so it has attracted
the ambition to travel upwards towards the closest astronomical
body. Our limited achievements in that department so far would
have been impossible had we no such near neighbour in space.

Science fiction is adroit at mixing fancy with actual or possible
science. Happily, our lives do not depend on it when we do so. Such

was not always the case. The publishing history of Johannes Kepler's *Somnium* in the seventeenth century proves as much. Kepler died during the Thirty Years War, his precious manuscript still unpublished. It appeared as a completed book in 1634. Among the astronomer's problems was the fact that his mother had been charged with witchcraft.

Somnium, or *The Dream*, represents scientific findings disguised as fantasy. The findings demonstrate Kepler's laws of planetary motion, which paved the way for modern science and astronautics. The fantasy may well have paved the way for Morghen's engravings, a century later.

Here is Kepler's picture of one of his two lunar races, the Privolans.

> The Privolans have no fixed abode, no established domicile. In the course of one of their days they roam in crowds over their whole sphere, each according to his own nature: some use their legs, which far surpass those of our camels; some resort to wings; and some follow the receding water in boats; or if a delay of several more days is necessary, then they crawl into caves.

Kepler's notes on *The Dream* are much longer than his story. In the excellent University of Wisconsin Press edition, *The Dream* occupies eighteen pages, and the Notes occupy almost one hundred and twenty pages. In Note 214, he explains,

> . . . water flowed in [to the country of the Privolans] at fixed times of the day. When it receded, I had the living creatures accompany it. To enable them to do so quickly, I gave some of them long legs and others the ability to swim and endure the water, with the proviso that they would not degenerate into fishes.

Kepler's mind was by no means free of mysticism; perhaps it was mysticism as much as observation and calculation which led him to discover the mathematical relationship between the distances of the planets from their primary and their orbital velocities. His laws of planetary motion formed a basis for all future astronomy, while from his third law Isaac Newton derived his law of universal gravitation. And from Kepler's way of populating his planet with plausible aliens—at least plausible in their day—we hardly deviate to this day. Even Filipo Morghen's creatures strive for some probability within context.

Advances in science in the seventeenth century brought new momentum to the problem of reaching the Moon. It was no longer a question of being wafted there by angels. Bishop Francis Godwin's hero, Gonsales, in his *Man in the Moone* (posthumously published in 1638), was carried thither by migratory gansas or geese. In that same year, another English bishop, John Wilkins, Bishop of Chester and a founder of the Royal Society, published *The Discovery of a Worlde in the Moon*, which discusses the possibilities of travelling to the Moon.

A generation later, the Italian, Francesco Lana, conceived more scientific means of transport. The vacuum pump was a recent invention. In Lana's *Prodromo* of 1670, his humble little wooden car or boat is elevated by means of four metal globes from which the air has been exhausted. Seated in this boat, the passenger is carried safely through space. The concept of space as a vacuum had been enunciated by Kepler but, happily for the fantasists, had not then taken root.

So we come to Morghen, the mysterious Florentine with the un-Florentine name. His so-called *Raccolta*, or *Collection*, purports to show some of the wonderful things observed by 'John Wilkins, the learned English Bishop, on his renowned voyage from the earth to the moon'.

Morghen's frontispiece shows two intrepid voyagers stepping from their machine. They have evidently returned from the journey of which we are about to have evidence. They greet two elders, devotees of book-learning, who appear to protest at the travellers' extraordinary tale.

The lunar vehicle is little more more than a flying chicken run. It has wings and a tail and observation ports. But of its method of propulsion we are given no clues, any more than we are later able to understand how H. G. Wells's time machine works.

The remaining nine plates show some interest in methods of propulsion. However, they are scarcely to be regarded as scientific speculations. They belong to a different and thriving eighteenth-century tradition, which takes little cognizance of the Royal Society's quest for sober truth, the *capriccio*. *Capricci*, or artistic caprices, offered an escape from the formal practices of drawing and painting. They allowed room for the imaginative touch, the flourish, the mystery. Probably the most famous *capricci* are Giambattista Tiepolo's, issued in 1799—which were later to influence Goya's *Los Caprichos* and formed the basis of my novel, *The Malacia Tapestry*.

The thematic origins of Tiepolo's *Capricci*, and his earlier *Scherzi*, while still cloaked in mystery, depict magical and mystical scenes. Italians had a craze for magic at the time. Filipo Morghen exhibits another side of this same coin. His lunar landscapes are magical whimsies, not intended to be taken too seriously.

Yet, over two centuries later, we can see reasons for paying these fancies a degree of attention. Their decorative qualities are as pleasing now as they were in Morghen's day. And we discern here a general wish for better machines—above all, a desire for a better form of motive power than a horse or a sail, which another half-century was to supply in the form of the steam locomotive. The industrial revolution which would sweep away the old world would then be up and running.

According to Morghen, the 'savages' on the Moon have certain advantages over terrestrial savages, not least in their means of locomotion. In their world, plentiful sunshine produces gigantic gourds but rather small animals. Even their largest wild beast resembles nothing so much as a spikey-haired mouse of generous dimension. Although creatures like terrestrial elephants are to be seen, they are little larger than rottweilers and of more benevolent disposition. It is true that the lunarians have gigantic birds to contend with, but these can be domesticated, or at least captured, if fed on the giant snails which abound.

The most horrific lunar lifeform is the winged serpent, a true anomaly of natural history. The serpent's wings sprout from a shaggy excrescence half-way along its body. The wings are large but rather delicate, insufficiently powerful to permit the serpent ever to be fully airborne. Its tail is doomed forever to trail along the ground. However, the serpent is a hardy creature and, when properly trained, will attack and overcome even the renowned smoke-emitting porcupine.

While speaking of the fowls and snakes inhabiting the Moon, we must not forget the parrots, kept rather as we keep them, for amusement, and the geese. These geese, interestingly, are all descended from the gansas which brought Gonsales of Bishop Godwin's legend here. They are highly regarded and often treated as pets, though some also find their way into the pot. They respond to drum beats, having a natural sense of rhythm.

Like us, the lunarians divide their society into classes. Those of the highest class have a singular privilege denied even royalty on Earth. Lunar sultans can command the assistance of Zephyrs, cupid-like creatures who live in the lunar clouds. Since these sultans travel in

Engraving from Filipo Morghen's *Raccolta*, showing 'Life on the Moon'.

carriages drawn not by horses but sails, they are able to summon the Zephyrs for means of propulsion, as we see in Plate 3.

In return, the potentates send up sweet incense to delight the senses of the attendant Zephyr.

Very little land transport is required. Most of the Moon is covered by shallow seas. Which is fortunate, since so much of the land is marshy and snakes abound. Here the lower orders have their own forms of transport: their boats move mainly by means of large bellows which have to be worked to fill the sails. Considerable labour is involved in this task. Naked slaves fed on snails are sometimes employed for the purpose.

Regular sailing services ply between villages along the coast. The habitations in these villages are provided by benevolent nature. Gigantic gourds grow abundantly on ricketty-racketty gourd trees. The gourds are easily hollowed out—providing as much as a year's sustenance for the average family—and then used as comfortable huts. It is convenient to fish from the windows of these gourd-dwellings. Sometimes the gourds are lopped from their parent tree; a rudder is attached, and then the occupants are free to sail where they will, fishing with net and trident, and smoking such of their catch as they cannot immediately eat. It is an idyllic way of life. Sometimes, fleets of gourd-dwellers circumnavigate the small globe just for the pleasure of it.

Little in the way of commotion or crisis disturbs the pleasant daily round. The one serious inconvenience comes in the shape of the mouselike creature, the snout-mouse, already referred to. The male of the species, on reaching puberty, grows a long hard corkscrew snout. With this snout, it amuses itself by puncturing holes in inhabited gourds—a fatal act in the case of the waterborne gourds, which are then liable to sink, along with occupants and smoked herrings.

However, the somewhat patchy lunar technology has come up with a weapon which, it is hoped, will deal with the snout-mouse for good and all. The Mouse-Splitter consists of a sharp blade which can be released suddenly on the unsuspecting animal. As it advances along a plank towards the bait, two infant gourds, down comes the blade, whack, and the snout-mouse is no more. The parrot cheers.

Morghen decorates the foregrounds—the footlights, one might say—of his stagey scenes with decorative foliage and creatures, rather in the manner of the charts of the period, such as the cartouches gracing maps designed by the illustrious Dutchman, W. J.

Blaeuw. Possibly Morghen was also Dutch; his is not an Italian name.

The result is a decorative set of copper-plates—yet not merely decorative. Just as no one has determined exactly when Tiepolo's *Capricci* were executed, so there is still discussion as to the precise dates of Morghen's small masterpiece.

Testament to their popularity lies in the fact that the prints went through at least three editions. Grant McColley, who has studied the problem, declares that

> the first of the three extant title pages . . . were printed during the period of 1764–1772, with the probability that the date of the first was 1766 or 1767, and that of the second 1767 or 1768. The third title page belongs to the years which follow 1784, and may have received its distinguishing alteration prior to 1800.

This 'distinguishing alteration' is of great interest, serving as it does as a marker of progress between the two dates of 1766 and 1784, as McColley has them. Much happened in that twenty-two year span.

Fresh interest in our neighbours in the solar system was aroused by Herschel's discovery of the planet Uranus in 1781. Could a way be found to travel in space? Two years after Herschel's discovery, the Montgolfier brothers sent up their first hot-air balloon. An exciting new means of progression had been discovered. An age of ballooning was heralded, though the hydrogen balloon sent up from Paris was torn and hacked to pieces by terrified peasants when it landed in a field, fifteen miles from its launch pad.

In 1785, Jean Blanchard and Dr John Jefferies, a wealthy American, crossed the English Channel by balloon, travelling hazardously above the sea from Dover to a forest near Calais. And in the third edition of the *Raccolta*, a representation of Blanchard's balloon has been added to the improbable wooden ship of the frontispiece. Morghen was bowing—perhaps a little reluctantly—to progress.

One other feature of that delightful frontispiece deserves comment. The wording changed between editions. To begin with, the collection was of 'the most notable things seen by the cavalier Wild Scull and Signor de la Hire on their famous voyage from Earth to the Moon'. Was there an Englishman of Morghen's acquaintance called Strangoar or Madhead? While we may never solve the riddle of Wild Scull, we know that de la Hire was an astronomer and mathematician living in the early eighteenth century.

Let the learned Marjorie Hope Nicolson take up the tale, as she does in her *Voyages to the Moon* (1948).

> In his first drawing, Morghen apparently associated the idea of an inhabited moon-world with La Hire, not aware that La Hire himself vehemently opposed the theory that the Moon might be inhabited. In the second 'edition', the voyager to the Moon has become no less a person than 'Giovanni Wilkins *erudito Vescuvo Inglese'*. And so John Wilkins, scientist and romancer-in-chief of seventeenth-century England returned in the eighteenth to revisit in Italy the glimpses of that moon he had discovered for his generation.

The work is dedicated to another Englishman, Sir William Hamilton, who was plenipotentiary in Naples from 1764 to 1800. Hamilton had a lively interest in all natural phenomena. He made twenty-two ascents of Vesuvius, witnessing the eruptions of 1776 painted by that great student of light and the Moon, the artist Joseph Wright of Derby. It is certain that Hamilton was acquainted with the mysterious Morghen; the DNB declares him 'the patron of Morghen the engraver'. Perhaps Wright was also acquainted with him. In Wright's *oeuvre* we see the Industrial Revolution getting into its stride. But only the mild breezes of the Rococo fill Filipo Morghen's imaginative sails.

These days, our imaginings may be more powerful. But they owe much to those who have forged the imaginative path before us.

KALIYUGA, *OR* UTOPIA AT A BAD TIME

Talk given at the Annual MENSA meeting in Cambridge

～～～～～～～～～～～～～～～～～～～～～～～～～～～～～～～～～～

Utopias were never popular. They've become even less popular this century. The reason's clear. Utopias are decent places where no international arms trade takes place, where IRA stands for Irredeemably Rational Arrangements, where Africa is a sort of vast health resort, and where Shakespeare is banned on the grounds that the fellow was mad enough to write gloomy plays.

How do we get to such decent states of grace from where we are now? Well, of course we can't. No way. We can hardly reform ourselves. Take prison reform; even with a sensible and humane man like Judge Stephen Toumim advising the government, we continue to build more prisons. We fear ourselves. We're a lot of ruffians, selfish, inclined to be greedy. What's more, every utopia reminds us that we are unfit to enter its portals, that first of all we have to transform ourselves inwardly before there's any chance of building a New Jerusalem—crikey, what am I saying? Look at all the racial and religious conflict surrounding the Old Jerusalem!—building a new paradise, a kind of Disneyland of the Psyche, here on Earth. Perhaps somewhere outside Barnsley.

So why bother you learned ladies and gentlemen with thoughts of utopia at this early hour?

One good reason might be because this is Kaliyuga. Kaliyuga in Hindu mythology is the present age of the world, the fourth age, characterized by total decadence. Decadence needs the purgative of perfection to taste on its over-ripe tongue.

A more personal reason is that I feel myself drawn helplessly, like moth to flame or fly to flypaper, towards writing a utopia myself. We all hope to see a better world, provided it doesn't spoil our holidays in

Corfu. And that as I see it is where we find the angel with the flaming sword barring the entry to our terrestrial pearly gates: we are naturally reluctant to surrender what we have gained for pie in the sky.

Some time ago, at the Oxford autumn fair in St Giles, a Christian booth was set up, where a man with a megaphone was inviting passing punters to join the Church of England. What he was saying as I hurried past was this: 'Join us now, join Christ! You don't have to give anything, you don't have to give anything up!'

Profoundly wrong, I thought. If you desire anything strongly, there are things you have to give up to gain it.

I suspect that to achieve utopia you have to give up technology, Big Science. This is what everyone suspects, and of course we don't like the idea. We are victims of—to coin a phrase—Techno-Tyranny. Technology isn't like religion. Most religions pay at least lip service towards helping the poor. Entry to church and mosque and synagogue is free. Entry into the company of G7 nations exacts a cost.

We know what that cost is. It's unspecifiable in terms of quality of life. Not just taxes, but—well, take two vital psycho-physiological payments which are being made by the whole world to keep 'Progress' on track. ('Progress' always comes in quotes these days, but quotes ain't handcuffs, and Progress is still a free man—free to tramp the Earth.) One of these down-payments is overdue: it's what you might call the Big Pollutant Bill. I refer to all the nuclear weapons lying around in Ukraine and god knows where else; plus all the other pollutants of land, air and sea. You're not primary school kids; you have the list in your heads.

The second psycho-physiological down-payment is what the world went through for forty years, that dismal stand-to we call the Cold War. Possible only because of state-of-the-art technology and the mentalities that shaped it and were shaped by it. I recall the genuine fears of my children as they grew up, awaiting the four-minute warning; the maimed kids in Romanian orphanages are more dramatic examples of the same bill of goods.

To be honest, I'm embarrassed to be saying this. You know it all already and I'm no expert. I'm a story teller and I retain a love of big machines and journeys to Mars and Alpha Centauri. But they have a price, and that price may be more costly than we realize. They stand between us and plans for better, less destructive societies.

Every age has a prevailing ethic or myth. In later ages, we're at a loss to understand what went on in earlier heads. What made men turn from hunting to the hard discipline of agriculture? Why did the Egyptians build those gigantic pyramids? Why did the Thirty Years War continue for so long? How could the Inquisition come about? Why did we undergo the Cold War and how did we survive it? Looking out through the bars of our 20th Century culture, we see that every age seems governed by a vast obsession—a kind of hive mind—which precludes the rationality of utopia.

Technology requires governments and large corporations to sustain it. But would we foreswear it? We think of dentistry and surgery and our computers and know that would be absurd. But it's not impossible to imagine that another age, living under another prevailing myth, might think and feel differently.

I realize I'm ill-equipped to write a utopia. Satire is more my line. I think of one of our recent utopianists, Aldous Huxley, the centenary of whose birth falls this year. Huxley wrote three utopias or dystopias. *Brave New World* is his most famous one, in which the processes of mass production are applied to biology. In *Ape and Essence*, a savage satire, the bombs have fallen and mankind has reverted to the primal ape; women have reverted to the oestrus cycle. These are works of the 1930s and 1940s. In the 1960s, towards the end of his life, Huxley wrote *Island*, a gentle utopia, where the things reviled and mocked in *Brave New World* are magically seen as positive: sexual promiscuity, drugs . . . *Island* is a hopeful vision, but to write it Huxley had to set aside the weapons he had wielded all his life, his sharp intellect, his wit, to give out with sweetness and light.

He made this sacrifice and, perhaps as a result, *Island* is not a complete success. But Philip Toynbee called it a gift of virtue and love. I believe that to be a correct judgement. We all need—wish, hope—to make a gesture of virtue and love at some point in our lives.

I suppose I began life as a Wellsian. Now I'm more a Huxleyan. Huxley takes care of the spiritual side. Huxley does not believe, as Wells came to believe, that a conspiracy of a few good-hearted businessmen and politicians could change the world. Indeed, he's sceptical about politics, saying at one point, that 'the great paradox of politics is that while political action is necessary, at the same time it is incapable of satisfying the needs which called it into existence'.

The same thought must have been in Samuel Johnson's mind when he penned that immortal couplet—and I intend to quote it again—

> How small, of all that human hearts endure,
> That part which laws or kings can cause or cure!

That being the case, it remains better to be ruled over by a weak John Major than a strong Napoleon. Strong rulers always know what is good for the nation, and what is good for the nation is rarely good for anyone but a few Top People and the heads of the armed forces.

From the 1940s onward, Huxley, seeing the world plunged into another war less than twenty-five years after the first, turned more and more to mysticism. When you mention mysticism, English audiences start to wriggle. Mysticism is so un-English that it gets confused with spiritualism. Perhaps they remember the embarrassing terminal state of Conan Doyle, who came to believe in fairies. When some practical joker in Oxford plastered the city with posters announcing that Conan Doyle would speak in the Town Hall on such-and-such a date on the subject of 'Sex in the Afterlife', the place was packed out—and it wasn't the Afterlife they wanted to hear about.

But mysticism is belief in or experience of a state surpassing normal human understanding. Most of us, I believe, know of such states, beyond what we call happiness. Ordinary worlds don't quite cover the case of such states, as Huxley found when writing *Island*, his labour of love. But after all, cosmologists and astrophysicists studying the origins of the universe are probing a similar state, beyond any normal human understanding. For them too, ordinary words are inadequate. Their computers must speak for them in mathematical symbols.

In the cultures developing since the Renaissance, it has become increasingly difficult to study mysticism, to be a mystic, to accept the discipline of mysticism. It seems to have no place in our supermarket economies. But supposing there is a real world 180 degrees away from our TV screens . . . Supposing we've got it all wrong. Supposing there is a specific reason, un-looked at, un-looked for, for the uproar we find around us in our societies . . . Supposing that we might escape the Era of Perpetual Entertainment—*fun*—and mature into beings who would wish to accept utopia for, not its boredom but—its excitement . . .

I find that hard to imagine. That's why I wish to imagine it.

Well, to remedy the weakness of Western religious organizations, many people turn to the less action-packed religions of the East, Buddhism and so on. Is there a hope there?

VR seems to be up-and-coming (he yawned). But what if we are already living only in a virtual reality, not in the real thing? Maybe this is a Philip K. Dick universe in which we are trapped with no way out.

Utopias could be the emergency exit.

Even as I say it, I know I don't want to live in a utopia myself. Is it because I was wrongly brought up, or is struggle genetic? Nature or nurture? Would I give up my Volvo estate so that a family in Rwanda could live in a nice bungalow? No. Not only am I selfish and possessive, because I couldn't afford a car till I was forty—I am sceptical about whether the nice Rwanda family would be able to keep that bungalow for five minutes. Once remove the routines of civilization, the laws under which we agree to abide, and a lot of people find it profitable, even enjoyable, to behave like brutes.

But if you step-up the routines of civilization, again the brutes break out.

Clearly it's a long way from here to utopia.

Utopia: Dream or Pipe Dream?

We know what utopias are. They are well-ordered societies where everyone gets a little more than their just deserts. Utopias are generally found at the end of a long journey, across the Atlantic or more recently across space. However, in a century like ours, scarred by wars enveloping the whole globe, totalitarianism, attempts to wipe out whole races, threats of nuclear annihilation, the classical utopia has taken a hammering and in has rushed the flourishing anti- or dystopia.

It would be a pity if proposals for better lives died. Karl Mannheim, in *Ideology and Utopia*, states that utopias are 'reality-transcendent', and their loss would mean 'the decay of the human will'. Why are they not being written? Have we run out of places to stage them in?

That could be the case. Ursula Le Guin's *The Dispossessed* of 1974 significantly moved utopia away from this planet to another one. Annares, because it is a hard world, is perfectly credible; but one might say that reality had crept in to the extent that it is no longer quite utopian, just as its antithesis, Urras, is not entirely dystopian. True, *The Dispossessed* is sub-titled 'An Ambiguous Utopia'. This blurring effect stands symbolically for the way the zeitgeist has turned its phantasmal back on utopianism. We're running out of convincing good places, in the same way that we have run out of Lost Races and the anthropophagi . . .

There have been a few utopias since *The Dispossessed*, published twenty years ago. One of the best, funniest, most pungent, of these is also by a woman, Charlotte Perkins Gilman. Her novel, *Herland*, resurfaced in 1979. This story of an all-women society hidden in the Amazon jungles was written during World War I and serialized in a magazine, to disappear—and reappear, shining and new, over half-a-century later.

Herland's benevolent socialist disposition is not always shared by more recent feminist writers of utopias. There was humour also, though of a harsher kind, in Margaret Atwood's very successful *The Handmaid's Tale*. Hardly surprisingly, lesbian-feminist utopias or dystopias are not far to seek. Sally Miller Gearhart's *The Wander-ground: Stories of the Hill Women* regards men and women almost as two species (an idea once developed as a joke in one of James Gunn's short stories—was it 'The Misogynist' in a fifties *Galaxy*?). Speaking as one who finds the idea of a world without women unbearable—like a planet without water—my preference is for the unjustly neglected *Armed Camps*, a novel of bitterly realistic sex war by the inimitable Kit Reed.

Perhaps utopias seem too static a concept, unlike dystopias, which contain their own momentum downhill. We are an age intensely on the move, still extending electronic networks, building more cities, more highways—which certainly aren't going to lead us to utopia. Or to ecotopia, a fashionable modern variant.

Ecotopias are a kind of half-way house towards—or perhaps back from—utopia. Generally speaking, as in Ernest Callenbach's *Ectopia* of 1975, we find only a partial rejection of the present day. Either our technologies are moderated somehow or somehow a steady-state economy has been reached. It doesn't need an economist to perceive that there's really no such thing as a steady-state economy—a steady-state economy is a declining one. A TV set lasts on average twelve years, a computer three years; of which item would you rather be the manufacturer? Obviously, if one commodity becomes less popular, you move to another line which is shifting faster. Digital watches are out, Swatches are in. This is known as 'market forces', and it is those same forces, rather than any deep wisdom, which inform our Western societies today. Being able to buy Mars bars as ice creams doesn't make us spiritually happier; it just makes Mars richer.

What about the other option, the utopia where somehow technologies are moderated, curtailed to a more human scale? That is to say,
people live closer to nature but still have dentistry; nanotechnology
but no cars; better eating habits but French wine; and of course
lashings of free love but fab contraception. This is the deep dream of
nostalgia, for a golden age, with all of today's perks and none of its
infuriating adverse trading balances. Transistor radios disguised as
old wireless sets.

Theodore Roszak's *Where the Wasteland Ends* of 1972, rejects
science entirely, and the world's 'sick infatuation with power,
growth, efficiency, [and] progress . . .' Of course, Roszak's book is
not SF. It inhabits that peculiar stratum with which we are familiar,
where books about the future and changes in society are labelled by
their publishers as being 'not SF'. 'Not SF' books occupy a stratum
between SF and Non-SF, and include such fictions as P. D. James's
recent *The Children of Men*, which bears an astonishing accidental
resemblance to my *Greybeard* from the same publisher thirty years
earlier, or Martin Amis's *Time's Arrow*, or Robert Harris's alternative
world, *Fatherland*.

A rejection of science and its burly half-sister, technology, carries
us over a category brink into post-nuclear holocaust fictions. These
were manifold; presumably they're now one with the Great Auk,
since the Cold War ended. They include such movies about mad
bikers as *Mad Max* and such series about mad horsemen as Robert
Adams's Horseclans novels, in which the USA has not recovered
from a two-day war, six centuries after the event. Is the world of
Horseclans a utopia? Well, of a kind, I suppose, if you have an IQ of
about 39.

But there's no departing from the meaning of utopia as 'a good
place'. A retreat into barbarism it is not. Aldous Huxley's utopian
island is placed realistically under threat. Though peace prevails
throughout most of the book, we are given to understand that
goodness is a fragile thing. In the last pages, the enemy invades. The
enemy is Indonesia—a pretty good guess.

In that respect, *Island* strikes a note of realism often lacking in
utopias. The whole problem with writing a utopia lies in that word
'realism'. How do we get from present mess to future perfection?
How do we credibly arrive there? H. G. Wells, that great artificer of
utopias, generally posited a war or other form of destruction, after
which humankind organized itself more tidily. Recently, wars have

become entirely too nasty for that sort of thing. Besides, wars and revolutions generally kill off the Kaminskis, the good guys, first.

It was Wells's perception at the beginning of this century that a utopia would necessarily have to be global. In a little book he wrote in the 1930s, called rather touchingly *What Should We Do With Our Lives?*, he supposes that at the right moment national states will be willing to abandon their frontiers. It was a pipe-dream. The desperate stand of the Muslims in Bosnia and the Chechens in Chechnya shows us what we would all do—and have done—were our frontiers threatened. So since Wells, utopias have shrunk faster than computers, from global embrace into Huxley's little threatened island. We have a clearer idea than did the Edwardians of the brutality and greed underlying even civilized states.

And there are other obstacles in the way of anyone wishing to write the next great new utopia. If you have read all the old utopias, Plato's, More's—which gave its name to the mode—Francis Bacon's, William Morris's, Butler's, Bellamy's, they conform to a pattern. These days we find that pattern rather boring. A newcomer arrives on the island, or wherever it is, and is shown around its wonders and its ideology. What is lacking is dynamism. We as readers are not involved because we belong to the wicked unreformed world and are forbidden to tread the new Eden. That lack of involvement proves fatal.

Of course, Doris Lessing's Canopus sounds like a utopia. But in her series of novels she never actually takes us there. The ideal world is hidden in distance.

As there is no model in the real world, so there are few literary models for anyone to follow who might attempt a utopia today. To be honest, the old utopias make disappointing reading. Viewed from the far side of our century with its dreadful blemishes, the innocence of the old utopias, from Plato onwards, strikes now as a shade fascist. You will remember George Orwell's unkind remark, made in 1941, when Britain was fighting Germany that 'Much of what Wells has imagined and worked for is physically there in Nazi Germany'. And Orwell stresses the parallels: the science, the steel, the concrete, the aeroplanes, and—above all—the order, the planning . . .

Order is the essence of utopia. You do as you are told, or you are persuaded that it is good for you to do as you are told, or you wander about in a drugged state not having to do as you are told. There's generally someone to keep an eye on you. Like the Samurai in *A Modern Utopia*. When it became Orwell's turn to write his dystopia, he had Big Brother watching everyone. The camera lens was turned on all of us.

What a sign of the times it is that that no longer seems sinister, as it certainly did when *1984* came out.

The big question in contemporary utopias is the relationship between humanity and technology. Perhaps it's a question of junk or be junked. Our societies don't improve at the same rate as our computers. You can't improve our vision by plugging in new revised parts, as you can in the Hubble telescope. In *Always Coming Home* le Guin presents us with Yaivkach, The City of Mind. Such cities are 'self-regulating communities of cybernetic device', therefore independent of the humans. Machine utopias. They explore 'the depths and superfices of the continents and seas, other bodies in the solar system including the sun', and so on into interstellar space. It sounds as if humanity—or at least *homo faber*, is becoming redundant. Perhaps that's where utopia must end. It's a loveless thought: those AIs going unsmilingly about their task of amassing knowledge, like a miser hoarding gold, caring damn all for daffodils, unmoved by sunsets, lacking the subconscious, just functioning—functioning forever, until all the stars go out or return into the primordial womb of fire.

But supposing one were rash enough to tackle a utopia in 1994. How to go about it? Perhaps the way to do it nowadays—I mean post-Derrida—is to abandon consecutive narrative and format it as a guide book on CD ROM. An imitation of the *Rough Guide to Switzerland*, for instance, complete with fake maps, video clips and stills.

Here's the sort of thing I mean:

Peace City. You are bound to like Peace City (pop. 200,000) the capital of Utopia. Peace City is the hub of our intellectual and vegetarian life. Best to visit in the month of May, when an exciting festival of Dance and Meditation is held around the huge maypole (150 ft) in Rejoicing Square. Choirs and children sing from dawn onwards. In January, called The Month of Cold Swims, Peace City is very picturesque, with deep snow everywhere.

To the West and South of the city lie the Unity Mountains (150,000 ft). Views of these mountains are not obscured because of the pleasant low-lying nature of Peace City's buildings, none of which is more than three storeys high.

Hotels. The chief hotel is The Peace and Parsimony Hotel (35 beds) on Maidenhood Avenue, almost opposite the marketplace, where you will be able to purchase your own handwoven towels, toilet paper, and soap for your stay. The market is open every day from six in the morning until dusk. Here you will find a splendid array of hand-crafted goods, from farm carts down to yoga mats. It's hard to realize that the colours in this vivid sight are all produced from vegetable dyes. The wicker handkerchiefs are unique to Peace City Market.

Walks. Since no mechanical vehicles are permitted within the confines of Peace City, you will enjoy strolling about the city. Sandals and cornplasters are available at many street corners. The fortunate inhabitants pay no ground rates, so the city spreads for miles in all directions. You can have really exciting walks, and are welcome to enter any residence on your way. Our houses have no doors, so remember to knock before you crowd in joyfully with your family. The occupants are sure to greet you with the traditional glass of warm water and sunflower seeds.

On your strolls, do not miss Rationality Park—acres of greenery adorned by immense statues of the men and women who founded Utopia. As a frivolous touch, flowers are grown in the north east corner of the park. Contraception Park, towards the North, has some rather naughtier statues, so best keep the children blindfolded, as a notice at the park entrance suggests. It is quite the custom to meditate in our parks, so take a mat with you. Wednesdays are Guru days.

Cuisine. After leaving the park, be sure to stop at the cafe amusingly called The Platitude Plateful. Hot food is available here at mid-day, most dishes ingeniously based on lentils. You'll be amazed at what can be done with the humble lentil! A non-alcoholic wine, 'Gravity', should also be savoured. Our spa waters are considered curative.

The best newspaper, crammed with local news and available on most street corners, is the *Conformist*, published every other Monday.

General Hints. Remember when visiting Utopia, you must leave your credit cards and cash behind. You can purchase caftans at the frontier post. Caftans are fun and compulsory wearing for all men and women visiting our carefree country. Sorry, no pets. We prefer hygiene!

*   *   *

Well, you see how it goes. Perhaps the truth is that we really find the whole prospect of utopia dull nowadays: would a utopia show *Schindler's List*? Despite which, we still carry utopian ideas within us. You will recall the song in Bernstein's *West Side Story*:

> There's a place for us, Somewhere a place for us . . .

A really good new utopia, spreading such warm and protective feelings round the globe, would be welcome any day now.

THE ATHEIST'S TRAGEDY REVISITED

An old Polish proverb says 'Watch the faces of those who bow low'.

Writers of prose are somehow considered as lower than writers of poetry. Perhaps it is for this reason they are more highly paid. As we plain slaves of the un-metred line bow to the poets, beware! Remember the Polish proverb. For sometimes we lard our prose (a word deriving from the Latin and meaning 'straightforward discourse') with steals from the poets.

We may even, if our characters are less than straightforward, insert the odd prose poem into our discourse.

Writers are still asked where they get their crazy ideas from. They are less often asked where they get their crazy prose from. In general, prose derives from all sorts of models long forgotten.

I would be unable to name all the writers—read when I was a boy or adolescent—who helped shape my idea of what prose should be. The roll call would include poets as well as novelists and essayists.

No idea can be presented to us unless it comes wrapped in words. The question is, which words. Sometimes, brevity is best. When Henry Ford announced that History is bunk, he was inspired (inspired but not necessarily correct). His apothegm is remembered and frequently quoted. Whereas, had an historian written an entire volume exploring the notion that the past, being dead, had no power to guide our activities; and that instead we should consider only the future (which, I take it, was what the inventor of the assembly line was suggesting), he would run a risk of not being quoted past breakfast time, or remembered past coffee break.

Science fiction writers on the whole present their ideas in the plainest possible terms. Style is clear glass, designed to be seen through uninterruptedly to the meaning. This is preferable if the idea is to disconcert the reader, or to offer something new. Cut glass, stained glass, equally admirable where apposite, is more the manner of a Bradbury, a Sturgeon, a Gene Wolfe, or an Iain Banks.

When the vampire is held captive in Suzy McKee Charnas' *The Vampire Tapestry*, Alan Reece says to those people looking into the cell:

> You are all confronting a lesson in the depths that lie behind the surface of every 'reality' of your daily lives. Think about this: you look into this room and you see a creature of human appearance. He looks back—and sees you with the immense contempt and cruel appetite of an immortal who feeds his endless life on your tiny lives.

Although the passage confronts us in plain terms with our mortality, it relates to and gains strength from the dedication in the preliminary pages of Charnas' book. That dedication is to the memory of Loren Eisley: 'his writing first opened to me the vast perspectives of geologic time'.

The Charnas thought is chilling; might one say, agreeably chilling? But there are countless ways to bring home to us, to familiarize us with, the mortality which encloses biological life. John Webster's Duchess of Malfi does so in elaborate language:

> What would it pleasure me to have my throat cut
> With diamonds? or to be smothered
> With cassia? or to be shot to death with pearls?
> I know death hath ten thousand several doors
> For men to take their exits; and 'tis found
> They go on such strange geometrical hinges,
> You may open them both ways: any way, for heaven-sake,
> So I were out of your whispering.

There is no idea which does not profit from being offered in appropriate language. How we judge what is appropriate depends on our intimate personal involvement with language, beginning on the day we are born, which is closely connected with the depth and variety of our reading. If we are scientists, we use scientific language, or possibly mathematics; if we are poets *manqués*, we use more 'poetic' language or possibly metaphor. If we live between these two stools, and are science fiction writers—then we must fend for ourselves . . .

The best of the hard science fiction writers know what to do. In

Gregory Benford's novel, *Mindscape*, two men are conversing, talking about a bloom disfiguring the ocean off the Brazilian coast. One of them, Kiefer, says that the oceanic food chain is threatened by over-use of fertilizer, and mentions manodrin.

> 'Manodrin [he says] is a chlorinated hydrocarbon used in insecticides. It has opened a new life niche among the micro-scopic algae. A new variety of diatom has evolved. It uses an enzyme which breaks down manodrin. The diatom silica also excrete a breakdown product which interrupts transmission of nerve impulses in animals. Dendritic connections fail . . .'

This language, to those of us who do not have to look up 'enzyme' in our dictionaries, is lucid. It conveys the idea that something strange is happening, that cause and effect is at work. Its sub-text reassures us that its writer is himself a scientist who knows what he is talking about. However, Benford is writing a novel, not a thesis. In order not to leave his readers behind, their fingers trapped in the 'e' pages of their dictionaries, he places this exchange next, when Kiefer asks Peterson if he has seen the bloom himself.

Peterson replies, 'I flew over it. It's as ugly as sin. The color terrifies the fishing villages.'

We are back safe in the world of common experience and common nouns, the bottom line of any kind of novel. And yet I cannot be alone in finding a magic in what seem to be ordinary English words in ordinary grammatical arrangement: 'The color terrifies the fishing villages' . . . Magic, of course, is inexplicable.

There is a pleasure in being mystified, to which SF writers regularly cater. Another expert in these matters is Greg Bear. In his novel, *Blood Music*, he tries to push language and comprehension to its limits. When Wittgenstein concluded his *Tractatus Logico-Philoso-phicus* with the proposition, 'What we cannot speak about we must pass over in silence', he certainly did not have *Blood Music* in mind.

Michel Bernard is invaded by noocytes, a cross between cellular structures and nanoprocessors. Bear graphically conveys the attempt at communication between Bernard and the invaders who are taking over his body.

> 'I'd like to speak to an individual' [he says]
> **INDIVIDUAL?** [they ask]
> 'Not just the team or research group. One of you, acting alone.'

**We have studied INDIVIDUAL in your conception.
We do not fit the word.**
'There are no individuals?'
**Not precisely. Information is shared between clus-
ters of ********
'Not clear.'

We identify with this remark of Bernard's. We are moving beyond humanity, where human language and understanding are breaking down. This Bear conveys with skill and economy.

Where does Bear's linguistic ability come from? It could in part derive from Alfred Bester, who employed typographical tricks when the going became rough. More likely, it comes from a lifetime of reading SF; in other words, it is custom, and has the ease of custom.

We do know what we are doing. Our prose is a part of our being. *Le style, c'est moi.* Even the earliest generations of SF writers, now often down-graded as 'hacks', aspired to a complexity of language. Besides such obvious names as Clark Ashton Smith, with his brocaded prose, one might mention Edmond Hamilton, Murray Leinster, and William Hope Hodgson.

Two of my earlier novels were written with the cadences of two admired—though contrasting—writers much in mind. *Greybeard* doffs its hat to Thomas Hardy, the whole range of whose novels I had read over the previous decade. I concurred with the sense he imparts of his characters being formed by nature, by the landscape surrounding them: though in my hands the greenwood tree has grown out of control.

By the time *Greybeard* was published—well, one's novels must sail in their own way down the stream of time, or sink—happily, thirty years on, the ship is still afloat in both hardcover and paperback—I had become enamoured of the French *nouveau roman.* Over and over, I watched the film on which Alain Robbe-Grillet and Alain Resnais collaborated, *L'Année dernière à Marienbad.* I was reading Michel Butor, Alain Robbe-Grillet, and others. Their drastic economies, their frugality, persuaded me that *Greybeard* perhaps carried a freight of more adjectives than modern traffic warranted. I made fast the mainbrace and wrote *Report on Probability A.* To my great satisfaction if to nobody else's.

Sometimes it is possible playfully to insert into a novel a passage which recalls, echoes, plays variations upon, something read and admired, perhaps memorized.

As an example, there follows a passage from my novel, *The Eighty-Minute Hour*, followed by the passage I had in mind, a wonderful piece of imagery from Cyril Tourneur's poetic drama, *The Atheist's Tragedy*, with its elaborate unfolding of clauses mimicking the flurry of waves up the shore.

There was a time when I had a passion for the dark plays of Webster and Tourneur, and saw most of them performed. This was how I doffed my hat to them, years later.

> After England and all but the granite hip of Scotland sank beneath thermonuclear bombardment, thousands of tattered human bodies—sodden and hairless as handkerchiefs—were washed ashore by mighty tidal waves, year after year, all along the western coasts of Europe, from Narvik and the Lofoten Islands in the north, from Jutland and the Frisians, from the rocks of Brittany southward, where the Medoc grapes grow, driven by furious new currents through Biscay, to appear informally dressed as Mortality in the charades at Biarritz and San Sebastian, and along the rainy beaches of Asturias and Galicia, right down to Lisbon and beyond Cape St Vincent, where one of the last time-nibbled deliveries of bodies was made as far afield as the estuary of the Guadalquivir, once the private hunting grounds of the Dukes of Medina Sidonia; there, herons, spoonbills, egrets, and birds fresh from nesting places in the permanent snowcaps of the Sierra Nevada gazed like museum-goers on the salt-pickled remains of the inhabitants of Southampton, Scunthorpe and South Ken, who were now part of some greater and more permanent snowcap. Even later than that, sometimes years later, arms still identifiable as arms, or children's hands resembling sleeping crabs, would be cast up in the Azores or on the black laval sands of the Cape Verde islands.

> Walking the next day upon the fatal shore
> Among the slaughtered bodies of their men
> Which the full-stomached sea had cast upon
> The sands, it was my unhappy chance to light
> Upon a face, whose favour when it lived,
> My astonished mind informed me I had seen.

He lay in's armour, as if that had been
His coffin; and the weeping sea, like one
Whose milder temper doth lament the death
Of him whom in his rage he slew, runs up
The shore, embraces him, kisses his cheek,
Goes back again, and forces up the sands
To bury him, and every time it parts
Sheds tears upon him, till at last (as if
It could no longer endure to see the man
Whom it had slain, yet loth to leave him) with
A kind of unresolved unwilling pace
Winding her waves one in another, like
A man that folds his arms or wrings his hands
For grief ebbed from the body, and descends
As if it would sink down into the earth,
And hide itself for shame of such a deed.

Recently, I saw a play several centuries older than anything written by Tourneur. There are reasons why I cannot name it, or say precisely where I saw it. It was a costume drama staged in a country suffering under virtual dictatorship.

The director of the play was a young and dynamic man, glittering, restless, clearly talented. I saw two of his productions; both were brilliantly staged, but it was the richly costumed earlier play which most powerfully impressed me.

Let us call the play *Madness*. It is, let us say, a sort of national play, as *King Lear* might be said (if the simplification were not absurd) to be a national English play. It was staged in the great national theatre. The chief characters were dressed in robes of deep reds and crimsons. They were heroic and statuesque. I must add that the impression the play made on me was heightened by the fact, having flown into the capital of that distant state, that I was there hardly an hour before being summoned to the theatre as a matter of some urgency. On arrival there, however, my escorts ushered me into an ante-room near the stage, where I was presented with a large meal, virtually a banquet.

We ate, we drank a dark Azeri vintage champagne. When I worried aloud about missing the performance, I was given evasive answers by my escorts: I would miss nothing, I was told. There were smiles about the table, and speeches. It was then after midnight. The great marble building wrapped us within its silences.

At last we were shown into the auditorium. It was deserted. Row after row of empty seats confronted us. We seated ourselves, a little clique of seven or eight people in the stalls. Music sounded. The lights dimmed. Majestic figures swept onto the stage and the drama began. The players had been told to wait until we were ready for them. I had left the real world behind to enter a world of pretence and darkness.

Later, I met the director in less formal surroundings, and dined at his table. There was some frank talk about the repression under which they suffered.

We discussed his staging of *Madness*. A thought which had occurred to me during the performance prompted me to suggest that he could stage Sophocles' *Oedipus Rex* in almost the same costumes; it would be startling and dramatic.

He became animated. He was a great admirer of Sophocles' drama, and longed to produce it. But that would be impossible under present conditions. Recall the dialogue between Oedipus and Teiresias. The latter says to Oedipus, 'Upon your head is the ban your lips have uttered! From this day forth, never speak to me or any others. You are the cursed polluter of this land.'

If the play were staged in the director's capital city, it would be interpreted as a criticism of the nation's leader. The theatre would be closed down. What might happen to the director and his family was a matter for speculation.

So Sophocles' two thousand year old play still has bite. There is still danger in art. And the powerful must still watch the faces of those who bow low.

But the life in *Oedipus Rex* cannot lie merely in its poetry, since we have no definitive translation and the play is reinterpreted every generation, generally in heightened prose. It is not the prose but the plot which sustains the life of Sophocles' drama.

And so it is with science fiction.

THE PALE SHADOW
OF SCIENCE

Address to the British Association for the
Advancement of Science

A venerable Oxford story tells of the college which received a large private bequest. In the senior common room, the Fellows were discussing how the money should best be invested. The Bursar finally said, 'Let's invest in property. After all, property's served us well for the last thousand years'. And the old Senior Fellow in the corner chirped up and said, 'Yes, but you know the last thousand years have been exceptional.'

We would probably all agree with the Senior Fellow. And we would probably agree that the years since the dropping of Little Boy on Hiroshima have been exceptional. We feel that civilization is going somewhere fast; therefore we ought to know where it is going. There seems to be no pilot on our speeding craft. So we turn to prediction.

Like ESP, to which it bears some relationship, prophecy has never become legit. Despite the commendable efforts of Nigel Calder in this country, Herman Kahn in the States, and so on, prophecy and prediction remain a happy hunting ground for astrologers and science fiction writers.

There is a kind of prediction called extrapolation, a nice scientific sounding word. How does it differ in fact from prediction? Well, you take all the known facts on a subject and simply double the number you first thought of. At least, that is how it seemed when 'futurology' became one of the in-words of the 1960s.

Extrapolation always sounds disarmingly sensible—a cool look ahead. Nigel Calder's experts in his 1964 symposium, *The World in 1984* (2 volumes, Pelican), were perfectly reasonable to extrapolate from that date that we would have a Moon base in operation by

1984. Had he got his experts together in 1944, none of them would have dared speak about a Moon base.

No Moon base yet exists.

Should we therefore consider the hypothetical 1944 panel more correct than their successors, twenty years later? That would be silly. Extrapolation is really a way of thinking about the present, not the future; part of the world-picture in 1964, much more so than of our present present, included a reasonable expectation of a Moon base within twenty years. The energy crisis and the recession had not then struck.

SF is another way of thinking about the future, and of the present masked as future. It is part of the function of some science fiction writers to keep on dreaming of Moon bases.

But not all science fiction writers. It is also the function of science fiction writers to be diverse.

The only way that science fiction can be justified is if it is good science fiction, not if its predictions turn out correctly. That is a literary matter.

Of course, some writers employ scientific ideas.

Suppose that I write a novel or a screenplay for a movie in which we have a hi-tech future world, where atomic-scale machinery is the norm. The application of technology and biotechnology has transformed human life. There are nanocomputers where switching times take a mere femtosecond (a femtosecond means a million times faster than a nanosecond, which is the billionth part of a second). Copies of oneself, clones, can easily be made, perhaps under a global health service, each clone enjoying its own life, but all separate lives able to merge their memories into one. These super-people would be almost immortal, with infinitesimal protein robots inhabiting their bodies, cleansing away poisons, making rapid repairs to any challenged organ. And when one super-person dies, resurrection is possible.

Dissatisfied still with the inadequacies of the planet itself, these super-people can transfer themselves into an immense simulator, into electronic impulses, where 'life' can proceed at many times the speed of our prosaic biological life. And to each other they are as 'real' as you and I. More real, perhaps, since their perceptions will have been greatly enhanced then: now, we see as through a glass darkly. [Note: in the future, such terms as 'life' and 'reality' will more frequently be used in the plural case.]

It is an imaginative scenario, the probability factor of which I have no means of estimating. Nor am I predicting. I have taken almost every item in this scenario from a work by a scientist, the well-known 1988 volume by Hans Moravec, *Mind Children: The Future of Robot and Human Intelligence*. Most SF writers must rely on similar sources. It would be ridiculous to claim anything in the above outline as 'my prediction', even were I to dress its elements up in a work of fiction a million words long.

Moravec's speculations are inspiring and exciting. They tickle the intellectual curiosity, which is a large part of the game, even when one is not enamoured of their basic assumptions. This is not to say that any foolproof scientific method has been devised which will make predictions more accurate than those of an informed writer's guesses.

In the nineteen-sixties, Herman Kahn's was a famous name. Kahn became director of the Hudson Institute in New York State. The Institute was dedicated to frameworking speculations about possible developments towards the end of the century, and was much consulted by government and industry. Herman Kahn and his associate, Anthony J. Wiener, produced a large book entitled *The Year 2000: A Framework for Speculation on the Next Thirty-Five Years* (1967). Twenty-eight of those years have now passed into history, and we are able to check the reliability of the Institute's speculations.

Kahn clearly states that his institute does not set out to 'predict'—the word is set in double quotes in the Preface—any particular aspect of the future. Nevertheless, his Table XVIII lists 'One hundred Technical Innovations Very Likely in the Last Third of the Twentieth Century'.

We would agree that #97 sounds convincing: New biological and chemical methods to identify, trace, incapacitate, or annoy people for police and military uses. (Though we'd argue that the more traditional clubs and electric shocks to the body remain in use over much of the planet.) Some items hit the target. #70, for instance: Simple inexpensive home video recording and playing. More reliable weather-forecasting—another hit. Widespread use of power-generating nuclear reactors: okay. More extensive organ transplanting: okay. And so on. But even I could have guessed that such items, incipient in the sixties, would be more fully realized by the nineties.

Some of the items on the list are very 'sci-fi'. Relatively effective appetite and weight control? Human 'hibernation' for long periods? Three-dimensional TV and movies? Direct electronic communications with the brain? Physically non-harmful methods of over-indulging? Interplanetary travel? Undersea colonies? Individual flying platforms? No way, baby!

#75 lists computers being generally available to home and business *on a metered basis*. Yet nothing about water being metered.

You may pay professional men very highly; they cannot operate a predictive sense which is not there. If God had wanted us to see the future he'd have given us a third eye.

This does not stop us wanting and trying to predict. It's part of an SF writer's stock-in-trade. But I understand the building which housed the Hudson Institute stands empty at present.

There's another aspect to the prediction business: we may not like what we find. Milton had a warning in *Paradise Lost*, which stands as the motto on the title page of Mary Shelley's *The Last Man*:

> Let no man henceforth
> Be foretold what shall befall him
> Or his children . . .

So science fiction writers and scientists have something in common. We would all go even further than the Senior Oxford Fellow and say that we expect the *next* thousand years to be exceptional. The build-up of population, the build-up of technology, of communication, of information, and the creation of complex social infrastructures cannot but bring immense changes in life and thought, in diet and behaviour, in birth and death, in knowledge and intuition, in speech and silence, in our whole perception of existence.

We know that . . . and yet the fine detail . . . Who will bet me a hundred pounds that there will be a Moon base in twenty years, in 2005? Who will tell me which way the pendulum of sexual morality will have swung by the time the Moon base is built? Who can tell me where London's fourth airport will be in 2005?

The relationship between SF and science is complex. It became more complex when the space age began and SF writers were invited out of their obscurity to explain trajectories and escape velocity and docking procedures to laymen. We were experts all of sudden: alchemists whose lead of fantasy had turned into the gold of knowledge. Ever since then, science fiction has had on the whole a better reception from scientists than from literary pundits.

This is very gratifying, but to my mind the thing should be the other way round. I don't mean that scientists should not take SF seriously as a form of literature in which the current developments and obsessions of the age are given in a dramatic airing, but rather that the *literati* should take it seriously for those same reasons—instead of ignoring it, as they do, because it doesn't conform to the conventions of the major nineteenth-century novels they have studied in the English schools of Oxbridge and Ivy League. Imagination is in short supply: a precious commodity that many fear.

A remarkable example of literary blindness could be observed in 1948, when Aldous Huxley published *Ape and Essence*, which deals with a nuclear catastrophe followed by the degeneration of humanity back to a stage where females undergo anoestrus. The novel also talks about despoliation of natural resources, long before conservation became a popular slogan.

In every respect, *Ape and Essence* is all that SF should be: it boldly elucidates a current dilemma in imaginative terms. Huxley's novel went to literary critics for review. None of them was capable of appreciating what Huxley was doing; they did not know how to read or process his book. Huxley got a bad, ill-informed press—and that in spite of his stature as a futuristic novelist, author of *Brave New World*.

Such illiteracy by the literates has led to a situation where science fiction writers court the scientists; they turn towards that audience as flowers—all except the difficult daffodil—turn towards the sun. It also leads them occasionally to address bodies before whom they feel themselves scarcely qualified to speak . . .

Frederik Pohl has been an assiduous speaker and lecturer between novels. At one time, he would accept invitations to address learned bodies on the population problem, which he regarded as the gravest issue of the 1960s. In the 1960s (if you remember) the nuclear issue had gone off the boil. Pohl told me he gave up at the point when he realized that he was beginning to enjoy painting a picture of doom. He relinquished the admired role of expert and returned to writing novels with a strong scientific content.

What is more dangerous is when writers start to regard their novels as if SF were in some way a branch of science. To do this, they may stress the predictive factor in their writing. For example, after the dropping of the atomic bombs on Japan, there were numerous stories warning against the dangers of fallout in future wars. Many of them predicted that radioactivity would cause mutations in the human race. Henry Kuttner forecast a sub-race of mutants, hairless and with telepathic powers against which the rest of humanity waged war. The idea sounds ridiculous now but given the date of origin, like the Moon base prediction of 1964, it wore an air of alarming scientific plausibility.

But science fiction novels are not scientific experiments which move towards a desired end to clinch a hypothesis. A science fiction novel should contain within it what Darko Suvin calls a 'posited novum', a new thing—whether object or concept—held up for our consideration. The novum may be, for example, an anti-gravity machine. The writer is under no obligation to tell us how it works. If he can tell us how it works, then he is wasting his time writing novels and his talent should be employed elsewhere. What he should do, though, is to give us some form of description, some bit of theory, so that we can almost persuade ourselves that we comprehend how the anti-gravity machine works. Then he can show us what effect his machine has on the world.

Ursula Le Guin's ansible is an instantaneous communication device as well as an anagram. It features in her novel *The Dispossessed*. We readily understand the need for such a device in a widespread galactic culture. Although we are not told how the ansible works, we know that it is one tangible result of Shevek's work on a unified field theory. Le Guin is not predicting the ansible; the important point about this posited novum is that it makes sense within Le Guin's own taoist thought, in a novel much concerned with utopian thinking and the difficulties of communication.

There can hardly be a less scientific concept, I imagine, than a time machine. H. G. Wells, who invented that blessed contraption, describes only its physical appearance, and that vaguely; the theory behind the machine's working is left even more vague. We know it works only because the prototype worked and disappeared into the future. Yet the novel, *The Time Machine*, is one of the most scientific of scientific romances, in that it dramatizes for the ordinary reader two of the nineteenth century's most profound discoveries: the great age of the Earth, and the principles of evolution. The Eloi and the Morlocks are not there merely to titillate and shock; they are there as examples of what we as a race might become, given time.

And of course *The Time Machine* is a morality, based in part on Kelvin's reformulation of the second law of thermodynamics. Let me remind you of the end of all things on Earth:

> The darkness grew apace; a cold wind began to grow in freshening gusts from the east, and the showering white flakes in the air increased in number. From the edge of the

> sea came a ripple and a whisper. Beyond these lifeless sounds the world was silent. Silent? It would be hard to convey the stillness of it. All the sounds of man, the bleating of sheep, the cries of birds, the hum of insects, the stir that makes the background of our lives—all that was over . . . At last, one by one, swiftly, one after the other, the white peaks of the distant hills vanished into blackness.

Here, imagination, scientific training, and a good prose style merge. The posited novum, the time machine, is a vital part of the story, but not the story itself. The story is not there to prove the machine exists. Literature and science work by opposite processes. The scientific method is to take particular instances and extract from them a general application which can then be demonstrated to apply to further instances. The method of literature, on the contrary, is to take a number of general applications, and embody them in a particular instance, which can then be felt to apply to other instances. Frederik Pohl and Cyril Kornbluth's *The Space Merchants* points to various ways in which advertising agencies lie to the public to fob off on them an indifferent product; the authors then show us the Fowler Schocken corporation selling the ghastly planet Venus to would-be colonists. We believe it. We know they'd sell real estate on Neptune as well, given the chance. But the literary method proves nothing, unlike a scientific experiment.

There is another way of looking at the two opposed modes of thinking represented by literature and science. Wells himself pointed to the distinction. He called the modes 'directed thought' and 'undirected thought'. We are all aware of the difference. In terms of human evolution we may suppose that undirected thought came first; undirected thought could be represented spatially as a ramble round and round a familiar object, perhaps seeing it anew. Whereas directed thought could be represented as walking towards a distant unfamiliar object for purposes of identification.

In *The Work, Wealth and Happiness of Mankind* (1913), Wells boldly entitles Chapter Two 'How Man Has Learnt to Think Systematically and Gain a Mastery over Force and Matter'. He speaks of undirected thought as imaginative play: close really to what we might now call a hypnoid state. He praises directed thought as leading to 'new and better knowledge, planned and directed effort'. Directed thought, according to Wells, enters philosophy with Plato and defines the scientific aspect of modern civilization.

It is doubtful if scientists today would endorse Wells's view of science as being purely the product of directed thought. His view too rigorously excludes the Eureka factor; it also excludes the character of the scientist. What is interesting about Wells's two contrasted modes of thought is that he employs them both, serially, in his fiction. The early SF novels—*Time Machine, The War of the Worlds, The Island of Dr Moreau*, up to *The First Men in the Moon* (1901)—are by common consent regarded as among his best and most enduring fictions. Their power lies in Wells's wandering around familiar objects and seeing them anew; he is trying to prove nothing; he investigates ambiguities and contrasts in the universe which he need not resolve. It is necessary that young Selenites be adapted to society; that process causes pain to the individual. That's the way things are, and there is no remedy. In those words of Samuel Johnson:

> How small, of all that human hearts endure,
> That part which law or kings can cause or cure.

In his later fictions, Wells attempts to produce cures. He switches to directed thought. The difference is marked. Gone are the ambiguities and balances we met on Moreau's island, the puzzle of the boundaries between human and non-human, between intelligence and reflex. In place of conundrums, instructions. We must submit to a world state for our own good. We must be governed by enlightened samurai. We must not have pets in our homes for health reasons. The mazes of human life are to be swept clean in exchange for a unitary answer. Mr Polly, Mr Kipps, Mr Lewisham, give way to Mr Britling, Mr Blettsworthy and William Clissold.

In short, Wells forecasts. 'The great general of Dreamland', as he once called himself, becomes a demagogue, the great spin doctor of humanity. As directed thought replaces undirected, we are addressed, but no longer enchanted. Wells gave up literature in an heroic attempt to save the world from itself.

The Shape of Things to Come was published in 1933. It is hardly fiction; it forecasts. For instance, the Modern State emerges after the 1965 Conference called at Basra by—yes, you guessed it—the Transport Union.

The Shape of Things to Come has been much admired for forecasting World War II. Writing in 1933, Wells almost gets the year of the outbreak of war right: 1940 instead of 1939. But his is not the war that was fought. The real war of Normandy, Anzio, Stalingrad, Iwojima, and Hiroshima was more savage than anything Wells describes; yet he has civilization breaking down as a result of war, because that suits his didactic purpose. Only on the rubble of yesterday can the Modern State of tomorrow be built.

It is impossible today to read *The Shape of Things to Come* with any patience, whereas the earlier fictions remain fresh. We value Wells as both imaginative novelist and prophet, but never as both together, for what is imaginative is not truly prophetic, and what is prophetic not truly imaginative. Wells taught whole generations that things were going to be different. It is a lesson we have thoroughly learned—though the War Office appears not to have done—but it was originally Wells's lesson.

In short, Wells's great early novels are examples of undirected thinking; his later propagandistic novels are examples of directed thinking. To go into the prediction business is to give up the best way of making an imaginative novel. The imagination always haunts ambiguity. Science, child of imagination, is dedicated to abolishing ambiguity.

Prophecies can, then, be ludicrously wrong. Of course they can also be ludicrously right. When an early telephone was installed in the office of the mayor of an American city, he was moved to prophecy. 'The day will dawn', he said, 'when every city in the United States will have a telephone.'

That's a story Arthur Clarke tells. One of the best-known prophecies of recent times is Clarke's famous projection of communication satellites in geosynchronous orbits, made in 1945. If Clarke could have formulated a means of delivering the satellites into their orbits—a means non-existent in 1945—he could have patented the idea. That would have made him, presumably, one of the richest men on the globe. This stunning piece of forecasting appeared as an article in *Wireless World*. Wisely so. Had Clarke written the idea into a story, a fiction, and published it in a science fiction magazine, his prediction would have had less force.

After all, predictions of a sort are two-a-penny in SF magazines. We SF writers have predictions the way dogs have fleas. They are the furniture of our future.

In any case, if you throw off a hundred predictions and two of them happen to be fulfilled, that does not make you a prophet, any more than a man shooting at a barn door a hundred times and hitting it twice can be called a marksman.

*   *   *

In sum, a novel of science fiction must succeed on its own terms as a novel, and not on some extra-literary terms. We still read *First Men in the Moon* with pleasure, not caring that the reality is otherwise. Prediction is a bad first priority for novelists.

If prediction is bad, can we turn the equation round and state that negative prediction is good? That holds true in at least one case—the case of Orwell's *1984*. Orwell was warning us; his forecast was apotropaic. Our real 1984 is probably less like the one Orwell imagined simply because he uttered his famous warning. But Orwell was a special case. We needed his warning because we believe the dangers of totalitarianism to be real; whereas we have not heeded John Wyndham's warning, and we remain totally unprepared for the triffid invasion. Prediction to be effective must deal with what is already in existence. Whereas most SF deals with something non-existent: from one of Italo Calvino's invisible cities the size of a pinhead to the vast intergalactic battles of Paul J. McAuley's *Four Hundred Billion Stars*.

And yet. Science fiction does have a relation to science, just as it does to literature. I only wish that the two cultures did not remain so far apart; then our bridges would be less difficult to build. Science fiction plays in that wonderful speculative world of possibilities which has been hard won since the days of the renaissance—a world of speculation always under threat. Science fiction is of immense importance when it is being its imaginative self, when it offers us a metaphor for the varieties of experience life offers. It should be about the future. And of course about human beings. When it gets involved with telepathic dragons, I'm lost.

A contemporary SF writer like Gregory Benford, a scientist working in astrophysics and plasma physics, writes highly imaginative SF which attempts not to bend the rules of science while treating of the unknown. In such novels as *Against Infinity* and *Across the Sea of Suns*, Benford presents a holistic view of science which is fructifying. Both novels point beyond our present problems to the numberless possibilities of the future.

DECADENCE
AND DEVELOPMENT

Despite its increased popularity over recent years, science fiction still carries a stigma, while the reading of it is regarded in many quarters, highbrow and lowbrow, as eccentric, to say the least. This fact has been remarked upon ever since science fiction came by its present name, and still deserves enquiry.

Accompanying the general despisal of SF goes a degree of uncertainty as to what it is. This uncertainty is not confined merely to those outside the charmed circle of its readership. SF readers and fans are equally undecided. The search for a definition has been long, arduous, and so far unavailing.

This may be because, in this century, the package of SF has been almost deliberately misleading. Like some politicians, its real nature has been lost under a projected image. This artifice has served to deceive not only those who refuse to read it and those who read nothing else, but also those who write it.

The packaging of SF was performed in the 1920s by Hugo Gernsback. Gernsback was a salesman. He published the first 'scientifiction' or science fiction magazines. For many people, Gernsback is supposed to have been the inventor of SF—strangely enough, since he reprinted in his pages stories written in the nineteenth century which were undeniably science fiction, such as H. G. Wells's *War of the Worlds*. However, one accomplishment, generally unacknowledged, was certainly Gernsback's: in the manner of all salesmen, he strove to label distinctively and homogenize the product. By this device the customer is guaranteed that the pat of butter he buys today will be identical with the pat he bought yesterday.

The device was a success. Readers applauded. They returned for more. Seventy years later, they are still returning for more. For more of the same. And that is what stifles SF. It should be a nonconformist literature. It should arouse and not stupefy. It should go against the grain of the ordinary. It does not fit on the assembly line.   -

Just look at those covers! The pornography of technology, the infantile dreams of the Conquest of Space—the baby's cry bringing what it most desires—all the elements satirized in Stanley Kubrick's film, *Dr Strangelove: or, How I learned to Stop Worrying and Love the Bomb*. It's a strange love indeed!

Basically, SF today has to conform: to public taste, to publishing formulas, just as it did back in Gernsback's day. A whole industry is dedicated to pinning it to its procrustian bed. For this reason, trilogies and series and sequels have become staple diet. The pats of butter have become bigger. And guaranteed low-calorie Instant Whip.

And what is the nature of the label slapped on the SF product? It's a literature of ideas. It's about the future, inventions, change, interplanetary travel, galactic empires, progress, big machines. It's technophile. Much SF is imperialist, near fascist, as the literature of the big machines must always be. Look at the covers. Jackboots are still popular, a fashion adornment.

And that's the sort of thing which puts off any ordinary sensible person.

A literature of ideas? The history of world literature suggests that the imagination of authors is seldom awoken by ideas or issues, but rather by themes in their unconscious which they cannot readily express except through the psycho-drama of their narrative. Emile Zola bestowed on his Rougon-Macquart novels a quasi-scientific framework of fatalistic heredity—a bit like Dorsai—much like any SF writer—and damaged them by his dogmatism. What really moved Zola was an obsession with injustice and degradation. As his biographer, F .W. J. Hemmings, says, 'it seems that when he [Zola] was writing he passed into a totally different state of being: private terrors, dreams of ecstatic sensual delight, abominable visions of nightmarish intensity, took temporary possession of him'.

Tolstoy's novel *Resurrection* has a strong didactic strain running through it, the theme of the impossibility of wicked men reforming others (a truly prophetic theme in view of the disaster which was to overtake his country two decades later). The American political economist, Henry George, is frequently quoted. Nevertheless, what really moved Tolstoy, what leads the reader entranced through a long novel, is the emotional activating incident, in which a nobleman serving on a jury recognizes in the prostitute brought forward for trial the virgin he seduced when he was a young man.

It is part of SF's gaudy misleading label that it predicts. Isaac Asimov claimed that the space programme of the 1960s vindicated all that the *Astounding* SF of the 1940s and 1950s stood for. But SF has no real predictive value, as I have argued. Disbelief, in the old prescription, may be willingly, too willingly, suspended, but true belief does not enter the bargain. The future is a barn door to fire at. Of course one shot in a hundred will not go wild. But our concern is less with accuracy than with that closed door.

Suppose one could accurately predict even the near future; the revelation would be dismissed as fantasy. In 1982 I worked with a movie director on a scenario based on one of my short stories. We considered the idea of a party of Western men going with androids into a Soviet Union which was breaking up under internal forces. We could not devise a way to make the dissolution plausible. Three years later, along came Mr Gorbachev with his themes of *glasnost* and *perestroika*, and in 1989 we saw the great edifice of the Soviet empire splitting apart under economic and ethnic dissonances. In went the West—true, with Coca Cola and McDonald's rather than androids.

Had we been gifted with genuine prophetic insight, and written in 1982 what happened in 1989, our screenplay would have been unacceptable. It would have been dismissed as fantasy.

Here is a remarkable example of accurate prophecy. Readers may perhaps recognize the writer.

> Communism is the secret name of the dread antagonist setting proletarian rule with all its consequences against the present bourgeois regime. It will be a frightful duel. How will it end? No one knows but gods and goddesses acquainted with the future. We know only this much: Communism, though little discussed now and loitering in hidden garrets on miserable straw pallets, is the dark hero destined for a great, if temporary, role in the modern tragedy . . .

The words were written by Heinrich Heine in Paris, in 1842. Can any SF forecast match that for psychological foresight?

So could it be that the general shunning of SF, its relegation to back pages and anachronistic magazines, is because of its false bright label?

If we survey SF in general, and include or not as we will the fantasy on which it has beached itself, or the horror into which it is sinking, we see it is only to a marginal degree concerned with the ingredients by which it is advertised: futurism, big ideas, high technology, hygiene, conquest, progress. (Of course these items often go into the general brew, just as there are writers who, deluded by the label, imagine they are the main dish.)

Instead, SF is about many more interesting and truthful matters, imagery, visions, disaster, oppression, hope: all factors which we might group together as anti-futurist.

Fans know this but feel prohibited from admitting it. For this reason, they allow such figures of darkness as Edgar Allan Poe and H. P. Lovecraft into the pantheon. Anne McCaffrey's dragons are welcome at the high table. The wild Iain Banks sits down with the pragmatic John Gribbin. The old Gothic bones show through the hi-tech skin—and not only in the writings of William Gibson.

A new friend has just read a novel I wrote in the 1960s, *Earthworks*. She exclaimed on its prophetic qualities, saying it was all taking place today. Yet what interested me so many years ago—although certainly I was informed on what was happening in the way of ecological desecration—was the traditional fascination SF has with ruins, with *Schädenfreude*, with raging melancholia, with new sensations.

Georges Charles Huysmans' decadent novel, *A rebours* (variously translated as *Against Nature*, or *Against the Grain*) was amazingly influential in the 1880s and thereafter. Its hero, Des Esseintes, influenced Oscar Wilde. Here is a science-fictional passage from Huysmans' novel in which, while bowling along in a cab in a Parisian downpour, he conjures up a vision of London:

> . . . In warehouses and on wharves washed by the dark, slimy waters of an imaginary Thames, in the midst of a forest of masts, a tangle of beams and girders piercing the pale, lowering the clouds. Up above, trains raced by at full speed; and down in the underground sewers, others rumbled along, occasionally emitting ghastly screams or vomiting floods of smoke through the gaping mouths of air-shafts. And meanwhile, along every street, big or small, in an eternal twilight relieved only by the glaring infamies of modern advertising, there flowed an endless stream of traffic between two columns of earnest, silent Londoners, marching along with eyes fixed ahead and elbows glued to their sides.

It's a vision. Exhilarating because so madly depressing. We recognize its similarities with the descriptions of a myriad fantasy planets on which the hero lands up, broke, to find people dehumanized, and some kind of megamachine of tyranny in charge.

The madness for large machines and larger ideologies is typical of last century and this. Yet it is with these bizarre manifestations of the human psyche that SF has chosen to identify itself. The crass fifteen cent optimism of the pulps has brought disaster.

And really, SF ain't like that—or only marginally. Its label does it disservice, its typical covers are cryptograms. In the main it is not at all for Development. It's for Decadence. It's Bester and Tiptree and Willis and Moorcock and Ballard and Kuttner and Sheckley and Harrison and Wolfe and Silverberg and Bisson and Di Filipo and Malzberg and Shepard, and anyone who thinks human nature is pretty awful but lovable, anyone who has had their writing rejected as 'downbeat', anyone who goes for hypersensitivity, strange tastes, the xenophile thing, nights of no moon, hubris clobbered by nemesis . . .

If only the people out there could see we're not really technological barbarians, horse-clans, unable to turn a phrase or the other cheek. The label's wrong, and has been wrong too long. Really, we are as decadent as anyone.

Space is just a slip of the tongue. We meant spice.

THE VEILED WORLD

A Lecture given to the Oxford Psychotherapy Society

We are misled into assuming that personality is continuous through-out life just because our physical beings, our bodies, appear to be continuous. This is not the case. Every cell in our bodies is renewed, changed, in the course of seven years. Why then should a more tenuous thing like personality be uniform and continuous?

We have documentation, birth certificates, medical records, pass-ports, all the stuff we carry about with us which spells continuity. However, a house may be continuously occupied, yet its occupants can change, and the Smiths sell up to the Joneses, even if the Joneses don't then change the wallpaper or tack on a conservatory. Our documentation—the kind of thing we may be required to produce if we are had up in court—consists of trophies of past time. It is no guide to our present state of mind.

Of course we have memories. But memory is also discontinuous. I distinctly recollect the joy of my third birthday, when I was given a red fire-engine almost as big as myself. I wore a smart woollen suit at the time. But this is not a true memory. I recollect it only because a photograph of me with fire engine under arm exists, my uncle happening to have had his camera out that day. That memory is purely external, an artificial aid. No application of thought will bring back any other fragment of that day. The birthday cake, if there was one, has totally disappeared. I retain in my head, as it were, only a clipping, not the whole newspaper.

I am as surely not that child as that child was not me.

The psyche is the generating house of our mental awareness, our spiritual well- or ill-being. Psyche follows psyche as snakes shed skin. I propose to call these successive psyches phoenix-personalities.

What if, in the hypothetical herbaceous borders of our being, personality is really a hardy annual, seeding itself, being reborn at appropriate seasons, and not the perennial we have been educated to suppose? Unlike perennials, nasturtiums and other annuals maintain continuity of species by yearly rebirth, seeding and death. Personality may require a similar cycle of renewal.

While our understanding of the universe has had to undergo vast revision during the twentieth century, this particular concept of ourselves as monuments through our own lifetime has scarcely been challenged. We are taught to regard our 'personality' as a road down which our awareness travels from cradle to grave. Not so. Our awareness is maintained only at constantly fresh perceptual levels by the phoenix-personalities. Not a road, but a series of—I speak metaphorically—helicopter flips.

As writers, we have to use ourselves as laboratories for the world. Such understanding as we have of other people's behaviour is based largely on our own behaviour, and our own perceptions. Even from this limited viewpoint, we can see how base and untrustworthy— and occasionally how noble and self-sacrificing—people are.

I clearly perceive, as I look back over my life, a series of successive selves. There they are, the hardy annuals, the portraits on the walls of that private gallery in our minds: the adventurous small boy, the unhappy lad at school, the macho soldier in the war, the wage slave, the lover, the traveller, the timid scribbler, the family man, and now the most unlikely avatar of them all—the established writer. These portraits bear family resemblances, yes, but the frames are more alike than the paintings. We may recall the people we knew and loved, the places where we lived. What we thought, what we said, the meals we ate—these are, mercifully perhaps, far less distinct.

Some of these phoenix-personalities, where the divisions between them are distinct enough, have acquired distinctive labels, which are widely accepted. 'The Teenager' is a well-recognized example, as is 'The Thirtysomething' and 'The Old Fool'. As Sophie Tucker taught us in her famous song, 'Life begins at forty'. We know the discontinuities exist but prefer not to know, as once we knew that smoking was bad for us and preferred not to know.

I think of phoenix-personalities as welling up, enjoying their day, sparkling and decaying, to give place to the next phoenix-personality. It's a dynamic concept in place of a static one, and therefore to be preferred. Deep 'below' them, of course, the archetypes continue to function, and may unknowingly promote change.

A word on the archetypes. The functioning of the brain remains more mysterious than the functions of the moons of Jupiter. Recent brain/computer analogies have been unable to shed light on its functioning, and are unhelpful. The unconscious psyche, that veiled world in which archetypes operate, is immensely older than humanity, being housed in an anatomy which, equally, is much older than we humans who have inherited it. Best known of the archetypes are the *anima* and *animus*, those parts of oneself in, respectively, men and women which function independently of ego-consciousness—and therefore exist beyond words and intellectual processes. We glimpse them in myth, puissant figures of Wise Old Men, Pure Virgins, Wizards, Animal beings . . .

According to Jung and his followers, who alone seem able to throw light on this mysterious world, the *unwelt* within which archetypes exist is a luminous darkness where the birth and death of individuals count for little or nothing. The pulse of time beats slowly. The nature of these—what should we call them?—autonomous semi-beings is so strange, so uncanny, that they may irrupt into consciousness when it becomes pathological. They form part of the material of schizophrenia.

It requires no great leap of understanding to think of the archetypes in some kind of hierarchical mode. One following another, they help to precipitate succeeding phoenix-personalities.

If I have a theory of fiction, it is that 'inspiration' must enter our writing for it to have any worth. Inspiration is difficult to define, except by negatives—it is that quality which a schoolboy's essay lacks. The definitions in the OED are suggestive. Inspiration means the drawing in of the breath (as if in surprise); also 'The suggestion of prompting (from some influential quarter) of the utterance . . . of particular views'. This prompting comes from the veiled world of archetypes.

However greatly we are 'conscious artists', something speaks through our lips of which we have no clear cognizance. In this way, we allow our characters to converse; and in this way we find, in the popular phrase, that certain characters 'take over' and seem to write themselves.

By giving this contained freedom to the motivating forces deep within us, that 'influential quarter' of which the OED makes mention, we hasten or reinforce the turnover of phoenix-personalities.

How many of my personalities through the years would have given a fig for that big red fire-engine? How many of them could have written *Somewhere East of Life*—or, in a different vein, *Hothouse*?

And of those two novels, the author of one could not then have written the other. The gulf between the authors is not merely one of time, but of experience and psychology.

When writing *Hothouse* in the early 1960s, I could by no means have conceived *Somewhere East of Life*. The 'I' who wrote *Somewhere East of Life* in the 1990s would have produced a dull pastiche had he tried to recreate *Hothouse*. Two different writers are involved: different skills, different friends, different wives, different attitudes to life.

A writer reinforces the discontinuities of his or her personality by writing different books. Novels can be a kind of forcing houses. They seal off old experience, and lead on to new perceptions. Experienced in this light, they generate tides of excitement in a writer's life. It is for this psychic excitement he or she is prepared to undergo weeks, months, eventually many years sitting more or less isolated at a desk. Successive phases give a so-to-speak evolutionary thrust to the psyche to go on developing. Perhaps that's what Carl Jung meant by 'individuation'.

'In the first half of life, a person is, and should be, concerned with emancipating himself from parents'—I quote from Anthony Storr's book on Jung[1]—'and with establishing himself in the world as spouse, parent, and effective contributor . . . Once a person has done so, then he could and should look inwards. Jung called the journey towards wholeness the "process of individuation". It is towards the study of this process that the thrust of his later work is addressed.'

Writing, being in some aspects a form of self-analysis, allows us a chance to create ourselves. In infancy, chance shapes character; in full adulthood, character shapes the chances.

Writers who write the same book to the same formula over and over are often the ones who achieve greatest financial success. Agatha Christie is an outstanding example. Readers, being deceived by tradition in this matter, are anxious, if only on a sub-conscious level, concerning their own unstable psyches; so they cling to the continuity of the Hercule Poirot novels, hoping, knowing, that one will be much like the next, will adhere to formula. For such readers, reassurance is all. For such readers, Sherlock Holmes must be called back from among the imaginary dead.

Everything exacts a payment. The writer engaged in what is comically called 'self-expression'—the will to explore his capacities to their full—may not become rich. The formula writer neglects the

1 Anthony Storr, *Jung: Selected Writings*, London, Fontana, 1983.

chance to achieve a real excitement (as opposed to publication and financial reward) and the contentments of individuation.

By these remarks I venture into the realms of philosophy and perhaps neurology; on neither subject am I qualified to talk. I have to speak from the security of a knowledge of my own self, born of years of seeking what particular meat should fill my next novel, and in what particular direction, from my limited viewpoint, I should look next. This is what I admire in Aldous Huxley: his restlessness.

Of course, we find that restlessness in Shakespeare.

We have long since accepted the idea of multiple personalities in one body; it is not unreasonable to posit multiple personalities along a different axis—the axis of time.

A recent understanding indicates that multiple personalities are generated almost invariably in children, generally female children, who have been sexually abused. Can it be that the not dissimilar gear-changes of personality may also be accentuated by some disturbance in childhood which directs the phoenix-personalities towards restlessness rather than reassurance? Perhaps they require reassurance, as most of us do, but cannot accept it as genuine when it comes along. There may be a certain warfare in the veiled world of the archetypes.

The concept of phoenix-personalities challenges most received notions of personality—and is none the worse for that. That the sun went round the Earth was a received notion for many centuries, and was overturned by Copernicus, to our better understanding of the universe in which we briefly live.

There are people who still reject the unnerving Copernican system. More reassurees . . .

Perhaps the cause of some types of mental illness is the failure of successive phoenix-personalities to be born. It is then that the archetypes irrupt. Sometimes we meet people who suffer from terminal boredom; their psychic machinery has stuck. Not all individuals have the fortune to reach full maturity. Circumstance may fall out against them.

It must be a fluke to reach such a maturity. Indeed, it is more than average luck if we grow to adulthood and manage to propagate our species. Most living things are less lucky. A bird may lay six eggs in a season; possibly only one reaches breeding fettle. Fish may spawn millions of eggs; a mere handful will survive to perpetuate their kind. This is another area in which humans are almost unique: in other species, breeding adults are passing rare. Successful writers are of course rarer still.

When giving interviews and suchlike, I am often asked what changes or developments I would like to see in the future. The expectation is perhaps that I will name some extraordinary techno-logical device, such as a matter-transmitter. In the technological line, I would like the future equivalent of a big red fire-engine, a private time-machine. To take a short stroll in Gondwanaland, to know Angkor Wat in the days of its glory, or Cleopatra in hers, or to visit Stonehenge when it was thatched, or to see Rome before the Vandals came a-knocking, to consort with the likes of Samuel Johnson, or even just to say Hello to Mary Shelley—all such goodies are highly desirable.

But what one really hopes for is some way in which the workings of our own minds become less obscure to us. It takes a long while to understand why we did such and such a thing in such and such a way. That lie, that evasion, that divorce, that failure . . . there was a reason behind it, but maybe not Reason itself. In moments of crisis, older things than the neocortex speak and act—speak up and act up—with the rapidity of a conjurer. The archetypes ride.

It is true that our brains are full of the evolutionary equivalent of fossils, yet there seems hope for us. The evidence is admittedly conflicting. Awful though this century has proved to be, we have learnt to be aware of our own destructive power, of something blind and impersonal in our natures, to which our recent forebears were wilfully unknowing. Not all but most.

We see in the case of the killers set against Salman Rushdie that a great many seemingly decent people will surrender their con-sciences to the ethics of the ant-heap, blindly agreeing, blindly doing what they are told to do. Yet at the same time people in Eastern Europe and the former Soviet Union, glimpsing daylight after gener-ations of oppression of one kind or another, emerge with perfectly clear ideas of sanity and decency. We do recognize truth, if intermit-tently.

So when the interviewer calls with his or her impertinent questions, my response is to say that we need to be less muddy. Only then will the centuries ahead be more lucid. Perhaps a surgical operation could be devised to generate new neural pathways through the brain: in order that we might more clearly comprehend the workings of our thoughts and the nature of our motives. And then, genetic manipulation could take the place of surgery.

Eventually, the human race would spend more time communing with itself, less time fighting with those demons, its neighbours.

There's wisdom as well as cynicism in the Russian proverb: 'Love thy neighbour, but build a fence'.

Much energy and money is spent in the modern world by people trying to understand why they are whatever they are. The demand for lucidity is strongly felt. It may become possible for a light to be made to shine down into the veiled world within. Or, not to trade in metaphors which spring from those regions, to be able to have conscious access to those semi-autonomous parts of our personality which at present communicate only in dreams, snatches, poems, paintings, and riddles. And, of course, in science fiction.

To speak of genetic manipulation to bring about a revolutionary change is one thing. But what would really help would be a revolution in education.

Our educational systems do not equip us—I know it's a cliché—do not equip us for life. What we all need at the age of puberty is not drugs or rock and roll but a Carl Jung in our lives: not just to teach us, but to interest us in the things that are truly interesting.

How would such developments affect my idea of discontinuity of the personality? Well, it might initiate us into enjoying these changes. Perhaps their cycles conform to that mystical figure of seven. As in Shakespeare's Seven Ages of Man. In which case, we should celebrate special psyche birthdays every seven years. It's boring always to be the same person.

I'm for blasphemy. I am for doubt and disbelief and all those uncomfortable things. We'll need them if we are to get far into the future in any useful way, instead of huddling in technological slums in a teeming overpopulated world.

I'm also for the shedding of god and gods. We need to understand ourselves, to come to terms with our own mystery, not the assumed mystery of some assumed godhead. God was mankind's greatest imaginative invention. We've got to survive without him.

A PERSONAL PARABOLA

Speech delivered at the Natwest Fundación, Madrid

At the conclusion of his survey of the origins of the universe, *The First Three Minutes*,[1] Professor Steven Weinberg remarks of the Earth, peaceful beneath the plane he is travelling in, how hard it is to realize what a small part Earth is of an overwhelmingly hostile universe. 'It is even harder to realize that this present universe has evolved from an unspeakably unfamiliar early condition.'

It is a modern dilemma: to have learnt so much about our environment that we are faced with its incomprehensibility. What existed before our universe was created remains a matter for speculation. In this abstruse area, scientists give way to mystics. Before the universe—was that a time of total purity, as the poet-saint Kabir seems to suggest?

'Behold but One in all things; it is the second that leads you astray.'

And the German seer, Meister Eckhart, also seems to speak up for nothingness, if not unity, when he says, 'The Godhead is poor, naked and empty as though it were not; it has not, wills not, wants not, works not, gets not'.

But for most of us, the world about us is too full of mystery and excitement for such asceticism ever fully to embrace us, or we it. Even if we have not Professor Weinberg's training and knowledge, we may be able to conduct our own line of investigation into what we see around us. Much of life can be spent studying to understand the world into which we are temporarily plunged.

One great interest used to be to venture into the great grey Communist world. Those trips entailed briefings beforehand and afterwards. And in Cold War days it was not unusual for one to be asked to carry out some small secret commission. The *frisson*, the foreignness, of those ventures behind the Iron Curtain was greater

---

1 I reviewed this book for the *New Statesman* in 1977, when Martin Amis was its literary editor.

than anything visits to Nice or Stockholm or Munich, those pleasant cities, could offer. An additional interpretation beyond mere conversation had to be pursued in Budapest and Moscow and Beijing, and the meaning behind the meaning sought out: the *sub-text*, as we now say.

In Stanislav Lem's novel, *Solaris*, scientists from Earth study the strange ocean planet of Solaris, endeavouerng to fathom its secrets. Data from the planet are sent back to Earth and stored in the Solaristics Library. The secret of Solaris may, eventually, be contained on Earth, in the library. But the library has become so vast that the secret is just as safe there as on the ocean planet.

A similar feeling could arise when sitting talking to friends in Zagreb, Chengdu, or Tirana: that the secret—the Secret—locking into and corrupting the Communist system was actually contained in the West: maybe even within one's own make-up. I have earlier quoted Vaclav Havel on that score.

Perhaps what reinforced the repressive nature of Communist systems, in Europe if not in China, was reaction against something in the West, or a correspondence with something latent in the West. Not merely the Western exploitation of labour and contempt for the poor, but the crass denigration of family life, and the commercializing of sex and many things which should have no commercial value.

It was always noticeable, for instance, that Russian children were fed a less frenetic and more peaceable diet of Kiddie TV than the vulgar and violent fare thrown at younger generations in London and New York.

This uneasy feeling of something missing, of an opportunity lost, haunted sensible people in both East and West. In a few more years, it will be difficult to remember the pessimism current in the West during the seventies. I recorded that pessimism in my novel, *Life in the West*. It even seemed possible that the democracies might collapse under monolithic pressure from the Eastern bloc. Although that bloc was in fact far from being monolithic, such was how many of us saw it, and how it intended itself to be seen.

To add to our discomfort, the propagandists of the Kremlin, and those who liked to sing the Kremlin's tune, in West as well as East, liked to say that really—*really*, that wonderful weasel word!—East and West were mirror images of each other.

In August 1976, an SF Convention, Eurocon III, was held in Poznan, Poland. Several Western writers attended, including friends of mine, Jon Bing and Tor Age Bringsvaerd from Norway, Sam

Lundwall from Sweden, Pierre Barbet from France, and several others. It was an educational experience.

During one of the forums, a group of communist speakers used the mirror-image analogy, claiming that little difference existed between East and West. With reference to science fiction, they argued that, just as they would be forbidden to publish a novel in which capitalism triumphed, so we in the West would be unable to publish a novel in which Communism prevailed.

As soon as I got home, I began writing *Enemies of the System*. It was published in hardcover in 1978. The sub-title of this short novel is 'A Tale of *Homo Uniformis*' (Man Alike Throughout). In its pages, a communist utopia is established, not only on Earth, but throughout the solar system, sustaining itself for many centuries.

A leading utopian, a woman called Jaini Regentop, explains the physiological basis for the success of *Homo Uniformis*. 'The endotomists established the fact that man's physiological structure comprised three governance systems which were in conflict. Owing to the rapid evolutionary development of man from animal, those governance systems were not entirely compatible . . . Our great endotomists and physiologists developed a method whereby those governance systems could be developed into one harmonious super-system. The three governance systems I refer to, by the way, are known as Central Nervous System, primarily a motor system, Autonomic Nervous System, primarily a sensual system, and Neocortex, primarily a thought system . . .

'To develop this more reliable super-system, the bio-shunt was introduced . . . [It] is a built-in processor which phases out much of the old autonomic nervous system or renders it subject to the direct control of the thought system. An obvious example is the penile erection, once an involuntary act . . . I frequently impress on my classes that the bio-shunt is the very basis of our great utopia.'

Like Kepler's *Somnium*, the kernel of my tale was wrapped in a fantasy, an ambush of lies. Like many inventions in science fiction, mine was no idle one, but based on a real and horrific Soviet formulation. Soviet medical students used to begin their Latin course with a statement: '*Homo sovieticus sum*' ('I am Soviet man'). These future doctors were taught that there were two strains of human being, *Homo sovieticus* and *Homo sapiens*. By the seventies, the ideologues declared they had created 'the motherland of a new and superior type of rational human being'—this is in 1974, in a book entitled *The Soviet People*, published by Politizdat in Moscow.

This book goes on to extol the conditions under which the New Man lives. 'His children go to kindergarten or school, his parents are treated by the best doctors; he himself has just received a new apartment . . . Scientists are concerned about clean air—and all this is for him, for Soviet Man . . .' However, the satirist, Aleksandr Zinoviev, took another view of the matter, saying, '*Homo sovieticus* has been trained to live in comparatively foul conditions . . .'

Anyone who visited the domains of the Soviet Empire with half a retina working could see that the truth lay with Zinoviev, not Politizdat. Contempt for human nature was matched by contempt for the environment. Nowhere on the globe is pollution worse than in parts of the USSR. Poor old *sovieticus* and his missus were choking to death . . .

Enemies of the System was published by Jonathan Cape in England and Harper & Row in the USA. It immediately received an enthusiastic review by Anthony Burgess. There were also several foreign translations. To date, the book has not been published in Russia.

I was happy to pass on by this book to doubters in the West the good news that our political and moral systems, faulty though they may be, are not and never were mirror images of those created in the darker recesses of the Kremlin. Resemblances . . . that's a different matter . . .

When people talk about 'the uses of science fiction', they generally lay emphasis on a supposed predictive faculty. My scepticism regarding prediction has been mentioned. But about SF's ability to pin down current falsehoods I have no doubt.

Somewhere on my travels I picked up the print which forms the frontispiece to this book of essays. As far as I know, it too dates from the seventies. It is very far from the art of Jim Christensen. By showing what one (unknown) artist thought of life under the Soviet system, with which he had to live, this artist provides what might well be an illustration for *Enemies of the System: A tale of* Homo Uniformis.

It is to be hoped no one mistook it for a vision of the future.

The first time my wife and I visited Madrid, over twenty years ago, Spain was a very different country from today's Spain. But we ourselves were very different people. A habit of change is inbuilt in nature. Out in the universe, primal fires still blaze. In the human anatomy, too, the heat is on.

Tomorrow I shall be speaking in one of the world's oldest universities, in Alcala de Henares, the birthplace of Cervantes. That's a humbling thought for any writer, not least a writer of science fiction. Or let me call myself by a less restrictive label, an imaginative writer; that places me more directly in a line of descent from Cervantes. SF is not universally well regarded. Of course, I take a different view, and hold that SF, at least in its platonic form, is the great new literature of this century, a fiction of developed nations best able to exemplify and dramatize the changes taking place about and within us.

However, SF will flourish without my defending it (as I have been doing for over thirty years). Instead, with typical writerly egotism, I shall say something about my own work, that ladleful of soup in the great cauldron of fiction.

Being a devotee of cause and effect, I believe there is a reason for everything, even for the universe itself. Perhaps that is why I turned to SF. Science fiction is a moral form in which, if you do *this*, *that* follows. But what prompts one to become a writer, to turn the world into words? It is strange that one's own thought processes should be obscure to oneself. Why is it that we do not know what is going on in our own heads? If I were given the task of reshaping the human race, I would attend to that matter first. We will return to this question.

One incentive to write was, for me, a repressed childhood. I was never allowed to answer back or question. As soon as I had a typewriter, I was free. Typewriters, and the computers which followed, never dispute. I embarked on writing—well, whatever I fancied . . . Looking back, I see that all those many books and stories represent a phantom outline of my life. Free-wheeling though they often are, they too have a reason. They obey the cause and effect of an interior climate. They are the fruits of what I am, and 'By their fruits ye shall know them . . .'

Our generations are extremely fortunate in the way that travel has become easier. Margaret and I travel frequently. My stories move round the globe and beyond. We can fly from London to New York in five hours in an ordinary jet, and faster than that in Concorde. Of course, in future these times will seem terribly slow. Or so we hope.

Time is being devoured, year by year. If you work with computers, you become impatient at a three second delay between programmes. But of course computers work extremely fast and imprisoned in their circuit boards is a zone where time holds quite a different meaning from the biological time as experienced within a human skull-case. No, hang on, there is more than one type of time in our skulls. We'll talk about that. Time's a great obsessive theme.

You hear people nowadays complain that whatever country they visit, they find there the things they found at home, a toy, a brand of whisky, a chain-store, a McDonald's restaurant. This is the inevitable consequence of mass travel. You also hear that people, nations, are getting more alike. That seems no bad thing. What people don't seem to talk about is how strange it is that individuals differ so greatly, one from another—brothers from brothers, daughters from mothers etc. The human race might easily have been more or less homogeneous, like a herd of deer.

I'm not talking about physical resemblances so much as inner lives. The circuitry in the human brain—no, that's a crass way of putting it—the neural pathways of the brain are formed early in life and cannot be rebuilt as easily as a circuit board. Priests and psychoanalysts (the high priests of our age) use rather crude screw-drivers, rigged up out of words and silences, to repair our thinking.

By a curious twist of evolution, we all contain a major paradox, too little commented upon: our own minds are not entirely open to us. This is what makes us, in Alexander Pope's words, 'Sole judge of truth, in endless error hurled; The glory, jest and riddle of the world'. Much of our thinking—our deep thinking—is obscure to us who think the thoughts. The phylogenetically ancient parts of our brain have a semi-autonomy which the cerebral cortex cannot quite bring under control. As a result, what we term instinctive behaviour is under the management of what Carl Jung has termed archetypes.

It's no comfortable discovery to realize these quasi-beings move within us on a time scale different from our own. The best known example of an archetype is the *Anima*, the dark woman in man, or the *Animus* in women. Archetypes are semi-independent signifiers which answer no call to die, from generation to generation. All our poetry and invention, as well as much of our difficulty in moving towards utopia, spring from this anatomical fact.

Fairy tales and stories of mythology deal with archetypal figures: the princess, the warrior, the wise old man, the mother figure, the cruel step-mother, the gentle knight, the prince transformed by magic, the beast that talks. These figures live their wraithlike exis-tence in us today, and no less in Fantasy. They may comfort us—or they may make our hair stand on end.

We might add to Descartes' famous dictum: 'I think, therefore I am; I don't think, therefore I bugger things up'.

One minor side-effect of this evolutionary paradox is a repressed inner life: an interior life which seems to flow below the surface of what, by consensus, we call real life. Below the surface and parallel to 'real life'. How widespread repressed inner life (RIL) is, we don't know. But clearly it is far from unusual. Every time we read or write a novel, we are releasing into our minds another layer of life apart from our own; but that's not what I'm talking about. Though the prevalence of fantasy shows how eager we are to enjoy something more that the plain diet of 'real life'.

Matthew Arnold wrote a fine poem about repressed inner life, 'The Buried Self'. Mary Shelley gives dramatic expression to the power of RIL when she speaks in her Journals of herself as one who 'entirely and despotically engrossed in their own feelings, leads—as it were—an *internal* life quite different from the outer and apparent one'.

To this startling remark many other similar ones could no doubt be added if you bothered to look. Perhaps the whole notion of *doppelgangers* sprang from this curious phenomenon of divided mind.

Here's a passage from Matthew Arnold's poem:

> But often in the world's most crowded streets,
> But often, in the din of strife,
> There rises an unspeakable desire
> After the knowledge of our buried life;
> A thirst to spend our fire and restless force
> In tracking out our true, original course;
> A longing to enquire
> Into the mystery of this heart which beats
> So wild, so deep in us—to know
> Whence our lives come and where they go.

'Our true original course . . .' What does he mean? Well, Arnold's idea was unwittingly echoed much later by Carl Jung. Jung perceived that we may, in the course of our mortal lives, work through many personalities, while the person into whom we eventually evolve may have been already present, latent, at birth. Amazing!

But everything is cause for amazement. We have a small grandson, Thomas, born last Christmas Eve. When you hold Thomas in your arms, you feel in one 12lb bundle the same wonder at human existence which a view of distant galaxies generates.

This sense of the miraculous—of the often unacknowledged—is one I have pursued in both SF and 'straight' fiction.

My novels form a parabola above the straight line of my lived life. They form a single-span bridge between 'real life' and the RIL, repressed inner life. After an early comedy of English society, they take off immediately into space, with *Non-Stop* and *Hothouse*, to planets or futures far away; though their subject matter mainly concerns evolution and origins, those hidden formats of our present days.

In the 1970s, the novels return to Earth briefly, to reminisce about a receding past; that is, World War II. Then off they go again, even further—this time in heavier vehicles, to a planet called Helliconia, a thousand light years away. This is the highest point of the personal parabola.

Of course I'm saying this for the purposes of this talk, in an attempt to make things clear. But you know that really life is subject to muddle and the accidental. While hindsight is notoriously prone to self-enhancement . . .

I loved Helliconia, with its long slow seasons lasting many hundreds of terrestrial years. It was a wonderful and real resort for my imagination; *this* happened, so *that* followed. Its construction lasted for seven of my years, roughly from 1978 to 1985. The dramas enacted on that planet are dramas of power and powerlessness such as we witness—are closely involved in—here on Earth, acted out through personae as vivid, as archetypical, as I could make them.

In the hours before a battle, generals can rehearse their strategies and act out their intentions in—well, in my day it used to be in sandtables; today they do it electronically. Whatever effect Helliconia had on my readers, the novels did much for me in the way of rehearsing and acting out on a small scale—indeed resolving—an inner war: my religious struggle in particular. The whole metaphysics of the novels are constructed in that way. The humans, who dread and hate the almost mindless *phagors*, the Helliconian winter creatures, in fact have evolved from being pets of the phagors, and once worshipped them as gods. I saw the phagors, timeless creatures without self-doubt or introspection, as archetypes.

This is all rather Jungian . . . But it possibly illustrates one metaphorical and valuable use of SF. Perhaps my readers' enjoyment of the three Helliconia novels would be spoilt if I let on that the phagors, by turn persecutors and persecuted, were designedly archetypal models! Quite rightly, too. They should remain part of my RIL, not transparently part of the story.

I have always believed that SF was potentially much much greater than its merely Gernsbackian technophile aspect; though in practice it is unable always to live up to Stapledonian aspirations.

The parabola of writing then brought me back to Earth. Not entirely unexpectedly. Everything has its omens. Preceding the Helliconias went a somewhat indigestible novel—full of startling virtues startlingly wrongly deployed—entitled *Life in the West*. *Life in the West* is not SF. Its whole complex matter came to me entire in a waking vision, as I stood on a shore in Sicily, staring out northwards over the Mediterranean at a departing sail. A remarkable moment. It was a gift, I believe a gift such as only hard-working writers are given; the penalty clause attached was that I had to go home and write the novel.

Two days after my return to Oxford, my mother died unexpectedly. I wrote *Life in the West* nevertheless, including in it a tribute to that strange lady I had both loved and feared.

Life in the West considers a global state of play, seen from the viewpoint of a slightly obnoxious character—my alter ego—Sir Thomas Squire.

The novel convinced me I was able to wed a novel of ideas, such as British literary critics shun, with a novel of character. It was with this conviction in mind that I embarked on the three Helliconia novels. That perhaps accounts for the way in which those three novels differ, one from another, in their construction. I was excited by the new power at which I had arrived.

During that period, I suffered from a malady which I sought to conceal, out of shame, from my wife and family. It was finally diagnosed as PVFS (Post Viral Fatigue Syndrome), a sort of CFS. Frighteningly, my memory was occluded. I found myself unable to remember how to drive round my home town, or keep in mind what day of the week it was. How I managed to write the Helliconia novels, I'll never know.

But all things are grist to the writer. We have to be our own laboratories. *Forgotten Life*, which flies in the wake of the Helliconias, takes up the theme of lost memory. All things connect.

Forgotten Life brought me back to the Here and Now of 'real life'. To Oxford, where Margaret and I have lived for over four decades.

Not simply to Oxford. Precisely to my character Clem Winter's consulting rooms at 13, King Edward Street. At that address I lodged when I first went to Oxford as a young man, after leaving the army. There I took up a new persona—a persona more adaptable to a civilized environment than that of soldier. The events in *Forgotten Life* are shaped in part by that experience—by dreams, fantasies of self-protection, and snatches of the past spicing and splicing our present.

The success of *Forgotten Life*, praised by such writers as Iris Murdoch and Anthony Burgess, was encouraging. While writing short stories and compiling the history of science fiction with David Wingrove, I was planning a third novel, *Remembrance Day*, which was published in 1993. In *Remembrance Day*, some characters from the earlier novels are given an extended life, just as King Jandol Aganol of *Helliconia Summer* has his spiritual life transformed in the succeeding *Helliconia Winter*.

Our personalities evolve throughout life. Writers can hasten by their writings what Jung calls 'individuation', provided the writings contain an exploratory element and reach towards what is fresh, unrehearsed. By paying attention to inner voices, one can achieve a synthesis between conscious and unconscious. It is part of the adventure of living, where physical and spiritual embrace. The buried self is unburied, the RIL uncaged, and a new centre, a midpoint of balance, is achieved. This startling and uncommon development can be assisted by meditation.

So into the mind came the notion of a quartet of novels which should pitch its tent in the middle of today's battlefield, and which should carry ordinary characters from the past, from the previous novels, into the near future. And of course they'd contain humour; jokes have a sharper edge when trouble's brewing.

Despite all I've said about inner life and so on, what strikes a reader first about *Life in the West*, *Forgotten Life* and *Remembrance Day* is their tangling with current affairs. They visit Jugoslavia (as was), Burma, Singapore, Czechoslovakia (as was), Russia and the USA. My interest in the emergent nations of Central Asia—those to the East of the Caspian Sea, Turkmenistan and so on—led me to write *Somewhere East of Life*.

It's a black comedy. *Somewhere East of Life* is about one Burnell. Poor Burnell has had the last ten years of his memory stolen. There's the memory theme again. The ten years have been edited down by pirates for a kind of futuristic video. Burnell's memories of his wife, Stephanie, which he holds sacred, are being sold as porn in the bazaars of Central Asia. So he goes in quest of copies, in Ashkhabad and elsewhere.

This novel, published in August 1994, completes the Squire Quartet. It also welds together contemporary novel and SF. And, with any luck, my own MPD character!

*   *   *

Behind the personal parabola lies a kind of quarrel with England.

In Thomas Love Peacock's novel, *Nightmare Abbey*, Mr Cypress, a caricature of Byron, says, 'Sir, I have quarrelled with my wife, and a man who has quarrelled with his wife is absolved from all duty to his country'.

When people have quarrelled with their native land, it generally entails a quarrel with their parents. So it was with me. In the Second World War, I was shipped out to the Far East on a troopship in 1943, being then under the age of nineteen. I've always loved that designation, 'Far East', and the remoteness it conjures up. The Far East was a good deal farther away in 1943 than it is now. Now, you may fly to Bombay in a matter of hours. In 1943, our troopship took one month to make the trip.

Being the opposite of xenophobic, I enjoyed my adventures in the East, or many of them. The fact remains that when you were despatched to distant lands on His Majesty's Service, the British Army issued you with *no promises about ever coming back*! It was an official expression of exile and indifference: of your expendability.

Supposing you survived the war in Burma, you still remained stuck out there, despatched to China, Hong Kong, or maybe Sumatra or Java, or some other trouble spot. I drifted around for over three years, maturing, rotting . . . And when eventually you were returned 'home', no one wished to know what had been happening to you, or what the countries were like you had visited. That part of your life remained perforce undigested. Nowadays, you would receive counselling after such a traumatic period.

From that exile I acquired a restlessness which probably surfaces in my writing. What have I seen or learnt on my travels? Many and many a time, the beauty of the world comes in and overwhelms our senses, like the first experience of love, or perhaps the last. The beauty of wild places, where even what is ghastly, the Kara Kum desert, the steaming volcanos of Indonesia, the Pacific in a rage, holds its own attraction, must be preserved for its sacredness to all life. An order of being is at stake. No one can say if Europe is more beautiful than China, or Rajastan than Scandinavia. All places have their own character. Such qualities can never be approached by VR, just as that characteristic of nature addresses something in us which words cannot convey. Words were meant for human business and do not carry as far into landscape as the faintest breeze.

Old towns too hold a gravity balanced between sorrow and delight. Oxford, Norwich, Stockholm, Toulouse, Sarlat, Munich,

Prague, Madrid, Budapest, Dubrovnik, Monemvasia, Istanbul—so many cities in Europe hold a wonderful quality compounded of architecture, industry, and centuries of human life. Time does its work there, provoking less destruction than villainous councillors.

Sometimes one comes close to animals, whose concerns are not with us humans—wildcats, snakes, monkeys, deer. One morning early, taking a walk in water meadows, I saw a coypu swimming in a water channel flanked by reed beds. She had a child clinging to her teat; it suckled as they swam along, causing hardly a ripple. This was in my native county of Norfolk. Now the great populations of coypu have been poisoned out of existence. They interfered with agriculture.

When coypu were still fairly common, I spoke to a farmer who had a coypu as a pet. He held the big rodent in his arms very affectionately, and fed it on Bassett's Liquorice Allsorts.

The coypu have gone. You visit many places where the animals have gone. Florida, for instance. The last white egret passed over Fort Lauderdale in 1990, flying south. What one mainly sees on one's travels is other people. Soon there may be only other people. Our numbers still increase. As do our cities.

We're unable to control our appetites, just like the apes from which we evolved. Gustatory, acquisitive, sexual appetites . . . One thing I liked about the East was its wild aspect. Sumatra when I was living there was quiet, full of animals and fruit and orchids and shade. People were thin then, just after the war. Even me.

I was so nostalgic for the East that when I first saw Indians or Chinese walking the streets of Oxford, I would follow them in order to hear once more the gutturals of Gujarati, the clatter of Cantonese.

I'd left England a child, to return as a man. I understood neither the currency nor the class system. My science fiction was a conduit for my estrangement. I cared more about Alpha Centauri than Ashby-de-la-Zouche. Estrangement is a reason for setting one's story in the future or in a far distant planetary system. And I say with pride that I was then one of a vanishingly small number of men who believed in the existence of other planetary systems, before such considerations entered the general intelligence. How many other writers, I wonder, have exorcized their alienation by moving their characters to a remote world, to Peralandra, Middle Earth, or the Wounded Land?

My early novels, such as *Nonstop* and *Hothouse*, carry coded messages concerning the East, distance, heat, the wilds, the jungles.

*   *   *

A novel's function is nebulous but definite. The novel is a literary construct with virtues specific unto itself, which can extend our imaginative boundaries and translate for us, perhaps, our everyday diet of 'real life' into a larger sphere which may not find ready expression in our lived lives.

My quarrel with England must have resolved itself or I would not have written my recent books. In those recent novels lies a hard kernel of truth, like a Brazil nut at the centre of a chocolate: the truth that we are spiritual beings, subject to revelation, such as the revelation in *Forgotten Life* which transforms Joe Winter.

We must change our lives. Mystical experience is more common than is generally allowed. It's difficult in the late twentieth century to find a suitable context for its expression. Mystical experience can interfere with careers.

But a writer doesn't have a career, only . . . pages and paragraphs. He or she is free to make a fool of his or herself, and to blurt out the truth. To—well, it sounds a bit religious, I know—to bear witness. With me, it has become a habit.

I take my leave with a quotation from *Lavengro*, written by a nineteenth-century author, George Borrow. Borrow was a marvellous independent man, born at Dumpling Green, within a stone's throw of my later birthplace. The passage is well-known:

> There's day and night, brother, both sweet things; sun, moon, and stars, brother, all sweet things; there's likewise a wind on the heath. Life is very sweet, brother; who would wish to die?

INDEX